Discovering English

V. E. LEICHTY
Michigan State University

Prentice-Hall, Inc.   Englewood Cliffs, N.J.

Library of Congress Catalog Card No.: 64-18185

Printed in the United States of America
[21592-C]

PRENTICE-HALL INTERNATIONAL, INC., *London*
PRENTICE-HALL OF AUSTRALIA, PTY., LTD., *Sydney*
PRENTICE-HALL OF CANADA, LTD., *Toronto*
PRENTICE-HALL OF INDIA (PRIVATE) LTD., *New Delhi*
PRENTICE-HALL OF JAPAN, INC., *Tokyo*
PRENTICE-HALL DE MEXICO, S.A., *Mexico City*

to Mary

Preface

In writing this book, my basic assumption was that the student would better understand conclusions about his language which he himself had developed than he would conclusions that he had studied in a text. In its first draft, the book consisted only of exercise materials, and these are still the heart of it.

In the exercises I have tried to provide materials that will require the student to observe his language as it actually exists and to develop generalizations from his observations—in other words, to create his own grammar. The function of the explanatory sections of the text is not to supply all the summaries or conclusions that might be drawn from the exercises, but rather to make some statements which may be explored and tested by the exercises. My concern is more with the development of habits of observation and analysis in the student than it is with the production of a complete and consistent grammar of English. If and when such a grammar is produced, I believe it will come from the transformationalists rather than from the structuralists; in no case is it likely to come from beginning students.

If the student is to observe and think about language, he needs terminology. The terms introduced in this book come from both traditional and structural grammar. This involves compromise. Though I recognize that the Fries' Class 1, 2, 3, and 4 words are not identical with the traditional noun, verb, adjective, and adverb classes, it has been my experience that the introduction of these nondescriptive and unfamiliar terms tends to confuse the student. For a similar reason, I have rejected Sledd's double classification based on forms and positions. Although I have introduced the Trager-Smith nine-vowel, multiple-diphthong theory, I have sought to avoid the endless discussions it can produce in terms of dialect and idiolect differences by noting only those vowel and diphthong phonemes that I commonly hear in the Midwest. Some instructors may feel the need to add to those provided or to substitute others. In any case, I should advise that the number introduced be kept to an absolute minimum.

I have devoted little space to the oral patterning of words and word-group structures, not because I feel that this is unimportant, but rather because I believe that such patterning can best be taught by the oral/aural method. The elaborate set of graphic symbols required to represent such patterning tends to confuse rather than to help the student. In addition, any thorough investigation of these patterns requires more time than is normally allotted to a beginning course.

Were I to predict that this method of studying language would automatically produce more effective writers, I should be less than honest. For many students the analysis of the medium, language, has no more relationship to the production of clear, thoughtful expression than the analysis of the medium, paint, would have to the production of incisive portraiture. Both are products of the mind that makes use of the media. The understanding of how our language functions has value in itself, regardless of whether or not the individual makes practical application of it. Yet the fact remains that the knowledge of media is essential to practical as well as to artistic production in any area of communication. It would be nice to predict, also, that every prospective high school teacher would be able to apply the knowledge he gains about his language to the teaching of composition and literature, but again, I would be less than honest if I did so. Some will find it an invaluable aid; some few will probably never see any real relationship between the medium and what can be produced with it.

For the more perceptive students who may be interested in such relationships, I have included some observation of language beyond the simple straightforward structure by introducing a few extensional and metaphorical uses and some of the wide range of substitutional possibilities that are available in English. To introduce such topics is, of course, to move from grammar into rhetoric, but if we are to observe language as we actually use it, this becomes a necessity. My hope is that such study will lead the student to further exploration of what has been done and can be done with the medium of language.

I have experimented with different methods of using the exercise

materials and have concluded that the method suggested on page
19 is quite feasible. Because it requires the student to synthesize his
findings, it reduces the amount of paper work for the instructor but
still permits him to spot false conclusions. In addition, it provides
practice in concise writing and develops topics for informed class discussion.

As will be instantly apparent to anyone acquainted with the field,
I am greatly indebted to a large number of people, for I have not
hesitated to adopt or adapt any ideas or examples that might help
to clarify the concepts I was trying to convey. I am, of course,
particularly indebted to Dr. Charles C. Fries and to Dr. Albert H.
Marckwardt. I should like to express my thanks to Dr. Harold Allen
for the concise and cogent criticism he offered when he read the first
draft manuscript, and to my officemate, Dr. Herman Struck, who
patiently discussed many points with me as I was doing the writing.
I also am indebted to the students who worked on the various
exercises and discussed them in class. I am quite sincere in repeating
the cliché that such virtues as the work may have are greatly owing
to these, for the most part, unnamed people, and naturally, I must
accept the responsibility for whatever faults are found therein.

I would also like to thank the individuals and publishers who gave
me permission to reprint copyrighted materials. These are acknowl-
edged as they appear.

V. E. Leichty

Contents

The Symbolic Nature
of Language

When a dog sees or smells hamburg he may think about past experiences with hamburg, and his mouth may water in anticipation of receiving some, but he has no sound that he can make which would signify hamburg and nothing else. Two people, however, at any time and under any circumstances, can discuss any food that they may have eaten in the past, food that they have never eaten, or food that they may expect to eat sometime in the future. No food has to be present in order to stimulate such a discussion, nor do the people have to be hungry. This difference between the animal and man is of tremendous importance; because he has the ability to use language, man can extend his thought indefinitely, not only into time and space, but even beyond them. He can communicate about things which are absent, about the absence of things, and even about things which never existed and possibly never will exist.

Because we live in a society which would be impossible without language and because we cannot recall a time when we personally could not use language, most of us are likely to take it for granted rather than to try to understand how and why it operates as it does. It is not often recognized, for example, that language is purely symbolic. We fail to recognize that *any* sound or combination of sounds could be used to represent *any* concept—that we use a certain sound or combination of sounds to represent a particular concept merely because there exists a general agreement among the users of a language that this sound or these sounds used in a particular linguistic situation should be the symbol for that concept.

Users of other languages have agreed similarly that a different sound or combination of sounds will symbolize the concept for them. For example, we use the word *girl* to represent a particular type of being; for the same type of being the French use *fille* (pronounced roughly *fee*), the Spanish use *niña* (pronounced *neén ya*), the Italians use *ragazza* (pronounced *ra gát sa*), and the Germans use *Mädchen* (pronounced *máid chen*). Each of these languages has other words to express refinements of this concept, just as we have *lass, maid, damsel, virgin, flapper, tomboy, bobby-soxer,* and other words relating to *girl* in English. We use these and many other words to emphasize and designate the different attributes of our concept *girl* that we have in mind at the moment of speaking.

But even within the same language area, different groups may decide to use different symbols to represent the same attribute of a concept, or they may decide to use the same symbol to represent different attributes or even to represent a totally different concept. In London, for example, the words *tube* and *underground* are used to represent what we call a *subway* in New York City; the British use the word *hood* for the roof of a car, whereas for us this term designates the metal covering over the engine. Even within our own country the names for many things may differ; the worm we use for bait is given the following names in different sections of the country: *fishworm, angleworm, earthworm, mudworm, eaceworm,* and *angledog*. A particularly large type that comes to the surface only at night or after heavy rains is frequently designated as a *night crawler*.

One principle of language should be clear by now: Any particular sound or combination of sounds signifies what it does simply because we agree to have it do so. If we agree to change a concept symbolized by a word, the word then comes to symbolize a new concept. And we frequently do make these changes. The words *knave* and *lewd* once meant *boy* and *ignorant*. The verb *to starve* once meant to die in any manner: if one were hanged, he starved; if he were killed in battle, he starved; and if he died of old age, he starved.

We are free, also, to change the oral symbol without changing the written symbol or vice versa. Thus some people pronounce *either* with the first sound similar to the *ea* in *beat*, whereas others pronounce it with that sound similar to the *i* in *bite*. The British pronounce *honor* and *connection* much as we do, but they normally spell them *honour* and *connexion*.

The Oral Symbol

Most of our words in English are made up of combinations of sounds. This is true even of some words that we spell with a single letter. The pronoun *I*, for example, as it is pronounced in most parts of the United States, is made by gliding from a sound similar to the sound represented by the *a* in *pa* to the sound represented by the letter *i* in *bit*.

When we associate a particular combination of sounds with a particular concept, it becomes the symbol for that concept. We cannot eat the sounds represented by the spelling *banana,* but we can eat the object that the sounds and letters symbolize. Because we associate the symbol and the concept symbolized so closely, we are frequently led to confuse symbol and concept in our thinking. A girl may wear bobby-sox without being a bobby-soxer. A man may subscribe to some of the concepts normally attributed to Democrats without being himself a member of the Democratic party, or he may be a member of the party without subscribing to all its ideals.

The Written Symbol

Man must have used oral language for millenniums before he found a means of writing. One of his early attempts at written communication was by drawing pictures. This was cumbersome, and he learned to use a simpler symbol to represent the picture— the head of an ox, for example, was enough to represent the whole animal. Further simplification resulted in a nonpictorial symbol such as $\triangle$. This particular symbol, positioned differently and modified slightly, became our letter A. Other groups of people, probably starting in much the same way, developed completely different types of written symbols to represent their sound symbols.

One need only glance at some Akkadian, Aztec, Chinese, or Egyptian writing to see how very different the types of writing have been. I. J. Gelb, who has made one of the most definitive studies of writing to date, traces the following stages in the development of writing: (1) pictures, (2) descriptive representational devices, (3) identifying mnemonic devices, (4) word syllabic writing, (5) syllabic writing, (6) alphabetic writing.[1]

In all written language, whatever its type, the written symbol is twice removed from the concept represented, for the written symbol is a symbol for the sounds, which, in turn, are symbols for the concept.

How We Learn Symbols

We normally learn the symbols that represent a particular object or concept by hearing the sounds in association with that object or concept. An English-speaking mother uses the sounds represented by the spelling *kitten* at the same time that she shows the animal to her child; when this has been repeated often enough, the word *kitten* becomes a symbol for the animal to the child, and when the mother says *kitten*, the child will look for the animal; if he wants the animal, he will try to repeat the word *kitten* to his mother. At first, he may apply the symbol to any animal vaguely resembling a cat, but gradually he acquires other symbols and he also acquires the ability to distinguish between different objects. Thus, by seeing many dogs and cats, and at the same time hearing the words used to represent these animals, he learns to apply the proper symbol to the proper animal. Not only does he learn to associate each of the symbolic words with a sense-perceivable thing such as water, an animal, or a chair; he also learns to associate words with concepts such as *good, bad,* or *truth,* which are not sense-perceivable. And long before he enters school he learns that certain words, such as pronouns, are associated with one person or thing at one time and with a different person or thing at a different time. After he has entered school, he learns to associate our written symbols with

[1] Dr. Gelb does not maintain that all writing passed through each of these stages. His point is rather that man has developed different means of writing, and that some of these appeared earlier than others. The student interested in this problem should consult his book: I. J. Gelb, *A Study of Writing: The Foundations of Grammatology* (Chicago: University of Chicago Press, 1952).

the sound symbols which he has already acquired. When he has done so, he has begun to learn to read and write.

Long before this occurs, however, he will have acquired the ability to use his language in several other ways that are extremely important. He learns that the word *animal* is used to designate not only cats and dogs, but also many other creatures. By putting an additional sound on *cat*, he finds that he can make this word symbolize more than one cat. He learns that the sounds *eat* represent not an object or a being, but an action. Soon he recognizes that the combination of sounds making up the word *ate* has a particular time relationship to the combination of sounds making up the word *eat*, and he realizes that a word such as *little* can be placed before words such as *cat* or *dog* to express a relationship of size. At a later time, he discovers that many words such as *truth, love,* and *life* represent abstractions that he cannot touch or measure. Many others could be mentioned here, but since it is one of the purposes of this book to help you isolate some of these various changes in the forms of English and to understand the function or functions each of them serves, it is neither necessary nor economical to try to mention all of them at this point. Before we leave this, however, it may be well to note that the child does not acquire the ability to use these distinctions of language in any fixed order; in fact, it is probable that no two children would follow exactly the same pattern in learning them. Nor does the child acquire all the possible variations used to represent a particular linguistic distinction at the same time. In fact, there are some distinctions that the particular individual may never acquire.

Abstract Relationships

The relationship that exists between the words *cat* and *dog* and the word *animal* has already been mentioned. Let us look at it more carefully to see what is actually involved. If you were asked to define *hamburg* you would probably say that it is a type of *steak*, or possibly that it is ground *beef* or ground *meat*. Or you might say that it is a type of *food*. A butcher might think of it as a part of his *stock* or *property*. In other words, we have numerous symbols or words that we can use to represent this product.

How then do we choose the one word or symbol that we wish

to use at a particular time? To answer this question we must first look at what is actually represented by these various symbols. The word *property*, for example, has literally thousands of possible referents. It may represent anything that is owned by someone: a house, a store, a suit of clothes, some furniture, a dog, a pencil, a piece of jewelry, or a pound of hamburg. The important concept expressed by the word *property* is not the object represented at a particular time that it is used, but rather the relationship (owner-ship) which exists between the person and the object. *Stock*, in the sense we use it here, is one kind of property; it is the kind that a storekeeper acquires with the purpose in mind of selling it or trading it to other individuals. Once again, it can represent almost anything. A grocer's stock consists chiefly of *food. Food* represents a particular kind of property or stock; it differs from other property or stock such as furniture or clothes in that it can be eaten. But the word *food* again represents a wide range of concepts as different as hay and hamburg. Among the possible concepts represented by *food* is *meat*. Meat may be part of a grocer's or butcher's stock and, as such, it is a part of his property; it is also a type of food. But its distinguishing characteristic is that it consists of the flesh of animals. Among the possible concepts represented by *meat* are *pork, beef, mutton, venison,* and so forth. Each of these represents meat from a different type of animal. But further distinctions are possible, not all of them parallel. *Beef* is a term we use to represent the meat from adult cattle, but if these same animals had been butchered while they were young, we would speak of their meat as *veal.* As subdivisions of the general concepts expressed as *meat, beef, veal,* and so forth, we have the possibility of designating the part of the animal from which the meat is taken: *heart, liver, brisket, steak,* and so forth. *Steak,* which comes from the back half of the animal, can also be divided into different types, again dependent upon the specific section of the animal from which it is taken. Here we have such terms as *sirloin, porterhouse, round, flank, T-bone,* and so forth. Finally, if any of this steak is put through a meat grinder, we call it *hamburg*.

Why do we need all these different symbols to represent what may be the same thing? The answer is, of course, that each word represents or calls to our attention a different attribute or characteristic of the object. When we have occasion to talk about these different attributes or characteristics, we have provided symbols for them. Each different symbol or word represents a different type of observation. Having a large number of symbols that we can apply to a particular object or concept, we are able, by choosing one, to refer to the exact attribute or characteristic of the object or concept that we wish to express. A major part of language is therefore a matter of classification. The child learns these multifold classifications chiefly by hearing them applied. As he learns the difference between a dog and a cat by seeing a number of dogs and cats, he also learns the names of these animals by hearing the particular combination of sounds that we associate with them. As he grows older, he learns general terms such as *quadruped* and *animal* and specialized terms such as *hound, spaniel,* and *terrier.* As we shall see later, this process of classification is further extended through the use of such linguistic devices as word-form changes and modification.

Suggested Readings

SECTION 1

Brooks, Nelson, *Language and Language Learning,* Chap. I. New York: Harcourt, Brace & World, Inc., 1960.

Brown, Roger, *Words and Things,* Chap. X. New York: The Free Press of Glencoe, Inc., 1958.

Hall, Robert A., Jr., *Linguistics and Your Language,* Chaps. III and V. Garden City, New York: Doubleday & Company, Inc., 1960.

Hayakawa, S. I., *Language in Action: A Guide to Accurate Thinking, Reading and Writing,* Chaps. II and VIII. New York: Harcourt, Brace & World, Inc., 1942.

Kluckholm, Clyde, *Mirror for Man: A Survey of Human Behavior and Social Attitudes,* Chap. VI. New York: McGraw-Hill Book Company, Inc., 1944.

Laird, Charlton, *The Miracle of Language,* Chap. IV. Cleveland, Ohio: The World Publishing Company, 1953.

———, *Thinking about Language,* Chap. II, Secs. 11 and 12. New York: Holt, Rinehart & Winston, Inc., 1959.

Langer, Susanne K., *Philosophy in a New Key: A Study in the Symbolism of Reason, Rite, and Art,* Chaps. II and III. Cambridge, Mass.: Harvard University Press, 1942.

Sapir, Edward, *Culture, Language, and Personality: Selected Essays,*
    ed. David G. Mandelbaum, pp. 1-12. Berkeley, Calif.: University
    of California Press, 1958.

Schlauch, Margaret, *The Gift of Language,* Chap. I. New York: Dover
    Publications, Inc., 1955.

The Sounds
of Modern English
—Consonants

As we noted earlier, two types of symbols are used in language: the oral symbols, which consist of sounds existing in time, and the written symbols, which exist in space and generally represent the oral symbols. In oral language, whether it be Urdu, Bantu, Hungarian, or English, sounds are invariably arranged in time sequences—that is, one following another. The order of their arrangement in any language is of supreme importance. Let us take, for example, the three sounds found in the English word *tip*. Arranged as they are in this word, they have one meaning. If we change the arrangement to *pit*, they will have a different meaning. Arranged as *pti*, *tpi*, or *itp*, they have no meaning, and in the arrangement *ipt*, they have no meaning in themselves, but may appear as part of the larger combination of sounds found in the word *equipped*.

The written language offers more variation in the possibilities of arranging symbols. In English, we normally arrange letters and words from left to right, but we can arrange them in other ways.

For example, in looking at the titles on the backs of books on my desk I see:

The

World

Through

Literature

Saint Joan

Teaching English Grammar

In other words, we sometimes write from the bottom up (British publishers seem to prefer this), sometimes we place one word below another, and sometimes we write from the top down (American publishers seem to prefer this). A cursory investigation of record envelopes and advertisements will show still other methods of arranging letters and words, such as from upper left to lower right. In many languages—Hebrew and Arabic, for example—it is customary to write from right to left; in others, a single symbol may represent the combination of sounds which makes up the syllable or word. We should have to define writing simply as being the making of a symbolic mark or marks upon what normally was a previously unmarked surface.[1]

In English, the specific mark or combination of marks represents a particular sound, combination of sounds, or sound pattern that recurs in the language. Our written symbols (letters) appear in spacial sequences; they represent or symbolize the time sequences of sounds used in our oral language. They also serve to indicate the pitch, stress, and juncture patterns which we apply to the time sequences of sounds that we use. Certain marks, such as the asterisk or the ellipsis periods, have acquired specialized meanings for the users of English. Other marks, such as the slant bars used by linguists to indicate phonemic transcription, convey no meaning to the general reader of English until their symbolism is explained.

Some early pictographic writing may well have been quite independent of the sounds of speech. Even today, numerals such as 2, 3, 4, 5, 6 are ideational representations for us—that is, we

---

[1] This definition would include painting as a type of writing, but it would not exclude the possibility of writing upon surfaces that have been previously marked in one manner or another.

can interpret them whether or not we chance to know the oral or the visual alphabetic symbols for such numbers in the particular language in which they appear. In like manner, many people use the abbreviation *e.g.* to represent "for example" without realizing that these letters are taken from the Latin words *exempli gratia*. The omission of the intermediate step in no way interferes with the symbolism, though it sometimes makes the learning of the symbol more difficult because the learner sees no relationship between the symbolic letters and the written or oral English words they represent.

For alphabetic writing, we should have one graphic symbol to represent each sound used in the language and only that sound, but this ideal is never achieved. To illustrate how far written English is from this ideal, let us examine some of the possible spellings we have for particular sounds and some of the possible sounds that a particular combination of letters may be used to represent. Consider the sound which appears at the beginning of the word *shoe*. This sound is also found initially in the words *pshaw, sugar,* and *schist,* and it appears medially in the words *conscience, machine, mansion, mention, mission, nauseous, ocean, special,* and *tissue.* Many of these words furnish examples of spelling conventions which have been borrowed from other languages rather than examples of attempts to represent the sounds used in pronouncing the words in English. *Pshaw* would be pronounced the same without the *p,* and many speakers use a pronunciation other than the one indicated here for some of these words—particularly *nauseous.* But it is undeniable that we rhyme *ocean* with *notion, mention* with *pension,* and so on, so we must admit that multiple spellings exist for the sound. Now let us consider the sounds represented by the combination of letters in the following words: *cough, hiccough, plough, though, through, tough.* In each word the sound appears in final position, and in each word we give it a different pronunciation. The *ough* spelling also appears medially in words such as *thought, fought,* and initially in *ought,* but here we can consider the *gh* as silent—that is, no sound appears between the vowel sound and the sound represented by the *t* in these words. On the same basis, the *gh* might be considered silent in *plough, though,* and *through,* for no sound appears after the vowel or diphthong sounds in these words. *Tough, cough,* and *hiccough* do end in consonant sounds. These examples should make it clear that if we are to discuss the oral language, we will need

to find some better means than spelling for indicating the sounds
we have in mind. We will need an·alphabet in which each symbol
represents one recognizable sound and only that sound.

If we begin to think carefully about an alphabet which would
have one symbol for *each possible variation* in sound, we find that
while this might be ideal, it is also impractical. A soprano might
make the sound of the letter *a* in *father* at the high *C* level and a
basso profundo might make it at the low *B*-flat level. These two
sounds would certainly differ in timbre as well as in pitch, and
they might or might not differ greatly in volume or loudness; yet,
despite these differences, there would be enough similarity in them
to allow us to recognize them as variants of the same sound. We
can therefore use a single symbol to represent all these possible
variations. For our practical alphabet, we will need symbols only
for those sounds which may be used to distinguish one word from
another in English. In the words *cap, map, nap, rap*, we find that
it is the initial sounds which distinguish one word from another.
In *ran, ram, rap, rat*, the final sounds are the distinguishing ones;
and in *bat, bit, bought*, it is the medial sound which distinguishes
one word from another. When we analyze words or syllables in
this way, we find that there are many variations in sound, quite
noticeable in themselves, which can be grouped together. When we
pronounce a word beginning with the /p/ sound, we normally
make this sound by opening the lips; quite naturally, this is followed by a slight explosion or blowing out of air before the next
sound is made. This we call an aspirated /p/. In some languages
aspiration is a feature used to distinguish one word from another;
in English it is not, so for our purposes a single symbol will serve
to represent both an aspirated and an unaspirated /p/. So, too,
the /m/ sound that begins the word *map* differs from that which
ends the word *ham*, and the /l/ sound we find at the beginning of
little is quite different from the /l/ sound we use at the end of this
word. But the /m/ and /l/ sounds found at the end of these words
are never used at the beginning of an English word, and those
used at the beginning are never found at the end. When our use
of sounds is so distributed, it is obvious that the distinctions between them cannot be used to distinguish one word from another.
Instead, they tend to complement one another, and hence constitute what we call a *complementary distribution*. Similar sounds
in complementary distribution may be represented by a single sym-

bol in our alphabet. A clearer example of complementary distribution can be found in our use of certain personal pronoun forms in standard English. We use forms such as *I, he, she, they* in subject position in our sentences, and the forms *me, him, her, them* in object position. If someone uses one of these forms in the wrong position, we consider this to be a substandard usage.

At times we may vary our pronunciation of a particular word or syllable. For example, we may pronounce the vowel sound in the final syllable of the word *wanted* sometimes with the vowel sound found in the word *bid* and sometimes with that found in the word *bud*. This we term *free variation*. For such sounds, even though they may be used interchangeably in certain words, we must have separate symbols, since quite obviously they provide the distinguishing feature of other words.

Before providing the alphabet that we will use, it may be well to distinguish clearly between the concepts of the phone, the allophone, and the phoneme. We can define the *phone* as the smallest unit of sound used in speech that we can distinguish as being different from all other sound units. If we were to listen carefully to any individual make the sound represented by *t* in *teen, tin, tan, tall, toll, tool*, we could perceive minute differences in these sounds which would be the result of the variation in phonetic environment provided by the different vowels that follow the sounds represented by *t*. We could recognize another group of very similar sounds which would appear in postvocalic position in such words as *beat, bit, bet, bat*, and still another group following an *s* sound in prevocalic position in such words as *steep, step, stop*.

Each of these groups of phones would make up an allophone of the *t* phoneme. The member phones of each allophone would not be freely substitutable for those of the other allophones—that is, they would be in complementary distribution. The *allophone* then could be said to consist of a group of phones that have phonetic similarity, but not phonetic identity. The actual differences in phones that make up a particular allophone are so slight that it would take an extremely highly trained ear to distinguish one phone from another. Even when we are contrasting a phone from one allophone with one from another, most beginning students will have difficulty in hearing a distinction. Yet, the initial /p/ in *pop* is made by opening the lips, whereas the final /p/ is made by closing them. This results in the production of slightly different sounds. But these sounds are not *significantly* different; in listening to a speaker, we pay no attention to their differences—that is, their differences are never the sole means used to distinguish one syllable from another or one word from another.

All of the phones found in the *t* allophones would make up the /t/ phoneme. The *phoneme* therefore consists of a group of phonetically similar phones that are *significantly* different from all the other phones that are members of any other phoneme that is used in the dialect. Actually, what we hear are the phones; what we pay attention to are the phonemes. If we were to listen very carefully to a number of different people say the word *bet,* we might be able to hear an equal number of slightly different pronunciations of the vowel sound in that word, none of which would be different enough to cause us to recognize this as some word other than *bet.* These different sounds would be the phones that would make up the /e/ phoneme for us.

Perhaps we can further clarify this by an analogy to color. The Optical Society of America in its book *The Science of Color* estimates that there are seven and one-half million noticeable differences in color.[2] Maerz and Paul, in *A Dictionary of Color,* provide fewer than four thousand names for these distinctions.[3] Most of us commonly use one to two dozen words to designate colors. There are many different shades that we would designate as red or blue or green. Similarly, there are many different phones that we would recognize as belonging to the /e/ or /a/ or /u/ phonemes. There are limits of tolerance for our pronunciation of the vowel sound in *bet* that enable us to distinguish it from the vowel sounds in other words such as *bit, bat,* and *but.* The vowel sounds we use in these words contrast with those we use in *bet,* and they therefore constitute different phonemes. The phone groups that make up a particular phoneme are called *allophones* of that phoneme. Thus, from our analysis above, we would say that the /t/ phoneme consisted of at least three allophones: the initial /t/, the final /t/, and a medial /t/ found between voiceless consonants and vowels. There are other variants of /t/ which we might dis-

---

[2] As stated in Roger Brown, *Words and Things* (New York: The Free Press of Glencoe, Inc., 1958), p. 211.

[3] A. Maerz and M. R. Paul, *A Dictionary of Color* (New York: McGraw-Hill Book Company, Inc., 1930).

cover, and as soon as any one of these was identified, it would also have to be classified among the allophones of the /t/ phoneme. A common method of identifying English phonemes is that of finding minimal pairs of words in which the sound elements are distributed in the same manner and in which there is but one pair of sounds in parallel position that differs significantly. This is the method followed above in our *bet, bit, bat, but, bought* group of words. This can be used as a means of establishing most of the phonemes used in any English dialect, but we do have a few phonemes for which there are apparently no such word pairs.

In this book the alphabet presented will be satisfactory for representing the sounds found in the speech of Midwesterners in the United States. Your instructor may find it necessary or convenient to introduce additional symbols to represent the sounds used by speakers from other areas or even some occasional idiolect difference present in the speech of a Midwestern student. If so, he will add such symbols to our basic list and identify the sounds represented by them.

We shall use an arbitrary division of the phonemic alphabet that has been made on the basis of those symbols which are already familiar to you and those which will probably be new to you. You should note, however, that although letters of the alphabet constitute the familiar symbols, in some instances these letters are used to represent sounds different from those you may normally associate with them.

FAMILIAR SYMBOLS

Consonants	Key Words	Semivowels	Key Words
/p/	pet, tip	/h/	hot, ear /ihr/ *
/b/	bet, tub	/r/	red, bar
/t/	tip, pet	/w/	wart, boat /bowt/ *
/d/	dip, pad	/y/	you, I /ay/
/k/	can, back		
/g/	go, bog	* For some speakers. Others would	
/f/	fun, cough	use the simple vowels in these words.	
/v/	very, Stephen	See Vowels.	
/s/	sit, kiss		
/z/	zero, dogs		
/m/	mother, ham	Vowels	Key Words
/n/	not, can	/i/	bit, Sydney, ear
/l/	let, call	/e/	bet, meadow
		/a/	father, bother
		/u/	put, book
		/o/	note, boat

Unfamiliar Symbols

Consonants	Key Words	Vowels	Key Words
/š/	shoot, ratio	/æ/	pat, back
/ž/	measure	/i/	just (adverb)
/č/	chew, catch	/ə/	putt, Cuba
/ǰ/	judge	/ɔ/	saw, bought
/θ/	thin, ether		
/ð/	then, either		
/ŋ/	sing, sink		
/hw/	when, whether		

We commonly combine a vowel sound with a semivowel sound with such rapidity that the result impresses us as being practically a single sound. These combinations we call *diphthongs*. The distinction between the simple vowel and the diphthong is often phonemic. Consider, for example, the following pairs of words: plot /plat/, plight /playt/; ha /ha/, how /haw/; saw /sɔ/, soy /sɔy/. Other diphthongs, /ih/ and /ow/ for example, are sometimes used in free variation with their initial vowel. That is, the distinction between /i/ and /ih/ or that between /o/ and /ow/ is not a phonemic one for most speakers. The six diphthongs provided below constitute a minimal list of diphthongs commonly found in Midwestern speech.

Common Midwestern Diphthongs

/ay/ bite   /ɔy/ boy
/ey/ bait   /aw/ bout
/iy/ beat   /uw/ boot

Theoretically, each of the nine vowels may combine with each of the four semivowels to form a total of thirty-six diphthongs, but no individual speaker of English uses all these. As was noted earlier, some additional diphthongs will undoubtedly be needed to describe accurately the sounds used by speakers of other dialects or possibly even some sounds appearing in certain idiolects of Midwesterners in the class. When your instructor recognizes a need for particular ones, he will introduce them. Our purpose here is merely to establish a minimal alphabet with which we can conveniently work. This we can do with the twenty-five consonant symbols and the fifteen vowel and diphthong symbols that have been provided. We could cut the list even more and eliminate such symbols as /hw/ and the various symbols for diphthongs, all of

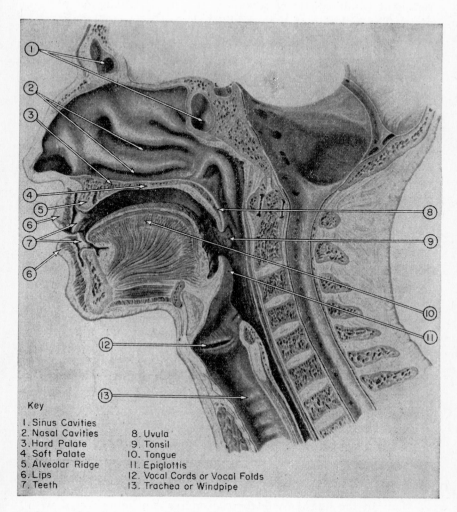

Key

1. Sinus Cavities
2. Nasal Cavities
3. Hard Palate
4. Soft Palate
5. Alveolar Ridge
6. Lips
7. Teeth

8. Uvula
9. Tonsil
10. Tongue
11. Epiglottis
12. Vocal Cords or Vocal Folds
13. Trachea or Windpipe

Median section of the face and neck. Right half of the head. Natural size. Reprinted with permission from G. Wolf-Heidegger, *Atlas of Systematic Human Anatomy* (New York: Hafner Publishing Company, Inc., 1962), Vol. II, Plate 5.

which are combinations of symbols already used, and all of which represent combinations of sounds which we have already recognized. The inclusion of these additional symbols as units is therefore merely a matter of convenience. Two other combinations of sounds and the symbols frequently used to represent them deserve some comment. There are in English a number of word pairs such as *ooze, yews; food, feud; booty, beauty;* which are distinguished one from the other by the absence or presence of /y/ before the diphthong /uw/. In the International Phonetic Alphabet and in many phonemic alphabets, this sound group is treated as a unit, and it may be so treated here if your instructor desires. The second combination is that consisting of certain vowel phones plus /r/, particularly when they appear in unaccented syllables (*medlar, lawyer, fakir, doctor, martyr*) or in monosyllables (*her, fur*). In some alphabets, the IPA symbol [ɚ] is used as a phonemic symbol /ɚ/ to represent this sound group.

The exercises throughout this book are based upon the assumption that, as a native speaker of English, you have been using your language with at least moderate success for many years. Their purpose is therefore not so much to teach you *how* to use your language as to help you discover how you actually *do* use it.

Do not rely upon the notions and rules that you may have acquired and memorized earlier in your academic career. If you try to use them as substitutes for thought and observation, you may experience considerable difficulty with these exercises. If, instead, you approach the exercises with care and with an open mind, you will find them not only easy to do, but also interesting in terms of what they will teach you about your language.

You will undoubtedly find some questions which are difficult to answer categorically. They have been posed deliberately in order to stimulate classroom discussion. When you come across such a question, note it carefully and raise the point in class.

Many of the questions in these exercises can be answered with a single word, such as *yes, no, eleven,* and so on. To arrive at such answers is but the first step in understanding the operation of your language. To get real value from each exercise, you should write a short paragraph in which you synthesize and summarize your findings. The following paragraph might serve as a summary of the discoveries you should make in working Exercise 2-1. Use it as a model for summaries of the other exercises. Note that it is not 100 per cent complete and correct—for example, we use a *pt* spelling in *ptomaine*, a *dh* spelling in *dhow*, and so on. Can we legitimately say that spellings such as *pt* actually represent the sound /t/, or would it be better to add a sentence to the summary saying that in many of these spellings, certain letters represent no sound at all?

Summary of Exercise 2-1

We make use of six consonant stops /p, b, t, d, k, g/ in modern English. Three of these /b, d, g/ are voiced, and three /p, t, k/ are unvoiced. In two /p, b/ the stoppage occurs at the lips; in two others /t, d/ it occurs when we place the point of the tongue against the teeth ridge; in the final two /k, g/ it occurs when we place the back of the tongue against the velum. Stops are used at the beginning, in the middle, and at the end of syllables and words. Two different spellings are used to represent the /p/ and /b/ sounds (ca*p*, ca*pp*ed) (ro*b*, ro*bb*ed), three to represent the /d/ sound (ba*d*, la*dd*er, darn*ed*), five each to represent the /t/ and /g/ sounds (ca*t*, *th*yme, ba*tt*er, tal*k*ed, cau*ght*) (do*g*, e*gg*, *gh*oul, *g*uarantee, catalo*gue*), and the /k/ sound may be spelled in ten different ways (*c*ow, a*cc*use, ba*cch*ante, *ch*aotic, ba*ck*, a*cq*uire, sa*cq*ue, bis*c*uit, *k*ing, li*q*uor).

Exercise 2-1   Consonant Sounds

1. How many different ways do we have in English of spelling the sound used at the beginning of the word *boot*? May it be spelled any differently when it is used medially or finally? When it is spelled with two *b*'s, are both of them pronounced? Always? Never? Consider *robbed, robbing, robbery.*

2. How many different ways do we have of spelling the sound used at the beginning of the word *pal*? How do we distinguish the sound normally represented by *b* from that normally represented by *p* when we hear it? Try pressing your fingers to your ears as you make these sounds. What do you discover?

3. How many different ways do we have of spelling the sound used at the beginning of the word *talk*?

4. How many different ways do we have of spelling the sound used at the beginning of the word *dog*? How do we distinguish the /t/ sound from the /d/ sound when we hear it? Does the same relationship exist between these two sounds as you found between

the /b/ and /p/ sounds? If you were putting them in pairs, which sounds would you place together?

5. How many ways do we have of spelling the sound used at the beginning of the word *cat?* How many ways do we have of spelling the sound used at the beginning of the word *girl?*

6. As you have probably noticed, these six sounds have already been grouped into three pairs for you. What parts of the mouth do you use in making the /p, b/ sounds? What parts of the mouth do you use in making the /t, d/ sounds? Try to describe how you make the /k, g/ sounds. Put your finger in your mouth as you make the /k, g/ sounds. Does the tongue touch any other part of the mouth? If so, where does the contact take place?

7. For how long can you continue the sound normally represented by the letter *m?* For how long can you continue the /p, b, t, d, k, g/ sounds? The term *stops* is used for these sounds; can you understand why? What is stopped? Is it stopped at the same place in making each of these sounds? Which are labial or lip stops? Which are alveolar or teeth-ridge stops? Consult the diagram of the mouth provided on p. 17. What kind of stops are the others?

8. Put your fingers on your Adam's apple as you make each of these six sounds. Do the vocal cords in your throat seem to vibrate more pronouncedly in making some than in making others? Which of the six sounds seem to be most heavily voiced? Which seem to be lightly voiced or unvoiced? Can any of these six sounds be made in isolation, or do you always make some vowel sound with them?

Exercise 2-2   Consonant Sounds

1. How many different ways do we have in English of spelling the sound used at the beginning of the word *son?* Is this the same sound that we find at the beginning of the word *cease?* Does this explain why the /k/ symbol was used to represent the sound found at the beginning of *cat?* Is the letter *c* used to represent any sounds in addition to the /k/ and /s/ sounds?

2. How many different ways do we have in English of spelling the sound used at the beginning of the word *zebra?* What sound appears at the end of the word *does?*

3. How many different ways do we have in English of spelling the sound used at the beginning of the word *shake?* Is this the

same sound we have in *son?* Is there any one-letter spelling for this sound?

4. How many different ways do we have of spelling the medial sound represented by the *s* in *pleasure?* Is this sound used at the beginning of any English words? Is it used as the final sound of any English words?

5. How many different ways do we have of spelling the sound used at the beginning of the word *chew?* Is there any one-letter spelling for this sound? Does the sound also appear medially and finally in English words?

6. How many different ways do we have of spelling the sound used at the beginning of the word *judge?* What sound is used at the end of this word? How is it spelled there?

7. Can these sounds be grouped on the basis of being voiceless or voiced as the stops could? Which would you place in each group? How do these sounds differ from the stop sounds we studied in Exercise 2-1?

8. Can two or more stop sounds appear next to one another in an English word? What sounds appear after the vowel sounds in *backed* and *bagged?* Can two or more of the sounds we have studied in this exercise, questions 1-6, appear in contiguity in an English word? Are there any large classes of English words that are affected by this problem of connecting sounds to one another?

9. What parts of the mouth are used in producing each of the sounds identified in Exercise 2-2? How does our method of making /t/ and /d/ differ from our method of making /s/ and /z/? Do /t/ and /d/ appear to be related to any of the other sounds of Exerise 2-2?

10. The term *fricative* is applied to the /s, z, š, ž/ sounds and the term *affricate* to the /č, ǰ/ sounds. Look up these words in your dictionary. Are they in any manner descriptive of the way these sounds are made? In what way do the affricates combine the characteristics of stops and fricatives?

Exercise 2-3   Consonant and Semivowel Sounds

1. How many different ways do we have in English of spelling the sound used at the beginning of the word *five?*

2. How many different ways do we have of spelling the sound used at the beginning of the word *very?*

3. How many ways do we have of spelling the sound used at the beginning of the word *thin?* Is this the same sound that we use to begin the word *then?* If not, how do they differ?

4. How many ways do we have of spelling the sound used at the beginning of the word *hat?*

5. How many ways do we have of spelling the sound used at the beginning of the word *wall?*

6. When we say the word *when,* do we begin with the sound mentioned in question 4 or that mentioned in question 5? Is the sound at the beginning of *when* a single sound or a combination of sounds? Are there any other spellings for it?

7. Do the sounds considered in questions 1, 2, and 3 above belong in the class of stops, fricatives, or affricates? Could any other sound noted in this exercise be classed with them? Does the sound of the beginning of *wall* belong with any of these groups?

8. Can any of the sounds we have studied so far stand alone as complete syllables? (Do not confuse the name of the letter or symbol with the sound expressed by it.) Which of the sounds in this exercise fit into the voiceless-voiced pattern?

9. Do we use our lips in making any sounds other than /p/ or /b/? What differences do you observe in your manner of making the /p/ and /f/ sounds? Do the same differences appear in making the /b/ and /v/ sounds?

10. What parts of our vocal apparatus do we use in making the initial sounds of *thin* and *then?* Do we use one sound or two at the beginning of each of these words?

11. Do we make use of the lips in making the /š, ž/ sounds? What part of the tongue do we use? What differences can you observe in your method of making these sounds and the method you use in making the initial sounds of *thin* and *then?* Compare these with your method of making the /s, z/ sounds. What parts of your mouth do you use in making these?

Exercise 2-4   Consonant and Semivowel Sounds

1. How many different ways do we have in English of spelling the sound used at the beginning of the word *me?* Is this sound identical with the final sound in *ham?* Can we use one symbol to represent both?

2. How many ways do we have of spelling the initial sound of the word *no?* Is this sound identical with the final sound in *sin?* Is it identical with the sound that appears before /k/ in *sink?*

3. How many ways do we have of spelling the final sound in the word *sing?* Do we ever use this sound at the beginning of words in English? What characteristics do these three sounds seem to have in common? Is the nasal passage open or closed when you make them?

4. Is the sound at the beginning of the word *little* identical with the sound that appears at the end of it? If not, how do these two sounds differ from one another? What happens to your lower jaw as you pronounce *little?*

5. Is the sound at the beginning of the word *rather* identical with the sound at the end of the word? If not, how do these sounds differ? What occurs in your mouth as you make each of these sounds?

6. Pronounce the words *leak, lit, lake, let, lack, lock, laud.* Does the initial sound differ in your pronunciation of these words? Try the words *keel, knell, knoll, call.* Does your pronunciation of the final sound of these words differ? What occurs in your pronunciation of the medial /l/ sound of *lily, Kelly, dolly, appalling?* Do you pronounce these words with one /l/ or two, or do you use one /l/ in the pronunciation of some and two in the pronunciation of others? If you use two, do you repeat the same /l/ sound or do you use different sounds? Are any of these /l/ sounds identical with the /l/ in *play, alms, wilt?* Do you pronounce the *l* in *talk* and *calm?*

7. Do you use the same initial sound in pronouncing *read, rid, raid, red, rat, rot, wrought, wrote, rut, rule?* Do you use the same final sound in *fear, far, for?* Is this the same final sound that you use in *medlar, lawyer, fakir, doctor, saviour?* Do you use the same sound at the end of all five words in this last list? Do you use one or two medial /r/ sounds when you pronounce such words as *horror* and *barrier?* Compare your pronunciation of *barring* and *bar ring.* What differences do you note?

8. Is the sound at the beginning of the word *young* identical with the sound at the end of the word *gory?* Would you class these as two variants of the same sound or as two different sounds? Are the differences you note here of the same type as those you noted in listening to your pronunciation of /l/ and /r/ sounds? In the sen-

tence, "Put the yoke on the yellow yak," do you pronounce the initial sounds of *yoke, yellow,* and *yak* differently? Compare this sound or sounds with the sounds we find in *canyon* and *onion.*

9. Is there more than one way to pronounce the sound represented by the letter *y* at the end of a word? Does this sound ever appear medially? Is the pronunciation of it affected in any way by the sounds that appear before or after it? Is it affected by the sounds that appear after it in other words? Consider *carry on, carry it, carry alcohol.*

10. Recognizable variants of the same sound make up the phoneme. List the phonemes we have studied in this exercise. In doing this, remember that we are dealing with sound—not spelling.

Exercise 2-5   Consonant Sounds

1. In Exercises 2-1, 2, and 3, some study was made of each of the following sounds: /p, b, t, d, k, g, s, z, š, ž, č, ǰ, f, v, θ, ð, h, w, hw/. Provide one or more words to illustrate the use of each of these sounds. Underline the spelling which represents the sound in each word. Are all of these sounds invariably used as consonants? If not, illustrate the vowel or semivowel use of those which are not.

2. In Exercise 2-4, the following sounds were introduced: /m, n, ŋ, l, r, y, i/. Are all of these sounds consonants? Determine whether each of these new sounds is voiced or voiceless. Can a voiced sound be pronounced without voicing? Whisper the following sentence and then say it aloud, holding your ears shut for both: "Just tell him what you think he can do." What do you discover about the sounds that are normally voiced? Can you voice the /t/ in pronouncing the word *time?* Which would be a more accurate description—to say that a sound is voiced or voiceless, or to say that it is normally voiced or voiceless?

3. Which of the sounds we have studied would you classify as stops? Which would you classify as fricatives? As affricates? As nasals? Which are left unclassified? Do the /h, r, w, y/ sounds have anything in common? Should /hw/ be included here? Try pronouncing pairs of words such as *we, whee; wear, where; ye, yacht; read, rod.* Can you understand why the term *glide* is used to describe these sounds? Is /h/ a glide? Why or why not?

4. Can you feel the air pass over your tongue as you make the /l/ sound? Does it pass over the top of the tongue or along one or both

sides? Is this true of all types of /l/ sounds? Does this explain why the term *lateral* is applied to the /l/ sounds? What happens in the front of your mouth when you make an initial /l/? Would you call this a lateral?

5. Can any of the sounds we have studied so far stand as complete syllables in English speech? If so, provide examples in which they do so.

6. Does the /h/ sound ever appear before or after consonant sounds other than /w/? Is there any other place in which the presence (or absence) of a /h/ sound before or after a consonant sound distinguishes one word from another in English? Is the letter *h* always pronounced before vowel sounds? Try to develop a generalization that will describe when we do pronounce it and when we do not.

7. Is the /i/ in *carry* a vowel sound or a consonant sound? Do we always pronounce it in the same way? Could it sometimes be pronounced to rhyme with the *e* in *me* and at others with the *i* in *hit*? How do you say it in the sentence, "Carry it home"? Can you use equal variation in pronouncing the words *beat* and *bit*? Does it appear possible that two sounds might be allophones of the same phoneme in some situations and phonemically distinctive sounds in others? Do you normally use either the /iy/ or the /i/ sounds for this final *y* spelling, or is the sound you use actually different from both of them?

Exercise 2-6   Consonant Clusters

The consonant sounds we have just been studying are frequently combined in forming English words. For example, note the combinations that appear at the beginning of the following words: *prim, brim, trim, dream, cream, grim, free, Vreeland, throne, shrank.*

1. Can /r/ be combined with any other consonants at the beginning of English words? Can it appear before as well as after the other sounds? Provide examples.

2. With what consonant sounds can /l/ be combined at the beginning of words? Can it appear before as well as after the other sounds?

3. With what consonant sounds can /w/ be combined at the beginning of words? Can it appear before as well as after these sounds? Provide examples. What sounds are commonly represented

by the spelling *qu* in English? Do we have the same sound or sounds in *quay* as we have in *queer?*

4. Can the /y/ sound be combined with other consonants at the beginning of words?

5. What consonant sounds may appear after the /s/ at the beginning of words? Do we have any clusters of three consonant sounds in words beginning with /s/? Provide examples.

6. How are the words *rhetoric, ptomaine, pneumonia, psychology, gnu,* and *mnemonic* pronounced? What does the spelling of these words suggest about the way they were once pronounced? Are these words native English words, or have they been borrowed from other languages? Consult your dictionary.

7. We also use consonant clusters at the end of words and syllables—in fact, we use many different combinations in that position. Some of these are combinations of two, three, and four consonants.

Examples: voiceless + voiceless	cats
voiced + voiced	dogs
voiced + voiceless	spelt
voiceless + voiceless +voiceless	rafts
voiced + voiceless + voiceless	sinks
voiceless + voiceless + voiceless + voiceless	sixths

Do we actually pronounce all four consonants at the end of such words as *sixths* and *glimpsed?*

8. Identify the consonant clusters found at the end of each of the following words and classify them according to the patterns suggested in question 7. Are there any that show patterns differing from these?

capped	glimpsed	bagged	help	bulbs
caps	churched	elf's	selves	elms
six	absorbed	clothed	gloved	gasped
cats	minced	chasms	lengths	cant
drenched	starves	orb	serfs	warned
backed	milked	ringed	rouged	work
robbed	mixed	rhythm	bergs	berthed
width	mulched	carl	lofts	barn
brads	purse	lunged	prince	burnt
judged	serf	cans	harsh	pitched

9. Add twenty-five other clusters of consonants that appear at the end of words and syllables to those provided in question 8.

SECTION 3

The Sounds
of Modern English
—Vowels
and Diphthongs

When a pianist strikes the *A* above middle *C* on a well-tuned piano he creates a tone which, if it were pure, would have 440 vibrations per second. If he strikes *B*-flat, the tone above it, the number of vibrations will be greater. A trombonist can produce a comparable tone on his instrument—that is, one that would also have 440 vibrations per second if it were pure—but he can also produce tones that would be the equivalent of neither *A* nor *B*-flat, but rather of something between those two tones. Normally we make no use of these tones in Western music, though of course the trombonist passes through their range in sliding from one tone to another.

As you make the sound represented by the letter *i* in the word *bit*, you will find that your lower jaw is raised so that your teeth are rather close together. If you try to continue or hold this sound and at the same time lower the position of your jaw as far as you can, you will generally find that after passing through various other sounds you will end with a sound similar to the sound represented by the letter *a* in *cat*. This transition is not a matter of jaw position alone. If you observe closely, you will find that you have also changed the shape of your tongue and the tenseness of your throat muscles.

Just as the trombonist can arrest his slide at a point between two

musical half tones, we could stop at various points on our scale between the *i* in *bit* and the *a* in *cat*, but most of us will make use of
three clearly distinguishable points on this scale of sounds: the *i* in
bit, the *e* in *bet*, and the *a* in *bat*. These sounds are commonly made
in the front of the mouth. Most of us will use at least two of the
three to initiate diphthongs. For example, we will make the *e* in *me*
by starting with the jaw nearly as high as it can go, and follow this
by lowering it very slightly and then raising it again. In the process
we glide from one of the sounds of the /i/ phoneme to one of the
sounds in the /y/ phoneme. This is the diphthong /iy/, the sound
most of us use in *me*. A similar phenomenon occurs when we make
the initial sounds of *ate*. We begin here with one of the sounds of
the /e/ phoneme and glide into one of the sounds of the /y/ phoneme. A simple method of checking this is to pronounce these
sounds as you hold your hand under your chin. You can generally
feel the movement of the jaw.

In working with the exercises in this section, it will be particularly important to take into consideration the entire spelling of
words. Note, for example, the difference between the spellings and
pronunciations of *mat* and *mate*. Here the difference appears to be
the presence of the so-called "silent *e*." In the pronunciations of
dove (noun), *dove* (verb), and *move*, we cannot possibly attribute
the differences in pronunciation to this *e*. In some cases, you will
only be able to say that a particular combination of letters is pronounced one way in a certain word and another way in other words
—for example, *say, said;* but *pay, paid; lay, laid.* If you wish to see
this clearly, make a large chart; on one axis list the sounds and on
the other list the different spellings you find for them. Words illustrating each spelling of each sound should be placed at the proper
points of coordination.

All the symbols that you will need have already been supplied
on pages 15-16, but you will have to combine some of these to represent some of the sounds we will be studying here. You will have
to combine two for diphthongs and, in some words, three for triphthongs.

Exercise 3-1   Vowel and Diphthong Sounds

1. How many different ways do we have of spelling the /i/
sound? Provide examples. Do you sometimes use this sound in

pronouncing the words *fountain* or *foreign?* If so, does it appear in the accented or in the unaccented syllable?

2. How many different ways do we have of spelling the /e/ sound? Provide examples. Does this commonly appear in lightly stressed syllables?

3. How many ways do we have of spelling /æ/? Provide examples. Do you use this sound in words like *an* or *and* when you speak rapidly? Try "I want an apple," or "Try and stop me."

4. How many ways do we have of spelling /iy/? How many of these appear only in words taken directly from some other language? Does the *i before e* spelling rule work in all cases? Provide examples.

5. How many ways do we have of spelling /ey/? Provide examples.

6. Do you pronounce the final sound of the word *happy* in an identical manner in the two phrases *happy hours* and *happy evenings?* Is this the /i/?

7. What vowels do you use in pronouncing the words *marry, merry, Mary?*

8. Do we ever use voiceless vowels? What happens when you whisper? Do you vocalize vowel sounds in whispers as you do in speech?

9. Write the following sentences in transcription—that is, use the symbols for the sounds rather than the conventional spellings for the words:

a. Peter bet six cents.
b. Place him in Elsie's seat.
c. His rate is fast.
d. We will see him at this rink.
e. Which mat is green?

Exercise 3-2   Vowel and Diphthong Sounds

1. Make the sound /i/; then make the sound represented by the double *o* spelling in boot. What difference do you notice in the shape of your lips? What differences do you find in the shape of your tongue? Is this sound combination which we represent by the double *oo* in *boot* made in the front or in the back of the mouth? Is it a simple vowel or a diphthong? Do you round your lips in making any other vowel sounds? If so, what are they?

2. How many ways do we have of spelling the /uw/ sound in English? Note carefully that the sounds in *food* and *feud* are different. Do we have a diphthong or a triphthong in the latter word? What sound follows the /f/?

3. How many ways do we have of spelling the /u/ sound in English? Do any of these spellings overlap those used to represent /uw/?

4. How many ways do we have of spelling the vowel sound in *note?* Do you use a simple vowel or a diphthong in making this sound? Does your vowel differ from the form you use before a voiceless consonant when it is followed by a voiced consonant?

5. How many ways do we have of spelling /ɔ/ in English?

6. How many ways do we have of spelling the /a/? Provide examples of each spelling for each of the sounds of this exercise.

7. When we speak in terms of spelling, we say there are five vowels in English: *a, e, i, o, u.* How many oral vowels and vowel combinations have we already distinguished? Does a diphthong constitute a phoneme? Is the *io* in the word *radio* a diphthong? If not, why not?

8. When sounds from the /h, r, w, y/ phonemes appear after vowels, should they be considered as consonants or as parts of diphthongs?

9. Should the final /l/ in *little* be considered a vowel or a consonant?

10. Sometimes the /m/ and /n/ phonemes appear as full syllables in rapid speech. In such instances, should we consider them as vowels or consonants? In the first sentence in this question, it would be better to speak of *sounds from* the /m/ and /n/ phonemes. Why?

11. Are there any other consonants that may appear as full syllables in English? Provide examples. Is it true that every English syllable contains a vowel?

12. Try to write satisfactory definitions for the terms *vowel, consonant,* and *syllable.*

Exercise 3-3   Vowel and Diphthong Sounds

1. How many ways do we have in English of spelling the sound /ə/? Do we ever use this sound in pronouncing the words *a* and *the?* When you pronounce the word *to* in normal speech, do you do

so with a sound from the /ə/ phoneme? From what other vowel phonemes do you frequently hear phones in unaccented syllables?

2. In what part of the mouth is the /ə/ formed?

3. What vowel sound is used before the /r/ in each of the following words? *murder, doctor, fakir, medlar, saviour.*

4. Does the /ə/ commonly appear in accented syllables? Provide examples.

5. Write the following sentences in transcription. In doing so, try to divorce the sounds from the spelling and record them as you would normally say them.

    a. We heard the bell ringing.
    b. Don't forget to get the dishmop.
    c. It was a pleasure to meet him.
    d. She should remember the date.
    e. We can't recall when we last saw her.
    f. What vegetables did your mother can?
    g. It was customary to call on the ambassador.
    h. The mission was easily accomplished.
    i. The cemetery was deserted.
    j. We were studying English word structure.

6. How many /ə/ symbols did you use in transcribing the above sentences? Was any other single symbol used as frequently as this?

Exercise 3-4   Vowel and Diphthong Sounds

1. Identify the sounds used in making the diphthongs which appear in each of the following words: *high, play, boy, bough.*

2. Which of the two words, *booty* and *beauty,* contains a diphthong? Do you have a simple vowel or a triphthong in the other?

3. Do we use diphthongs in pronouncing *pa, saw,* and *blow?* If so, of what sounds are they composed?

4. Are there other places in your speech in which you find you use diphthongs or triphthongs? If so, describe them. Pay particular attention to words that end in vowel sounds.

5. If we consider /r/ to be a semivowel, what do we have in words such as *fire* and *hour?* Compare the words *gnawer* and *nor.* What differences do you find?

6. Are the sounds of the phonemes /l, m, n/ and /ŋ/ in such words as *pile, rhyme, fine,* and *sing* as vowel-like as the /r/ in *fire* and *hour?* Reconsider your definitions of vowels and consonants.

7. Do we use any words in English that are made up exclusively of vowels? Do we use any that are made up entirely of consonants? Should we consider forms such as *I'm, I'll,* and *can't* as one word or two words? How do we use them in oral speech? Is this an adequate test?

8. Is the length of the vowel normally used to distinguish one word from another?

9. Write the following sentences in transcription.

a. I want you to buy some household equipment.
b. Do you believe that feuding is dead?
c. The Christmas play was well produced.
d. The boys like to play in the snow.
e. We are counting on you to build the fire.

Suggested Readings

SECTIONS 2 and 3

Bloch, Bernard, and George L. Trager, *Outline of Linguistic Analysis,* pp. 10-52. Baltimore, Md.: Linguistic Society of America, 1942.

Fries, Charles C., *Linguistics and Reading,* Chaps. V, VI, and VII. New York: Holt, Rinehart & Winston, Inc., 1962.

Trager, George L., and Henry Lee Smith, *An Outline of English Structure,* pp. 11-35. Washington, D.C.: American Council of Learned Societies, 1951.

Whorf, Benjamin Lee, *Language, Thought, and Reality: Selected Writings of Benjamin Lee Whorf,* ed. John C. Carroll, pp. 220-32. New York: Technology Press of Massachusetts Institute of Technology and John Wiley & Sons, Inc., 1956.

SECTION 4

Some Clues
to Meaning

Many people, when they think of grammar, think of certain expressions as being "correct" and of other expressions as being "incorrect." Or they may go back to some previous experience with grammar and think of it as a series of definitions for the parts of speech or some complicated line drawings called sentence diagramming. Grammar, as we will use the term, will impinge upon all of these areas, but, actually, it will be none of these things. Instead, we will try to make some analysis of our language in the hope that we will come to know how we understand one another when we use it. In other words, we will attempt to isolate and to describe those aspects of the language that provide meaning for us.

We frequently hear the question, "What does this word mean?" Such a question is rather silly, for most words have more than one meaning. For example, if I choose a column at random from my desk dictionary, I find the letter *h* used as a symbol or abbreviation for fourteen different words. Continuing down the column, I find four possible meanings for *ha*, two for *Habakkuk*, two for *haberdashery*, two for *haberdasher*, two for *habergeon*, two for *habile*, two for *habiliment*, two for *habilitate*, twelve for *habit*, two for *habitant*, two for *habitation*, three for *habitual*, and two for *habitu-*

33

ate. Of the twenty-five entries in the column, only six have one
meaning listed. Of these six, three are names of persons or places,
one is an abbreviation for such a name, and the others are *habeas
corpus* and *habitable.*

A little reflection will therefore show that any attempt to classify
words on the basis of meaning is likely to involve us in overlapping
classes. *Habitat* and *habitation* have one meaning in common—a
place of abode—but the second meanings differ widely from one
another. If we work with meaning alone, we will have to put the
same word in different classes. How complicated this might become
is easily illustrated. People *run* for offices; they *run* races; they *run*
ads in newspapers; they *run* bills at stores; they *run* blockades; they
run horses; they *run* risks; they *run* fences along their property;
they *run* rope through pulleys; they *run* second or third in a race;
they *run* metals together. In addition, their noses *run;* the colors in
their clothing sometimes *run;* streams *run;* fish *run;* machines *run;*
and shelves may *run* around the walls of a room. Even now, we have
hardly begun to explore the possible meanings of *run.* We can have
a *run* on the bank, a *run* in our hose, or a *run* of bad luck. We can
score a *run* in baseball or go fishing in a *run* in the meadow. If I
stop at this point, it is not because I have *run* out of examples. The
American College Dictionary lists one hundred and four possible
distinctions of meaning for the word. We must conclude, therefore,
that any attempt to classify words on the basis of their meanings
will be doomed to failure at the outset. Just as the individual sound
has no significance until it is placed in a pattern of other sounds, the
individual word can be said to have no precise meaning until it is
placed in a pattern of other words. This is true even of names: consider Abraham *Lincoln* and *Lincoln,* Nebraska. Yet the possible
meanings of a word are limited by tacit agreement of the group of
people who use it, and if anyone uses a particular word to express
a meaning other than those tacitly agreed upon, he runs the risk of
being misunderstood. In England, people have *ladders* instead of
runs in their hose, and British politicians *stand* instead of *run* for
election. The Englishman who uses the words *ladder* and *stand* for
these concepts may not be understood by Americans; the American
who uses *run* may not be understood by Britishers. In other words,
a word has only those meanings which the users of the word are
willing to accept for it.

The meaning we have been talking about is called *lexical* meaning. It consists of all the meanings the users of a language are willing to apply to a particular word. Now let us take a look at another type of meaning, which we will call *positional* meaning. If we take three words: *John, Mary,* and *hit,* we can place them in six different positional relationships: John hit Mary, Mary hit John, hit John Mary, hit Mary John, John Mary hit, Mary John hit. It should be noted that the form of each of the words remains constant; the only variation is in their position. But as soon as we hear or read the first two of these combinations, we know that the message is a statement or a question about the occurrence of an action. The respective positions also tell us which of the two is the doer of the action and which is the receiver of the action. The lexical meanings tell us that both the doer and the receiver are probably people, and that the action is of a particular type. The falling or rising intonational pattern at the end of the word group in speech (or the use of a period or a question mark in writing to indicate this variation in intonational patterning) will tell us whether we are to consider the word group as a statement or as a question.

If we look at the third and fourth combinations, we find that these may express a different kind of idea, but only if they are spoken with the proper intonational pattern or written with the proper conventions of capitalization and punctuation. Instead of being statements about the occurrence of an action, they may become commands for one person to do something to another (Hit Mary, John. Hit John, Mary). Again, the positional and intonational patterns not only tell us this, but they also identify which of the two persons is the doer and which is the receiver of the action.

As we shall learn later, intonational patterns are made up of varying combinations of stresses, pitches, and junctures. One might call them "the punctuation of oral speech." These patterns can make drastic changes in the meaning of sentences even when the word position within the sentence is invariable. A clear example of this may be found in the following sentences which are varied only by punctuation in writing and by intonational patterning in speech. "The teacher," said the superintendent, "is wrong." The teacher said, "The superintendent is wrong." In like manner, it would be possible to make commands of our original two declarative sentences by varying the intonational patterning in speech and the patterns of capitalization and punctuation in writing. (John, hit Mary. Mary, hit John.) We have therefore recognized a third clue to meaning—

a clue from intonational patterning in speech and from the nonverbal conventions of capitalization and punctuation in writing.
This we could call *intonational* or *conventional* meaning, but because the word conventional is likely to be misunderstood, we will
refer to such meaning as *intonational,* keeping in mind that by this
term we mean also the nonverbal conventions of writing which are
used to symbolize the verbal intonational patterning. We see also
from our examples that when a conflict exists between positional
and intonational meaning, the latter takes precedence over the
former. In most English sentences, the positional pattern and the
intonational pattern tend to reinforce one another; however, it is
possible to speak or write sentences which would express utter nonsense if word position alone were considered, but which do convey
meaning as soon as the proper intonational pattern is used. "John
where Mary had had had had had had had had had had been correct" is such a sentence. If we make use of certain conventions of
writing to indicate the proper intonational pattern, it can make
sense: "John, where Mary had had *had had,* had had *had; had had*
had been correct." Written punctuation at its best, however, is a
very inadequate means of indicating intonational patterning such as
we use in oral speech.

Ordinarily, the fifth and sixth positional patterns of our variations—*John Mary hit* and *Mary John hit*—would be considered to
be nonnormal English or meaningless patterns. But if we think of
these as being uttered in a particular situation, such as one in which
the first person named is a spectator at a baseball game in which
the second person named is a participant, we find another meaning
for them. The first word in this situational pattern identifies the
listener, the second identifies the doer, and the third, the action.
(John, Mary hit! Mary, John hit!) Thus we can recognize a fourth
clue to meaning which we might call *situational.* It should be noted,
however, that situational meaning also involves intonational changes
in speech and changes in the conventions of writing to represent
them. Seldom do we find a change in meaning indicated by a single
clue.

Up to this point, no change has been made in the forms of the
words used for our illustration. Now let us change some of the forms
slightly to see what the results will be. Instead of saying, "John hit
Mary," let us say, "John hits Mary," or "Johnny hit Mary." In such
sentences the position still indicates the statement about an oc-

currence, but the addition of the *s* to *hit* changes the meaning of the time of action and of the frequency of the action, and the addition of the *ny* to *John* leads us to assume that John is probably a child or a young man. Thus, differences in the forms of words are also capable of conveying differences in meaning to us. We will call this type of meaning *formal*.

There are still other clues to meaning in English. One of them is the function word. If we say, "John got hit," "John got to hit," and "John got a hit," we are expressing a different meaning in each sentence. The only changes made are the addition of *to* in the second sentence and *a* in the third, but these slight changes produce considerable differences in meaning. In the first sentence, something happened to John; in the second, John had an opportunity to do something; and in the third, John did do something. The addition of these little words has therefore contributed clues to meaning for us—a type of clue we will call *functional*, since these words are generally designated as being *function words*. Such words are often omitted from newspaper headlines, and sometimes the result is an ambiguous message, such as *Fire Burns Fast*, which could be either a simple statement of fact, a statement about a particular fire, or an order to discharge someone named Burns.

There are other clues to meaning which we will group under the general heading of *extensional* meanings. The one characteristic which these have in common is that we must recognize a meaning different from the literal meaning. In some instances we achieve this by substituting the part for the whole; in others we substitute one object or action commonly associated with another for the other. "He rode off on his *wheel*." (He rode off on his bicycle.) "She sets a good table." (She is a good cook.) In still others, some comparison is implied. "Her brother John is a rat." (John and the rat share certain unspecified characteristics or qualities.) "The machine gun barked from the hill." (The noise of the gun, like the barking of a dog, provided warning of its presence.) In still other situations, there may be no apparent relationship between the literal and the extensional meanings, though presumably there must have been some such relationship at one time, for if not, the expression would never have developed. An example of this is "Put that in your pipe and smoke it." (You must accept the situation whether you like it or not.)

Intonational patterns and situational contexts also contribute to extensional meanings. We would, for example, use different intonational patterns to express the literal and nonliteral meanings of "She is a good girl," and the sarcasm of the instructor's caustic "You're early today" might go unrecognized if the situation were not one in which the particular student addressed was habitually late to class.

Obviously we cannot discuss the different variants of these patterns or clues to meaning all at one time. We shall therefore deal with them one at a time, paying little or no attention to the presence or absence of others in the unit being discussed. We shall begin with some of the positional patterns, and try to observe at the same time the forms that words take in these patterns.

Suggested Readings

SECTION 4

De Saussure, Ferdinand, *Course in General Linguistics,* eds. Charles Bally and Albert Sechehaye, trans. Wade Baskin, pp. 134-39. New York: Philosophical Library, 1950.

Francis, W. Nelson, *The Structure of American English,* pp. 222-34. New York: The Ronald Press Company, 1954.

Fries, Charles C., *Linguistics and Reading,* Chap. III. New York: Holt, Rinehart & Winston, Inc., 1962.

———, *The Structure of English,* Chap. VII. New York: Harcourt, Brace & World, Inc., 1952.

Smith, Henry Lee, *Linguistic Science and the Teaching of English.* Cambridge, Mass.: Harvard University Press, 1956.

SECTION 5

Syntactic Functions,
Position Patterns,
and Normal Forms
of the Noun

Most of us who learn to recognize the various parts of speech and the various parts of the sentence do so in the same way that we learn to recognize various animals or objects—by hearing or seeing enough of each and having the name for each provided for us. Once we have identified one of these units, we can then begin to examine the forms it may take, the ways in which it may be used, and the environments in which we are likely to find it. That is what we shall be doing here.

The most easily recognizable syntactic function of the noun is that of being the subject of the sentence. In all but a few types of statements, the subject appears at the beginning of the sentence. We will consider the subject as any word or word group that can be fitted into the blanks left in the sentences provided below.[1] Actually, in these sentences the position of the subject does not vary from one sentence to another within each group. The examples are provided only that we may examine some of the different concepts which may be expressed by the subject, and thus squash at the beginning the notion so commonly held that the subject is invariably

---

[1] This method of identifying word classes and syntactic functions by their distribution or position was suggested in Leonard Bloomfield, *Language* (New York: Holt, Rinehart & Winston, Inc., 1933), Chap. XII, "Syntax," pp. 184-206. It is more completely developed in Zellig Harris, "From Morpheme to Utterance," *Language*, XXII (1946), 161-83. Dr. Charles C. Fries' use of this method in his book *The Structure of English* (New York: Harcourt, Brace & World, Inc., 1952) has so popularized it that these frames are now frequently referred to as the "Fries Frames."

the actor. Parentheses are used around *the* to indicate that this word, or a substitute for it, may or may not appear before the word used as the subject. In some sentences a word of this type is required, in others it cannot be used, and in still others the writer has the alternative of using it or not as he sees fit. In the latter case, his use or nonuse of it will indicate some difference in meaning. For example, we can say, "Mary is good," in which case we omit the word. If we want to say something about one boy being good, we will have to use such a word—"The boy is good." But we have our choice of saying "Cake is good," meaning cake in general, or of saying "This cake is good," meaning a particular cake.

Sentence Frame	*Concept Expressed by the Subject*
(The) _____ is good.	that which is described
(The) _____ is a mason.	that which is classified
(The) _____ is the man.	that which is identified
(The) _____ runs.	that which acts
(The) _____ has a book.	that which possesses
(The) _____ was built.	that which results from action
(The) _____ was given to him.	that undergoing action
(The) _____ was given a book.	that to or for which the action is undergone
(The) _____ was owned by him.	that which is possessed

In certain types of questions, the subject will appear after the verb.

Is (the) _____ pretty?
Has (the) _____ a book?
Who am _____?
Which are (the) _____?
What are (the) _____?

In other types of questions, the subject will appear after the first auxiliary verb.

Do (the) _____ think so?
When will (the) _____ come?
How can (the) _____ be recognized?

In still other types, the subject will appear before the verb.

What _____ did that?

There are a small number of words in English which, when placed at the beginning of a statement, require that the subject appear after the final verb. Exceptions to this requirement will be discussed later.

Rarely can (the) _____ go alone.
Hardly had (the) _____ appeared, when . . .
Seldom has (the) _____ been seen.
Scarcely were (the) _____ removed, when . . .
Nor can (the) _____ be said to be . . .

The function word *there* and the adverbs *there* and *here* may pre-empt the position of the subject in statements, and the function word may also do so in questions. It should be noted that as a function word, *there* does not express spatial location. When the function word is used, the subject will appear after the final verb word.

Will there be (a) _____?
There will be (a) _____ on the corner.
There must have been (a) _____ at the corner.

When the adverbs *there* and *here* are used, there are alternative positions for the noun subject, but if a pronoun is used as subject, it must take the position before the verb in statements. These forms are not used to begin questions.

There goes (the) _____.   There (the) _____ goes.
Here comes (the) _____.   Here (the) _____ comes.
There *he* goes.
Here *it* comes.

A second common syntactic function of the noun is that of object of the verb. We generally recognize two major types of objects: the direct object and the indirect object. A common meaning conveyed by the direct object when the verb is an action verb in the active voice is "that which receives the action of the verb or results from the action of the verb"; a common meaning conveyed by the indirect object under similar conditions is "that to or for which the action of the verb is undergone." As either of these objects may be transformed into subjects of the passive voice verb, the same general meanings may be conveyed by that structure. A common meaning expressed by the object of an active voice verb of possession is "that which is possessed." This may also be expressed by the subject of the passive voice of such a verb.

In statements in which the verb is in the active voice, if there is but one object (the direct object), its position will be immediately following the verb. When two objects are present in an active voice statement, whether they be construed as direct and indirect objects or as two direct objects, both will appear after the verb, but their positions in relation to one another may be varied by adding a preposition to the sentence.

The boy hurt (the) _____ .
The boy taught (the) ___x___ (the) ___y___ .
The boy taught (the) ___y___ to (the) ___x___ .

Third, the noun may be used as the predicate noun. Some other names given to this are predicate nominative and subjective complement. The general meanings provided by the predicate noun are: (1) identifier of the subject noun, or (2) namer of a class to which the subject noun belongs. In statements, the position of the predicate noun is that immediately following the verb. The verb used in such sentences will be one expressing a concept of state of being or condition rather than one of action or motion.

John is the _____ .
The girl is a _____ .
Roses are _____ .

A fourth syntactic function of the noun is that of being the so-called object of the preposition. Actually there is no relationship between it and the direct or indirect object of the verb, though in certain situations the preposition and its object may serve as an object of the verb. Most commonly, the function of the preposition is that of connecting its noun (object) to a word or word unit in the sentence; the function of the prepositional phrase (the preposition and its object) is most frequently that of identifying or of limiting the word or unit to which it is connected.

The man in (the) _____ is my father.
We stood at (the) _____ .
On (the) _____ , the class did well.

Fifth, the noun may complement the object. As object complement, the noun expresses the result of the action of the verb upon the object. When a noun is used in this way, it will have either the same referent as the object, or it will name a class into which the object is placed by the subject; hence it serves to identify or classify the object. Its position is following the object, and it may or may not have a noun determiner before it.

The chairman appointed John (the) _____.
We made John (a) _____.
They made John (a) _____.

It may also be introduced by a preposition, by the infinitive *to be,* or, occasionally, by the common form of one of the other linking verbs.

They chose John (as) (the) _____.
We thought John (to be) (the) _____.
That made John (appear) (the) _____.

When the verb is in the passive voice, the "receiver of the action" or "that which undergoes the action" serves as subject. When this passive voice construction is used and the word in object position expresses "the result of the action" instead of "that to or for which the action is undergone," we still have a complement (this time of the subject of the passive voice verb), to which we give the name *retained object complement.*

Lincoln was elected _____.

Sometimes nouns expressing concepts of location in space or time will appear immediately following the verb. In some situations, these may be connected to the verb by a preposition; in some we must use the preposition, and in others we cannot use it.

Henry works *Wednesdays.*
Henry works *on Wednesdays.*
Henry went *to college.*
Henry went *home.*

Nouns commonly appear in two other functions and positions: as noun adjuncts before other nouns (table lamp) and as appositives after other nouns (the baker, John). The appositive construction is normally set off by commas in writing and by intonational patterns of stress and juncture in speech. Some borrowed compound nouns and a few recently created compounds place the adjunct after the noun it modifies (Knight Templar, Lake Michigan, Operation Bootstrap). These and the adverbial nouns discussed immediately above will be considered in greater detail later.

Earlier, in our study of sounds, we encountered the term *free variation*. It was used to describe a situation in which there was an observable difference in the sounds found in a particular position or environment, but we noted that this difference was not used to distinguish a pair of forms from one another. In like manner, we may find other parts of speech occupying any of the positions we noted here for the noun, and we will find many of these to be normal positions for other parts of speech as well as for nouns. We do not, however, use the term free variation to designate the situation we find here. For our purposes, it will be sufficient if we accept the subject position in the statement as the key position for the noun. Later, when we consider possible substitutes for the noun, we will see that other parts of speech may sometimes be used as nouns, but by that time we will have found means of distinguishing these from true nouns. We will say, therefore, that any word which can be fitted into the blank in the frame sentence, "(The) _____ is/are good" will function as a noun—that is, it will be a noun or a substitute for one.

One means of separating nouns from their substitutes in this position will soon become apparent. Nearly all English nouns will have two forms, one of which will be used before *is* in such a frame, and the other of which will be used before *are*. This change or addition, we call an *inflection*. One characteristic of the inflection is that it can be applied to a large number of words, and these words will all be members of the same part of speech or form-class. A second characteristic of the inflection is that it is used to express a particular concept—in this case, the concept of plurality or more-than-oneness. We soon find, also, that inflections expressing a particular concept may have more than one form.

The Morph and the Morpheme

The term morph is from the Greek and has the general meaning of form. In any language, certain sounds and certain sequences of sounds will recur and can be contrasted with other sounds or with other sequences. If a foreigner were trying to learn our language by listening to us, he might hear us use the words *oxen, sunken, oaken, brighten* and many others which happen to end with that combination of sounds. He might therefore conclude that this combination of sounds /ən/ represented a unit which was attached to other units. If he listened long enough, he would certainly hear *ox, sunk, oak,* and *bright* used without the ending on them. This would reinforce his conclusions that this sound sequence was indeed a unit which could be added to the end of other units. He would be right, and he would have identified a morph or form of English.

As he learned more about these words, he would find that, although the *en* on oxen represented plurality, that on sunken was customarily used only when we wanted to place the verb form *sunk* before a noun as a modifier, that we used either the name *oak* or the form *oaken* in that position as a modifier (an oak table, an oaken bucket), and that, when we placed this ending on *bright, soft,* and many other adjectives, it was a means we had of forming verbs. Eventually he would learn that the word *oven* could not be separated into /əv/ (of) and /ən/. Thus the form /ən/ when it is found in the same position or distribution on a word does not always have the same function. When our foreigner was able to place a meaning of plurality for /ən/ in *oxen*, he had identified this morph as belonging to a morpheme. But he would soon find that we had various other ways of indicating this particular meaning. To mention but a few, we put an /s/ on *cat*, a /z/ on *dog*, an /əz/ or an /iz/ on *dish*, and nothing at all on *sheep*. Different morphs are added to different words to indicate plurality. All of these different morphs plus any other means we have of indicating this concept of plurality would constitute a morpheme. Our foreigner would also learn that he could not use these forms interchangeably—that we cannot add /s/ to *dish* or /ən/ to *cat*. Thus the variant forms are in complementary distribution. Each of these forms would constitute an allomorph of the noun-plural morpheme. But in the case of *dishes*, at least, our foreigner would hear some people say /dišəz/ and others say /dišiz/, or he might hear the same person use one pronunciation at one time and the other at another. The allomorph therefore may be constituted of more than one morph, and these morphs do not have to be in complementary distribution.

Our pattern of structure here parallels the pattern of structure we used with the phoneme, the allophone, and the phone. In our study of the phone and the phoneme, we found that the term *phone* was used to represent any recognizable sound of speech, whereas the *phoneme,* while it might at first encounter appear to be a single sound, in reality consisted of groups of related sounds, which were termed its *allophones.* The morpheme consists of one or more allomorphs; the allomorph consists of one or more morphs. A particular morph or a particular allomorph may, however, be a member of more than one morpheme. The /s/ we add to *cat* in oral English may represent *cat's* as well as *cats.* The meaning of the sound on the two words is certainly different. Just as we hear the phone but pay attention to the phoneme to which it belongs, so we hear or see the individual morph, but we get our meaning from the morpheme to which it belongs.

The morphemes we have been talking about are segmental morphemes, that is, they are made up of segments of sound. We will see later, however, that the way we join sounds together, even when they appear in the same sequence (oxide, ox-eyed), the stress we put upon them in speech (pérvert, pervért), and the pitch we use at the end of a series (Mother→)(Mother↗) all contribute to meaning. These are superimposed upon the string of segmental phonemes; they are called suprasegmental morphemes.

If we look more closely at our segmental series of morph, allo-morph, and morpheme, we can observe certain characteristics which will help us to define them. To begin with the morph, we can ob-serve that it is the minimal unit that is capable of expressing mean-ing. We can divide the word *oxen* into *ox* and *en,* but we cannot further subdivide this word. When we look at the allomorphs of a particular morpheme, we find that these are semantically identical (they all express the same meaning) and that they are found in complementary distribution. Phonetic similarity is not a quality of the allomorphs; they do not have to sound alike, though in many instances they do show a degree of phonetic similarity. When we look at the morphs making up a particular allomorph, we find that these have some degree of phonetic similarity, but they are not phonetically identical. (/s/ and /z/ are phonetically similar in all qualities except voicing, but they are not phonetically identical.)

We recognize two varieties of morphs: bound and free. A bound morph is one that we use only in combination with some other morph or morphs. The /z/ in /bɔyz/ is such a morph. A free morph is one which may be used alone. By definition, it is therefore a minimal word. The word *boy* is a free morph. But many minimal words are composed of more than one morph. The word *electrocute* is composed of two bound morphs: *electro* (originally meaning *amber*, but now meaning "pertaining to or caused by electricity"), and *cute* (which has been taken from the word *execute* in its sense of "killing legally" and hence now expresses the idea of *to kill*). It is interesting to note that neither of these forms originally had the meaning now attached to it. The Greek word for amber came to be used as the root or morph for all our "electrical" words because amber collects static electricity when it is rubbed.

Before leaving this topic, it may be well to note again that two forms which happen to be identical in speech, such as the homophones *red* and *read*, do not belong to the same morpheme because they convey different meanings, and that two quite different sounding morphs, such as /iz/ and /ən/, may be members of the same morpheme because they do convey the same idea. We should also recall that a word like *boy*, spoken with a rising tone at the end, might be a question you would ask of a new father; with a falling tone, it might be the response the father would give to such a question as "Is it a boy or a girl?" If the word were spoken with a level tone at the end, it would provide a means of calling to a child whose name you did not know. Thus, *boy*, which we would normally say constitutes a segmental morpheme in itself, might here provide the basic sounds for three different suprasegmental morphemes.

Turn now to Exercises 5-1 and 5-2 for practice in working with these concepts.

Exercise 5-1 Noun Plurals

1. Write the plural form for each of the nouns provided in the lists below. Then write both the singular and plural forms in phonemic transcription.

A.	B.	C.	D.
cat	cab	potato	deer
cap	bed	play	sheep
tack	dog	bee	trout
cough	cave	boy	dozen
	lathe	cow	Japanese
	car	ewe	series
	pal		
	ram		
	can		
	sing		

2. What differences do you note in the pronunciation of the plural inflections for groups *A* and *B?* Does a similar difference exist between the inflections for plurality in groups *A* and *C?* How do you account for these differences? Recall what you learned about voicing. What is peculiar about the plural of *dozen* as compared to the plurals for other words in group *D?*

3. Write the plural for each noun provided in the lists below. Then write both the singular and the plural forms in phonemic transcription.

E. base	*F.* dish
bridge	buzz
maze	leech
	bass (singer)

4. What differences occur in the spelling of the plurals for groups *E* and *F?* Do the pronunciations of the plural inflections differ for the two groups? Can any of these be given more than one pronunciation? What phonetic generalization can you make about such plural endings?

5. Follow the directions given in questions 1 and 3 for groups *G, H, I,* and *J.*

G. man	*H.* wife	*I.* ox	*J.* thesis
woman	wolf	child	phenomenon
tooth	loaf		alumnus
goose	life		cherub
foot	reef		
mouse	brief		
louse			

6. Describe the differences in spelling and pronunciation that occur in forming the plurals for group *G.* Note particularly what occurs in forming the plural of *woman.* Look up some of these words in an etymological dictionary. Does this help to explain their forms? What is meant by the word *umlaut?*

7. Do all the nouns in group *H* form their plurals in the same way? Consider both spelling and pronunciation.

8. Consult your dictionary for the origins of the plurals for the words in groups *I* and *J.* Do we have any other ways of forming the plural for any of these words?

Exercise 5-2 Noun Plurals

1. Provide two plural forms for each of the words in groups K and L. Then write the singular and both the plural forms in phonemic transcriptions.

K. ton   L. hose
   dozen   index
   beau
   seraph
   stadium
   heathen
   focus

2. Are the differing plural forms for groups K and L used to represent the same or different concepts? Is this true of all of them? Are the two forms for the plural of *hose* plurals for the same morpheme, or are they plurals for different morphemes which happen to be homonyms and homographs?

3. What is the plural form for *traffic?* Is there a plural for *arithmetic?* What meaning does the word *arithmetics* convey to you? Do we have singular forms for the words *measles, mumps,* and *scissors?* Should *athletics* and *mathematics* be put into the same class with these words?

4. Do such words as *audience, class,* and *congregation* represent singular or plural concepts? Are they singular or plural in form?

5. Are there plural forms for such words as *food, water, truth, duty, English, sugar, salt,* and *pepper?* If so, what does each plural indicate?

6. How do you form the plurals of compounds or word groups such as *spoonful, passer-by, bypass, Knight Templar, son-in-law, Governor of Michigan?*

7. Summarize in your own words the various ways we have of forming the plurals of nouns in English. Consider both the spelling and the pronunciation.

Derivational Suffixes

When we begin to make substitutions of words in the subject position of our formula sentence, we find numerous words that appear to have endings in common. For example, note the following:

audacity, capacity, mendacity, rapacity
accuracy, delicacy, efficacy, fallacy
Dunciad, dryad, *Iliad*, triad
blockade, escapade, lemonade, masquerade
baggage, language, savage, voyage
denial, recital, refusal, trial
assistance, brilliance, defiance, distance
beggar, liar, scholar, medlar
coward, dunkard, drunkard, wizard
anarchy, hierarchy, monarchy, oligarchy
adversary, dictionary, functionary, secretary
acetate, consulate, mandate, senate
agitation, decoration, flirtation, starvation

Obviously, what we have here in most of these words are bound morphs being used as parts of the words. It is necessary to say *most,* because in one case we have mere chance spelling. There are quite a large number of such morphs. The list provided does not even include all those that begin with the letter *a.* A little experimentation will show that these differ from inflections in that each of them can be applied to only a very limited number of words. They differ from inflections in another way also. The variant forms of an inflection express the same meaning; the forms used in the examples above have no meaning in common. And, in some words, more than one of these morphs could be added to the same stem. For example, we could have *blockage* as well as *block-ade,* but we can't have *lemonage* or *masquerage,* nor can we have *baggade* or *languade.* A little investigation also shows that even the identical form cannot be depended upon to express the same meaning in two different words: *blockade* expresses the result of the action of blocking, while *lemonade* designates a type of drink made with lemons. The *-ade* in these words must therefore be considered as belonging to two different morphemes. The *-ar* in *medlar* is unrelated to the other *-ar's*.

These endings are called *derivational suffixes* because through their use we derive words from root morphs or from stem words. Before we can investigate exactly how this is done, we will need some means of identifying the other parts of speech.

We have already noted that any word which will fill the blank in the frame "(The _____ is/are good" will function as a noun, and also that one characteristic of most nouns is that they will have a plural form which will be used before *are* in such a frame. We shall recognize the verb as being any word other than *not* which will fit in the invitational frame, "Let's _____." When we come to consider the verb in greater detail, we shall see that all verbs have a common or base form which appears in statements after any of a particular group of auxiliaries or verb determiners. Among these are the auxiliaries *could, shall,* and *should.* (A statement is a group of words expressing an idea with which it is possible to agree or to disagree.) This common form of the verb is the form that is used to name the verb, and it is also the form that will appear in the "Let's _____" frame.

In affirmative statements, we can recognize the verb as being:

1. Any word that will fill the blank in the following frame: "(The) noun could _____." (In certain sequence sentences such as the response to a question, the auxiliary may appear as a substitute verb, thus creating a pattern similar to the first frame shown below.)

2. The words *is, are, was,* or *were,* or any other word that will fill the blank in any of the following frames. As we shall see later, verbs can be classified according to their use in a particular structure as being intransitive linking verbs, intransitive nonlinking verbs, or transitive verbs. No single type of verb can appear in all these test frame sentences, though in a few instances a single verb form may appear in more than one type of verb usage and hence in more than one of the frames.

(The) noun _____.
(The) noun _____ good.
(The) noun _____ quickly.
(The) noun _____ (the/a) noun.

If the noun preceding the verb is singular in number, the verb will be *is* or *was* or will take either of two inflections: one to indicate third person singular present indicative ($/s/$, $/z/$, or $/əz/$, $/iz/$), or one to indicate past tense (for all regular or weak verbs $/t/$, $/d/$, or $/əd/$, $/id/$; for irregular or strong verbs a wide variety of forms). If the noun preceding the verb is plural in number, the verb will be *are* or *were,* the common or base form, or it will take the inflection to indicate past tense. The verb may occupy other positions in the sentence, and there are forms of the verb which will not fit in the test frames which are provided above, but we will reserve our discussion of these forms and of the details of the inflections mentioned above until we can concern ourselves with the verb in detail.

Modifiers are customarily divided into two major classes—adjectives and adverbs. One characteristic of the modifier is that in normal use it is related to a word or word group called the head. One traditional method of distinguishing adjectives from adverbs has been in terms of their heads. Words modifying noun heads were said to be adjectives; those modifying verb, adjective, or adverb heads were said to be adverbs. Another traditional method of classifying these words was based on the meanings they expressed. Words answering such questions as *Which one? How much?* or *How many?* were designated as adjectives; those answering questions such as *Where? When? Why?* or *How?* were classed as adverbs. As we shall see when we consider modification in detail, these methods of classification produce considerable overlapping. A second problem arises when we find other parts of speech used as modifiers.

The important thing in a structure of modification is not the classification of the modifier, but rather the recognition of the head and of the relationship or relationships that exist between the modifier and its head. Forms and/or positions will enable us to distinguish most words that would normally be classified as adjectives from those that would normally be classified as adverbs, but neither form nor position nor a combination of the two will enable us to arrange *all* those words in two mutually exclusive lists.[2] Nor can we arrange them into mutually exclusive lists by working from the form-classes of the heads to which they are related or by noting the meanings attached to the modifiers.

Yet, even considering the reservations stated above, we find that most words normally classified as adjectives in grammars and dictionaries will fit in both blanks in the following frame, though we would not, of course, use the same word in both positions in one sentence.

---

[2] Some grammarians have used a combination of the *-er, -est* inflections and the *-ly* derivational suffix as criteria for setting up two mutually exclusive lists of modifiers, but such a classification excludes many words normally classified as adjectives or adverbs from either or both lists. See Archibald A. Hill, *Introduction to Linguistic Structures* (New York, Harcourt, Brace & World, Inc., 1958), pp. 166-72; or James Sledd, *A Short Introduction to English Grammar* (Chicago: Scott, Foresman & Company, 1959), pp. 79-80.

(The) very _____ noun is/are very _____.

A few words, such as *main, chief,* and *principal,* will appear as modifiers only in the position before the noun, and there only when *very* is removed from the test frame.

Most words normally classified as adverbs are commonly found in final position in the sentence. This, however, is of little help in identifying them because (a) nouns, verbs, or adjectives may also occupy this position; (b) most adverbs may also occupy other positions; and (c) intensifiers such as *very,* which are traditionally classified as adverbs, will not take this position.

In order to identify the adverb in final position we must apply one or more of the other criteria that have been noted above. We can take, for example, the frame "(The) noun is/are adjective." In such a frame, the noun will serve as a head for the adjective modifier. If to this construction, a new word is added at the end, it will serve as an adverb, although it may be identifiable as a member of some other form-class such as the noun or the verb. But this is true only if the adjective in the new frame "(The) noun is/are adjective _____" continues to be a modifier of the noun subject. If it does not, such a frame might produce a sentence such as "The girls were good scouts," in which the adjective would be a modifier of the noun which followed it. One test for the adverb in such a frame is that of changing its position to initial position in the sentence. (The girls were happy there. There, the girls were happy.) In other frames, such as "(The) noun arrived _____," it will again be necessary to recognize the modifier-head relationship before we can classify the word which will fill the blank. If this word is related to the noun, as in "The man arrived tired," we must classify it as being adjectival (though not as being an adjective); if it is related to the verb, as in "The man arrived there/then," we must classify it as being adverbial (though again not as being an adverb).

Some characteristics of the adverb, such as form, multiple use, and mobility, will be considered later. Before leaving the adverb, we can also note that in the majority of sentences in which an adverb appears, it is grammatically unnecessary—that is, the sentence containing the adverb would be a complete sentence without it. Like all of the other tests that have been considered, this one is by no means infallible, for we certainly find sentences such as "John is here," in which the adverb is an essential part. We also have constructions such as *turn in* and *put off*, in which what is normally considered to be an adverb is a part of the verb unit. Most of these combined verb units express concepts quite different from those expressed by the simple verb. (Turn your papers. Turn in your papers.)

Despite the fact that the frame tests will not work in all cases, they do provide us with some help in identifying the majority of words belonging to each form-class or part of speech.

Now let us return to our problem of derivational suffixes. If we consider the group of words, *audacity, capacity, mendacity,* and *rapacity,* we find that these will all serve as nouns, but we have another group of words quite clearly related to these that will serve as adjectives—*audacious, capacious, mendacious,* and *rapacious.* A little dictionary research will show us that the initial sections of these words can be traced back to Latin forms. So too can the endings, both for the nouns and for the adjectives. If we try to find contemporary English words such as *mend, rap,* or *cap* in these, we find that the meanings these short contemporary words convey are totally unrelated to the meanings conveyed by the complete words with which we began. Obviously, then, these free morphs are not used in making up the longer words. We must conclude that each of these -*acious* and -*acity* words is made up of two bound morphs. In addition, as we have already noted, the -*acity* words will most commonly be found in noun positions, taking noun inflections, if any, and being modified by words normally used to modify nouns; the -*acious* words will most commonly be found in adjective positions, the heads they modify will normally be nouns, and if they themselves serve as heads, their modifiers will be of the intensive class or of the *more-most, less-least* function word-class.

Now let us look at another group. We have *denial, recital, refusal,* and *trial.* Alongside these we can place the words *deny, recite, refuse, try,* which will fit into verb positions. We might say, then, that this group of nouns is derived from verbs.

This seems simple enough, but now let us look at *assistance, brilliance, defiance,* and *distance.* Here we can find the related verbs *assist* and *defy,* but there are no related verbs for the other two words. We also have the words *assistant, brilliant, defiant,* and *distant,* but before we jump to conclusions and say these are all derived adjectives, let us try them in our adjective frame. When we do, we find that the last three will fit the frame, but the first will not. We cannot use *very* before *assistant* even when assistant is functioning as a modifying word. We will have to consider it then as a noun, for it will fit into the noun frames, or as one of the special group of adjectives such as *main, chief,* and *principal.*

Two principles have just been illustrated here: (1) Certain derivational suffixes may be combined with either bound morph roots or full-word stems (*acetate, consulate*), and among full words, the stems may represent varying parts of speech (*escapade, lemonade*). (2) The same derivational suffix may appear on more than one part of speech: arrival (noun), national (adjective); agitate (verb), candidate (noun). *Separate* looks as though it has the same form (*-ate*) for both verb and adjective, but when we pronounce these forms, we find that they differ.

We must observe one more thing. A word may contain more than one derivational suffix. To the word *nation,* for example, we may add the suffix *-al* to make the word *national.* To this, we may add an additional suffix *-ist* to form the word *nationalist,* and to this, a further suffix *-ic* to make the word *nationalistic,* and to that, still another suffix *-ally* to form *nationalistically.*[3] And our original word *nation* is itself composed of a bound root and the *-tion* suffix. To any of these words that would serve as nouns, we could add a noun inflection. This inflection would always appear at the end of the word, regardless of how many suffixes the word might contain (nation*s,* national*s,* nationalist*s*).

Now we are ready to turn to Exercise 5-3 to see what further things we can learn about derivational suffixes.

Exercise 5-3   Derivational Suffixes

1. From what type of base (root morph or word stem) is each of the following nouns derived? When the base is a word stem, as what part of speech would this stem normally serve?

---

[3] The suffix here is really *-ly.* The suffix *-ical* is sometimes used as a parallel form to *-ic.* In some words the meanings of the two forms are practically identical (poetic, poetical), in others they vary (an economic policy, an economical policy). Frequently, when spelling conventions require the *-ical* form before the *-ly* suffix, the *al* section of it is not pronounced (/næšnəlistikli/).

autocracy	engineer	cigarette
docker	hostess	appendicitis
politician	Benthamite	heroine
catholicism	dukedom	sultana
pianist	boyhood	czarina
friendship	piglet	seamstress
teamster	lambkin	suffragette
widower	duckling	roadster

2. Which of the endings on these words indicate gender or sex? Which indicate people? Which may be either people or things? Which indicate abstractions? Which indicate spatial areas? Which indicate temporal areas? Which indicate smallness or youth? Which indicate illnesses?

3. We learned in Exercises 5-1 and 5-2 that, with a very few exceptions, the /s/z/əz/ (-s, -es) plurals could be placed on all English nouns. Is this true also of the endings that appear on the nouns in the list above? Can we use more than one of these endings on a single noun—that is, can we form such words as *teamsterette* or *engineeress?* If we add a plural inflection to any of these nouns, would it be added before or after the derivational endings?

4. From what type of base is each word in the following list derived?

storage	agreement	creation
reliance	walking	spinster
player	conversation	growth
deportee	reversal	diffusion

5. Are any of the endings found on the words in the list for question 1 also found on words in this list? If so, do the two words have the same type of base? Does the particular derivational suffix appear to signify different concepts when it appears on words with different types of bases? Would there be any possibility of classifying some of the base words from the second list with the majority of the base words from the first list? Why or why not?

6. Are there any derivational suffixes on words in the list for question 4 that represent people? Which of them represent verbal ideas? Which represent the idea of an agent? Is the agent represented necessarily human? What other kinds of ideas are represented by words in this list?

7. From what type of base is each of the following nouns derived?

independence	redundancy	nationality
darkness	youngster	socialism
height	depth	socialist

8. Are any of the derivational suffixes found on words in this list also found on words in either of the two earlier lists? Does the suffix signify something different here than it did in either of the other lists? Would there be any possibility of classing the bases of words from this list with those from words on one of the other lists? Why or why not?

9. From what type of base is each of the following nouns derived? Does the base have any meaning in itself? When the base happens to correspond to a word, as in the word *tailor*, can we derive the meaning of the word from the meaning of this base word plus the meaning of the suffix?

tailor	grocer	dentist
doctor	deism	verity

10. The list in question 9 is very short. Find at least ten additional nouns that would fit into it. Make use of derivational suffixes which appear on words in the other lists—for example, *elocution*.

Compounds

Most of us are certain that we know a word when we hear one or see one. Yet, when we are required to provide an adequate definition for the term *word*, we often encounter considerable difficulty in forming one. Superficially, most of us think of a written word as being a meaningful group of letters separated from other groups of letters appearing to the left and/or right of them by a space greater than that used to separate the letters within the groups from one another. A little investigation will show us, however, that we do not group or separate words in oral English in the same manner that we do in written English. In fact, we are very inconsistent in our patterning of words in written English, as can be seen from the following sentence: "One never pulls the *bowstring* with his *bow hand*." In this sentence, the words *bowstring* and *bow hand* may both receive the same type of stress and juncture patterning in oral English, but in written English we write the word solid in one case and as two units in the other. We even make use of a third distinction in writing. We have not only *bluebottle* flies and *Blue Ridge* mountains, but also *blue-sky* laws.

In oral English, we distinguish words quite carefully by our use of stress and juncture patterns. In the sentence "There is a dog-house behind the brick house," we use a different stress pattern for *doghouse* than we do for *brick house*. It is possible to recognize more than four degrees of stress in ordinary speech, but for practical purposes, the recognition of four is generally adequate—at least, this is enough for the beginner to observe.[4] The symbols normally used to indicate these four degrees of stress are (´) for primary or loudest stress, (ˆ) for secondary stress, (ˋ) for tertiary or soft stress, and (˘) for weak stress or unstressed sounds. When we use these symbols to indicate the stress we place on *doghouse* and *brick house*, our patterns are dóghoùse and brîck hoúse. For the word *longshoreman*, the pattern would be lôngshoŕemăn. Stress patterning also enables us to distinguish between pérmìt, pervêrt (nouns) and pèrmít, pèrvért (verbs). In such situations, stress patterns constitute phonemic differences; hence, we can have stress phonemes.

Stress patterns are commonly accompanied by patterns of juncture. The concept of juncture is a complex one. If we think of it simply as the length of time between sounds, we will be oversimplifying. Juncture is rather the manner in which we move

---

[4] Actually, there is a considerable lack of agreement among linguists about this whole area of suprasegmental phonemes. Some observers point out that we use five or more degrees of phonetic stress in certain phrases; others feel that only two degrees of stress are phonemic. There is a similar lack of agreement about variations in juncture, and there is no absolute agreement on even the segmental phonemes. Many of these contrasts are extremely difficult to recognize when the word or phrase is used in isolation. (Try, for example, to say "flying planes" as you would say it when it precedes "is dangerous" and then as you would say it when it precedes "are dangerous.") Yet there can be no question that we do make use of contrasts of stress, juncture, and terminal pitch in our ordinary speech. Anyone who is interested in investigating the problems of this area more thoroughly would find it worthwhile to consult the *Texas Conferences on Problems of Linguistic Analysis in English* for 1956, 1957, and 1958. Transcripts of these conferences were published by the University of Texas (Austin, 1962).

from one sound to another. It is also our choice of sounds for the inception of a syllable or word.

Juncture is dependent upon which sounds in a group we use as initiatory sounds and which we use as release sounds. Consider the transition from one sound to another in *sore, sawer,* and *saw her.* In the author's idiolect, identical sounds are used for the first two of these combinations—/s/ /ɔ/ /r/—but in the first word, the transition from the second sound to the third is very smooth, whereas in the second word there is a release after the vowel /ɔ/ and the initiation of a new sound with the semivowel /r/. In rapid speech this also provides the pronunciation of *saw her* in "I saw her yesterday." In slower and more precise speech, there is a distinct release of the vowel /ɔ/ and a distinct /h/ at the beginning of *her.* Juncture therefore represents not only the space of time between sounds, but also the choice of position for inception and release of sounds. It is what enables us to distinguish between "an ice box" and "a nice box," or "it swears" and "its wares."

It is this combination of stress and juncture patterns that enables us to distinguish orally between such phrases as *a good looking glass* and *a good-looking glass.* In writing, such situations are often unmarked by punctuation of any kind. Consider the sentence "They are frying chickens," first with *they* having *people* as its referent, and second with *chickens* as its referent.

Just as we found stress to be a phonemic and morphemic distinction in forms such as *pérmit, permít,* we find juncture used phonemically and morphemically in "it scares" and "its cares." In most situations, however, we will find stress and juncture patterns supplementing one another rather than creating distinct differences individually. In more simple language, two identical series of sounds may represent different concepts when they are used with different stress and/or juncture patterning.

Exercise 5-4   Forming Compound Nouns

In the last three exercises we have learned that nouns may be derived by adding certain suffixes to other nouns, to verbs and adjectives, or to roots (combinations of sounds) which are not in themselves full words. In addition, we should have observed that use of derivational suffixes is not confined to the development of nouns alone; it is also used to form words belonging to other form-classes. Keep in mind that the addition of prefixes is as common as the addition of suffixes. In other words, we create two-unit words in all of the following manners:

free morph + free morph	green+house, base+ball
free morph + bound morph	young+ster, man+hood
bound morph + free morph	en+rich, re+turn
bound morph + bound morph	electro+cute, ortho+dox

1. From what combination of morphs is each noun in the following lists formed? When any unit of a word is a free morph, indicate the class of word (part of speech) to which it would normally belong.

     A. railroad, rooftop, weekend, coalshed, football
     B. blueberry, high chair, hot dog, White House, hothead
     C. upshot, onset, overhead, underdog, downdraft
     D. walkout, tie-in, kickoff, run-in, dugout
     E. playboy, crybaby, pay dirt, lock step, shut-eye
     F. short-cut, long run, hard-sell, deadbeat, high jump

2. Do these lists contain all the possible combinations that are used to form compound nouns? Consider *bootblack, evergreen,* and *looking glass.* Can you identify still other types of combinations? What do we have in *midshipman?*

3. Use an etymological dictionary to look up the origins of the words *lord, hussy, daisy,* and *bonfire.* Have changes in meaning accompanied the changes in form for all of these words? Would you be justified in considering the first unit of any of them as a free morph? While you are at the dictionary, look up the words *don* and *doff.* Is the phenomenon we are considering limited to nouns?

4. How would you form the plural of each of the compounds listed in question 1? Would you ever use endings such as *-en, -ren,* or any of the foreign plurals? Would you use any of the umlaut plurals, such as we have in *feet?* What occurs when one of these words forms the final unit of the compound? Consider *black sheep, field mouse, dormouse, charwoman.* In what way does *ottoman* differ from these?

5. When an inflection is of the type that would be applied to a new word that comes into the language (either through borrowing

or creation), we speak of it as a *living* inflection; when an inflection is no longer applied to new words, we speak of it as a *dead* inflection. Which of the plural inflections we have studied are living inflections? How would you form the plurals of the following words, which have been borrowed or created in relatively recent times: *blitzkrieg, nazi, fascist, sputnik, VIP, payola?* Look up the plurals for *dormouse* and *titmouse*. In what situations do we continue to apply dead inflections? Are we consistent in this usage?

6. Can you think of any new word to which you would add *-th* to form a noun such as *wealth, growth,* or *health?* Can you think of any to which we might add *-ness?* Do we appear to have living and dead derivational suffixes as well as inflections?

The Genitive Inflection

In addition to the inflectional forms used to designate plurality in nouns, we have another noun inflection—the genitive. In one sense this is an inflection of the noun because it is placed upon nouns, but in another sense it does not seem to be an inflection of the noun because, once it is placed upon the noun, the most common use for that noun becomes that of modifying another noun, rather than that of serving as subject, object, predicate noun, or objective complement. Still, we frequently do find genitive nouns or substitutes for them, such as *mine*, fulfilling any of the varied syntactic functions of the normal noun.

In English speech, the form of the genitive is indistinguishable from the form of the plural for most nouns. While we write *boys, boy's,* and *boys',* we pronounce all three of them /bɔyz/. The few nouns that have unchanged plurals in English also have but two forms; in these nouns, however, the contrast is between the common and the genitive case forms (/siyp/; /siyps/). A few nouns have three forms; in these, we have no contrast to indicate case in the plural (/wayf/, /wayfs/; /wayvz/). Only a few nouns have four forms; these present clear contrasts for both number and case (/mæn/, /mænz/; /men/, /menz/).

Like the regular plural inflection, this genitive inflection is varied in speech; it may be /s/, /z/, or /əz/, depending upon the quality of the sound that precedes it. Unlike the plural inflection, it expresses a wide variety of meanings although it has no irregular forms. This could be advanced as another reason for doubting that it is a true inflection. Older grammars generally speak of the genitive as being the possessive case. In actuality, probably no more than 40 per cent of genitives express possession. Some other concepts expressed by the genitive are: place of origin (the moon's light); species, type, or that for or by which an object is used (men's gloves); measure (a day's drive); relationships such as part to the whole (the bicycle's sprocket); material (the coat's wool); location (Lansing's post office); loose association (the family's dentist).

Like the indirect object, the genitive can be expressed periphrastically—that is, the concepts normally expressed by the genitive can also be expressed through the use of function words. Thus we have the choice of using the cup's handle or the handle *on* the cup, *from* the cup, etc. We are often inclined to use this periphrastic genitive rather than the inflected form because it permits us to express our ideas more accurately. Occasionally we make use of both the function word and the genitive inflection. We have, for example, such forms as "a friend *of* father's," or even "a friend *of* my father's."

In forming the plurals for word-group nouns which are composed of a head word plus a prepositional phrase, we normally add the plural inflection to the noun head (sisters-in-law), but place the genitive inflection at the end of the group noun (sister-in-law's, sisters-in-law's). The same generalizations apply to other phrasal nouns, hyphenated or unhyphenated (passers-by, bystanders; passer-by's and bystander's).

Although it is common to add more than one derivational suffix to a word in English, we normally do not add more than one inflection. Again, the genitive appears to be an exception to this generalization, for it may be added to words which already are inflected as plural; we have already seen this from such examples as the men's hats, the oxen's horns, my sisters-in-law's friends, and the passers-by's comments.

In many situations we make one uninflected noun modify another simply by placing it in the position before the other (the *noun adjunct*). In certain constructions, the uninflected noun adjunct may be used for the same concept which would be expressed if the genitive noun were used instead (the *truck* load, the *truck's* load; the *table* top, the *table's* top). When the noun adjunct primarily indicates type or species, it will *not* substitute for the genitive (the *child* mother, a *stone* house, the *glass* bowl).

Words substituted for genitive nouns may take the genitive inflection. (The aged *people's* woes were many. The *aged's* woes were many.) The personal pronouns and the *who* pronoun have forms which will serve as genitives. For some of these the form is unique (*mine, yours, hers, ours, theirs* are used only as pronouns); for others, it is used to express different concepts. (His and *whose* may be used either as pronouns or as noun determiners or, if you prefer, as genitive adjectives. *Whose* may also be used as a question, starting pronoun, or adjective. /its/ is the same in speech for "*its* back" and "*It's* a back.") Certain noun determiners are also said to have a genitive form; for these plus their nouns, we may make use of the pronoun substitutes as illustrated below.

	My hat is blue.	Mine is blue.
	Your hat is red.	Yours is red.
Sue's hat is green.	Her hat is green.	Hers is green.
Joe's hat is black.	His hat is black.	His is black.
	Our hats are brown.	Ours are brown.
The girls' hats are pink.	Their hats are pink.	Theirs are pink.
	Whose hat is gray?	Whose is gray?
The dog's tail is short.	Its tail is short.	

Theoretically, the form *its* may serve as a noun substitute, but we seldom use it as a subject or object. The genitive nouns may also be used to replace the nouns they modify (Sue's hat is green. Sue's is green.). These substitutes will be discussed in greater detail after you have completed Exercise 5-5.

Exercise 5-5 Genitive Inflections

1. Do you have the feeling that *blackberry* is one word or two? What about the following words or word groups? *upshot, hot dog, brother-in-law, attorney general, Governor of Michigan, dog in the manger.*

2. If you were speaking of more than one of each of the above terms, where would you add the pluralizing inflection? Does this suggest a test of whether each expression is one word or more than one word?

3. When you wish to indicate that a book belongs to Jack, how can you do so? Is there more than one way of doing this? If you were indicating hats belonging to different men, what form of the noun would you use? Is it also possible to use the function word *of* for this purpose?

4. Go back to the list of nouns provided in Exercise 5-3 (pages 56-57) and decide with which you would prefer to use the *'s* /s, z, əz/ inflection and with which you would normally use the function word *of*. Would you normally use one form with all of these?

5. Where would you place the genitive inflection on nouns listed in groups *A-F* of Exercise 5-4 (page 60)? With which of these nouns would you use the *of* construction? With which could you probably use either construction?

6. Try to make a valid generalization about where it is most natural to use the genitive inflection and where it is most natural to use the function word construction.

7. Can the genitive inflection be used to express anything except possession? What is expressed by each of the genitive inflections in the following sentences?

   a. The General's letter containing our orders arrived today.
   b. The General's letter from the Secretary of War just arrived.
   c. The letter containing Lincoln's autograph is the General's.
   d. The truck's load shifted.
   e. The egg's shell was broken.
   f. The cup's rim was fragile.
   g. The family's doctor is out of town.
   h. The child's mother was very angry.
   i. The train's tracks were smooth.
   j. It is only a stone's throw from here.
   k. She bought a dollar's worth of material.
   l. Chicago's stockyards are not as large as they once were.

8. Instead of using the genitive construction, *Chicago's stockyards,* we can use another construction, *the Chicago stockyards.* Can this type of construction be substituted for each of the genitives listed in question 7? Provide examples of its use. When it can be so used, are the meanings expressed by the two constructions identical in all instances?

9. What relationship exists between the form of the genitive and the form of the plural for most English nouns? (Remember we are concerned with sounds.) In what types of nouns is the genitive identical with the plural form? In what types does it have a form

different from that of the plural? Which has the fewer variations in form—the genitive or the plural? Can we add both a genitive and a plural to all nouns? When it is possible to add both a genitive and a plural suffix to a noun, in what order do we add them?

10. Can we use the genitive inflection with all of the nouns provided in the lists in Exercise 5-3? in Exercise 5-4?

11. In modern usage we frequently see units such as *Pikes Peak, teachers college,* or *boys camp* written without an apostrophe. Should these be considered as genitives despite the fact that the apostrophe is omitted?

12. Many of you have probably learned to call the *'s* /s, z, əz/ inflection the *possessive.* Do you still consider this an adequate term? Recheck your responses to question 7 before answering.

13. Do any classes of words other than nouns have genitive forms?

14. What phonetic variations are there for the genitive inflection? Describe the situation in which each is used.

Noun Determiners and Substitutes for Nouns

When we first discussed the noun, we used a frame with the word *the* in parentheses to indicate that this word or a substitute for it might or might not be required before the noun. *The* is but one of a fairly sizable group of words which may appear before nouns and serve as noun determiners. What they actually determine is not the noun itself, but rather the noun function. Many nouns are commonly used without a determiner. For example, we say "*John* is happy," "*Hell* is a village in Michigan," "*Wheat* is a grain," and "*Dogs* are carnivorous."

However, when an adjective is substituted for a noun, we use a determiner to indicate its new function. This distinction may be clearly observed in our use of some of the -*ing* words which may be either adjectives or nouns. If I say "Charming is an unusual occupation," I will be using the word *charming* as a gerund or verbal noun. This word will not pattern with *very* in such a usage. Now, if I change my sentence and say "The charming are often dangerous," I have used an adjective as a substitute for a noun. I have indicated its noun function by placing a determiner before it (in fact, if I were to omit the determiner, the sentence would

become senseless), but I can still recognize its adjective nature
by the test of inserting *very* before *charming*—"The very charming
are often dangerous."

A list of words commonly used as noun determiners will be found
in question 5 of Exercise 5-7 (page 71). To these must be added
the cardinal numbers from three to ninety-nine and a few other
words, such as *yonder,* which may occasionally serve as noun determiners. We shall identify the noun determiner as being any
word which will substitute for *the, a,* or *an* in the position before a
noun.

We have already noted (page 42) that the choice between
the and *a* or *an* before *singular predicate* nouns indicates our use
of these nouns as identifiers, or as designators of classes to which
the subject belongs.

> Henry VIII was *the* king.
> Henry VIII was *a* king.

Our choice between the use of *a* and the use of *an* is determined
by sound differences rather than by semantic or syntactical variants. We use *a* before words beginning with *consonant sounds,*
an before words beginning with *vowel sounds.* However, *the* used
before a singular or plural *subject* noun generally indicates a total
subclass whenever the predicate noun indicates a larger class, of
which the subclass named by the subject is a member.

> *The* dog is *a* quadruped.   *The* flowers are roses.

We can note further that *a* and *an* are used only before the singular form of nouns, whereas *the* may be used before either singular
or plural forms. *The* points out or specifies a particular unit or
particular group. *A* and *an* are less definite; they indicate *any*
unit of the class named. If we admit some exceptions and some
overlapping, we can divide noun determiners roughly into those
that may substitute for *a, an* and those that may substitute for *the.*
Thus the groups that are sometimes called genitive nouns and
genitive adjectives (John's, Helen's, my, your, and so on) belong
to the *the* class, whereas the numerals belong to the *a, an* class.
(But numerals above *one* are used with plural nouns, whereas
a and *an* are used only before singular nouns.)

As soon as we look carefully at our use of these determiners, we begin to find a number of other complexities. We should realize that many of these markers may stand as substitutes for nouns, whereas certain others will not function in this way. Thus we may say "*All* is/are good," "*Both* are good," "*Each* is good," "*Much* is good," and "*Those* are good," but we cannot say "*The* is good," "*Your* is good," or "*Every* is good." Next, we can note that some of these (for example, *much*) will pattern only with singuar forms of the verb, while others (e.g., *many*) will pattern only with plural forms; several (*this, that, these, those*) have different forms for patterning with singular and plural forms of the verb. (As noun determiners, of course, these pattern with the singular or plural forms of the noun.) Finally, we can identify some that will not themselves function as nouns (*my, our, your, their*) but which have related forms that will so substitute (*I, me, mine; we, us, ours; you, yours; they, them, theirs*). These related forms will not function as noun determiners.

We must observe, also, that although these words function as noun markers or determiners, most of them are not without meaning in themselves, and often the distinction between the noun determiner and the modifier of the noun is very debatable. Some markers indicate the grammatical concept of number; others are exact quantifiers; some are gender indicators; others indicate person; and some indicate more than one of these concepts.

We also find that we use more than one noun marker before nouns in certain situations (*all the* boys, *both her* friends, *the two* girls, *some more* sugar), and that modifiers of the noun may appear between the noun marker and the noun itself (her *girlish* figure, the *blue* coat, a *Bogen* tuner). The following markers may appear after *all* or *both*, but not after any of the other markers on the list: *the, my, your, his, her, our, their, these, those. This* and *that* may appear after *all*, but not after *both* (except in the special situation of the compound, such as "Both this book and that pencil").

As we have seen, some determiners will also serve as noun substitutes and others have related noun-substitute forms. A series of definite relationships also exists between subclasses of nouns and the type or types of substitutes used as replacements for them. Most of these substitutes are personal pronouns and have distinct forms to represent (1) the noun used as subject, (2) the noun used as object, and (3) the genitive adjective or genitive noun combined with the noun head and used either as subject or object (*I, me, mine; he, him, his; she, her, hers; we, us, ours; they, them, theirs*). *You* and *it*, however, do not change form to indicate the object relationship (*you, yours; it, its*). Only one other word in the English language, the pronoun *who*, has separate forms to indicate such case relationships; the forms of this word (*who, whom, whose*) may be combined with *-ever* and with *-soever*.

The various groupings that can be based on our choice of substitute words provide us with a means of identifying certain subclasses of nouns. One of these subclassifications is that of *gender*. In many languages, gender represents an arbitrary grammatical classification —for example, in Spanish, *mesa* and *mano* (table and hand) are feminine, but *zapato* and *dedo* (shoe and finger) are masculine. In modern English, gender is almost identical with sex. Thus we have words of masculine gender representing males (*rooster*), words of feminine gender representing females (*vixen*), common gender representing both males and females (*people*), and neuter gender representing sexless things (*iron*). However, we still use grammatical gender in a few situations; we refer to the sun as *he*, or to the moon, a ship, a country, or certain machines as *she*. A second subclass is that of the collective noun—a word which represents one group in its singular form and two or more groups in its plural form. A third subclass of nouns we might term "defective" because they lack either a singular (scissors) or a plural form (traffic).

Nouns may be divided in still another way—in terms of their patterning with a different set of determiners. Certain nouns represent abstract concepts or masses that we measure rather than count. These nouns will pattern with the determiner *much* (*truth, education, water, sugar,* or *stone*). Other nouns represent concepts that we count rather than measure; with these we use *many* (*people, tables, books,* or *shoes*). Most noncountables also have a plural form with which we use *many*, but when we use them this way we indicate either different types, individual units, or examples of the material or concept. Thus we may have *much sugar,* but we do not have very *many sugars* (cane, beet, and maple sugars) in this country. Or we can say "There is *much stone* (are *many stones*)," "I did not learn *much algebra* though I opened *many algebras*," "His sayings contained *many truths,* but did not provide as *much truth* as I would have liked." For our defective words and for plurals which represent masses, we indicate the unit by supplying another noun head and using the defective noun as the object of a preposition in a phrase modifying the head (a *pair* of *scissors*, a *box* of *berries*, a *lot* of *traffic*, a *case* of *mumps*); we also use this method for indicating units of the singular mass words (a *piece* of *stone*, a *cup* of *tea*, a *surge* of *ambition*).

Nouns are commonly classified as representing abstractions or concrete objects. Concrete nouns represent things which we can touch. Abstract nouns represent ideas or qualities. We abstract the concept of *heat* from our various experiences with things which may provide this quality—stoves, fires, the sun, and so on. Actually, of course, any word that represents a classification is abstracted. *Dog*, for example, is an abstraction for *Pekingese, greyhound, dachshund, terrier, cur*, etc., and each of these is an abstraction for the individual dogs that make up the particular breed or group. In this sense, the class-naming noun is like the phoneme. We never see the prototype, but only see examples of it; we never hear the phoneme, but only hear phones which belong to it.

Still another division is that between common and proper nouns. The common noun represents the class, the proper noun the particular person or place within the class. Thus we have *countries* (common), but *France, England,* and *Sweden* (proper); we have *people* (common), but *John, Mary,* and *Rose* (proper). It is sometimes said that there can be no plural for a proper noun. Technically this is true, for as soon as we use such a noun in the plural, we are setting up a class of people or places. When we do so, we continue to capitalize them in writing to indicate their proper noun origin. ("I have three *Marys* in my eight o'clock class." "For a while, it looked like we might have two *Congo Republics* in Africa.")

Finally, we can divide nouns in terms of their components. *Blackberry, forget-me-not,* and *hot dog* are compound nouns—that is, they are made up of more than one word; *desk* is a simple noun; *humanity* is a derived noun.

In addition to the personal pronouns and those determiners which may also appear as substitutes, we make use of nouns to refer to other nouns when the meaning would be vague or unclear without the presence of the referent. (The will divided the property among the heirs. John's *share* was a six room house.) We will make note of other types of noun substitutes when we consider the other parts of speech and the parts of the sentence in greater detail.

Exercise 5-6   Gender

1. In Exercise 5-3 we noticed that endings such as *-ine* and *-ess* were frequently used to indicate feminine gender. How many genders do we recognize in English? In what way is gender, as we use it, related to sex? Is this true of other languages also? Do we ever use what might be called "grammatical" gender in English?

2. Indicate the gender of each of the nouns in the following list.

man	audience	cattle
stone	sheep	table
ram	vixen	stallion
goose	steamship	chicken
mare	drake	automobile

3. Supply the feminine form that corresponds to each of the following masculine or common gender nouns. Do we have more than one form for some of these?

abbot	brother	comedian
hero	widower	landlord
host	executor	billy goat
actor	aviator	wrestler
god	alumnus	sheep

4. Supply the masculine form that corresponds to each of the following feminine or common gender nouns. Do we have more than one form for some of these?

lady	laundress	seamstress
aunt	doe	hen
mare	cow	turkey
goose	suffragette	sow
bride	maid	bitch

5. Indicate the gender of each of the italicized words in the sentences which follow. What problems do these examples raise?

   a. *Man* has used language for untold ages.
   b. *Everyone* must hold *his* own ticket.
   c. The captain of the ship brought *her* into port.
   d. The dog wagged *its* tail.
   e. The baby hurt *its* head.

6. Does gender appear to be most frequently expressed by derivational suffixes or by word selection? Are gender and sex completely synonymous in English?

Exercise 5-7   Noun Determiners

1. To what word-class (part of speech) are words such as *old*, *good*, and *poor* normally assigned?

2. Are the words in the following sentences being used as members of their normal word-class or as nouns? Name two things that you considered in classifying them.

   a. The old have few wants.
   b. The good die young.
   c. The poor are always with us.

3. The word *the* is called a noun determiner. Whenever this word is used in English, a word functioning as a noun will appear after it. Test the accuracy of this statement by writing five sentences containing the word *the*. Can other words appear between the noun determiner and the noun? If so, what function do these words serve in the sentences you wrote?

4. Is the word *want* normally classified as a noun? How is it used in sentence *a* of question 2? Does the word *few* appear to be a noun determiner in this sentence? What else helps to determine the word-class of *wants?*

5. The words below are commonly listed as noun determiners. To make the list more complete, we would have to include the cardinal numbers three to ninety-nine. Can you supply other words which may be used as noun determiners? Are genitive nouns ever so used?

a	enough	much	some
an	every	my	that
all	few	neither	their
another	her	no	these
any	his	one	this
both	many	other	those
each	more	our	two
either	most	several	your

6. Which of the words listed above may be used only with the singular form of nouns? Which may be used only with the plural? Which may be used only with noncountable nouns?

7. Which of the above words can be used as substitutes for nouns? Which cannot be so used? Do any have related forms which can be used as substitutes for nouns? Are these other forms ever used as determiners? When these words are used as substitutes for

nouns, do we ever use another determiner with them? With which ones is another determiner required? Which never use one?

8. Do we ever use more than one of these substitute-determiners before a noun? If so, what combinations may be used? Is there a fixed order in which they must appear? What is the largest number that may be put together before a noun? When a series of two or more substitute-determiners is used, may other words intervene between them and the noun?

9. In our study of the noun, we have noted plural inflections, genitive inflections, derivational suffixes, and noun determiners. Do plural nouns, genitive nouns, or derived nouns ever function as determiners for other nouns?

10. Can the words *little* and *yonder* be used as noun determiners? Does either of them function as such in the following sentences? How does each function in the other sentences?

   a. He paid little attention to what was said.
   b. He was a cute little boy.
   c. Yonder house is the one where they used to live.
   d. They went off yonder.

11. Do you find any qualifying adjectives such as *beautiful* among the noun determiners? Do you find any quantifying adjectives? Is *little* used as a quantifier in either of the sentences provided in question 10? What function is performed by words such as *my* and *your*? What function is performed by the words *this* and *that*? Classify the determiners listed in question 5 according to other functions they might serve.

12. In question 3 the statement was made that a word functioning as a noun always appears after *the*. Is this true of all determiners? Is it true of any of the other determiners?

Suggested Readings

SECTION 5

Francis, W. Nelson, *The Structure of American English,* pp. 162-220 and 237-52. New York: The Ronald Press Company, 1954.

Fries, Charles C., *The Structure of English,* Chap. V. New York: Harcourt, Brace & World, Inc., 1952

Harris, Zellig S., *Structural Linguistics,* pp. 136-64 and 179-95. Chicago: University of Chicago Press, 1951.

Hill, Archibald A., *Introduction to Linguistic Structures*, Chap. X. New York: Harcourt, Brace & World, Inc., 1958.

Hockett, Charles F., *A Course in Modern Linguistics*, Chap. XXXI. New York: The Macmillan Company, 1958.

Lees, Robert B., *The Grammar of English Nominalizations*, pp. 124-73. Bloomington, Indiana: Indiana University Research Center in Anthropology, Folklore, and Linguistics, 1960.

Sledd, James, *A Short Introduction to English Grammar*, pp. 79-81. Chicago: Scott, Foresman & Company, 1959.

Whitehall, Harold, *Structural Essentials of English*, Chap. XII. New York: Harcourt, Brace & World, Inc., 1951.

SECTION 6

The Verb

Words normally designated as verbs fall into two classes: full verbs and auxiliaries. *Full verbs* express lexical meanings; *auxiliaries* express grammatical meanings.[1] In some senses, the uses of the auxiliaries are very similar to the uses of the noun determiners. They serve as markers for the full verb and, in certain situations, are used as substitutes for it. Like determiners, more than one auxiliary may appear before the full verb, and when more than one does appear, the order of their appearance is fixed.

There are some verbs in which the common or naming forms of full verbs are identical with those of auxiliaries. It is generally said

---

[1] In our study of the noun, we noted that certain forms tended to recur with great regularity and that these forms had associated with them certain meanings which could be classified under the general headings of *number* and *case*. As we study the verb, we again find a series of recurring forms, but we also find a series of word groups or phrasal forms which recur again and again; the specific meaning which may be attached to these word groups does not appear to be a part or a product of their individual lexical meanings. Thus the present tense forms of the verb *to be*—*am, is, are*—do not in themselves express futurity, nor does the form *going*, but if we place one of these forms of *to be* before *going* and follow this phrase with an infinitive, we certainly express the idea of futurity. (I am going to leave.) If the *to be* forms are changed to *was* or *were*, the resulting meaning is quite different. It may imply that something did not occur. (They were going to leave.) Again, this is a meaning which is not one of the lexical meanings of any word used in the sentence. In different structures these same meanings may be expressed lexically. (I leave *tomorrow*. They did *not* leave.)

74

that these verbs serve both as auxiliaries and as full verbs; but because these verbs, when used as auxiliaries, do not express the lexical meanings normally attributed to them as full verbs, I think it is better to say that we have two verbs—the auxiliary and the full verb—which happen to correspond in form. Some examples of these dual verbs are *can, will,* and *have.*

Most grammars list ten auxiliaries as being *modal* auxiliaries because the chief function of these verbs is that of expressing a group of grammatical concepts which are included under the general term *mode* or *mood.* Two of these modals, *can* and *will,* have corresponding full verbs, and therefore illustrate the generalization made in the above paragraph. The full verb *can* (to put in cans) has the forms *can, cans, canned,* and *canning;* in writing, the auxiliary has but one form, *can;* in rapid speech it is commonly /kin/ or even /kən/, though we may give its vowel full quality /kæn/ to express emphasis. The full verb *will* also has four forms: *will, wills, willed, willing.* The auxiliary has but two in writing—*will* and the contraction *'ll* (in speech, this contraction is normally no more than a syllabic /l/, and it may be used to represent either *will* or *shall*). Three other auxiliaries—*have* (past tense), *should,* and *would*— share a contracted form of *'d* in writing and /d/ in speech (I*'d* gone. I*'d* go if I were you.)

The ten verbs generally listed as modal auxiliaries are *can, could, may, might, must, ought, shall, should, will,* and *would.* Of these, as we have already noted, *can* has one form in writing but several in speech, and *shall, should, will,* and *would* use two forms in writing and two in speech. The others are one-form verbs. *Ought,* however, operates in a manner different from the others. In standard Midwestern dialect we normally do not use two of these modals in the same verb unit, and when we make use of one of them with a nonmodal auxiliary, the modal will appear before the nonmodal. With the exception of *ought,* the form of the verb following the modal will always be the common or naming form of the verb, regardless of whether this verb is being used as an auxiliary or as a full verb. (They may *have* been here. She will *be* coming. We may *go.*)

Ought requires that the sign of the infinitive, *to,* appear between it and the following verb—again regardless of whether this following verb word is being used as an auxiliary or as a full verb. (We ought *to have* gone there. She ought *to eat* more.) *Ought*

differs from the other modals also in that we frequently find it used
in the position of the second verb in the verb phrase, although this
usage is by no means universally approved. (We had *ought* to go.)
I myself have heard hundreds of examples of this or a similar usage,
but I can recall hearing only one use of any of the other modals in
that position. An aunt of mine used to use the expression, "I just
might could," to signify "I may be able to do that."

Another verb which appears to have quasimodal use is the verb
used to. This verb is quite distinguishable from the verb *to use.* In
speech, we use the /s/ for *used to* and the /z/ for *to use.* (Did he
/yuwstə/ be so mean? Did he /yuwz/ "to be" in the sentence? He is
/yuwstə/ books. He has /yuwzd/ two books. We /yuwstə/ know
them well. They /yuwstə/ visit us frequently.) Like the modal
auxiliaries, this verb has no form for the third person singular of the
present indicative and no form for the present participle. We do
not use it after *have,* so we could say that it has no past participle
form. After *do,* our tendency is to spell it without the *d,* but we retain the /s/ in speech even in this situation. Like other auxiliaries
which are followed frequently or invariably by infinitive forms with
the sign, the juncture between *used* and *to* is normally closer than
the juncture between the *to* and the following verb form. (I
/hæftə//now/. We /ɔtə/ /layk/ that. They /yuwstə//siy/ him.)

With the exception of the eleven verbs just discussed, English
verbs have inflected forms for the third person singular of the present indicative, for the past tense, for the present participle, and for
the past participle. The verb *to be* is very irregular in that it has
eight forms: *am, is, are, was, were, be, being, been.* A few other irregular verbs have zero inflection for the past tense and past participle (*cast, cast,* has *cast*); a few others have zero inflection for
the past participle (*run,* ran, have *run*); and some verbs have
alternate inflections for the past tense and/or the past participle.
The details of such irregularities will be observed when you complete the exercises on the verb.

We sometimes confuse what is expressed by the verb with what is
expressed by other parts of the sentence. This seems to be particularly true of the relationship we call *time.* Although English verbs
have but two simple tense forms—the present and the preterit, or
past—grammarians frequently list a fairly sizable number of tenses.
All these tenses except the simple present and the simple past in
English are *analytical*—that is, they are formed through the use of

auxiliaries, and hence are composed of more than one word. One of the numerous functions of tense (simple or analytical) is that of expressing time relationships, even though time relationships may be expressed by some other word in the sentence. In the sentence "He will come tomorrow," time is indicated both by the verb form *will come* and by the word *tomorrow*. If we say, instead, "He comes *tomorrow*," time is indicated primarily by the lexical meaning of *tomorrow*. Time, in other words, is not always clearly indicated by tense forms.

Similar situations exist with regard to other concepts which may be expressed by the verb in certain structures. The concept of *condition*, for example, is expressed by the verb forms in the sentence "*Should* he *come*, give him this," and by a function word in the sentence "*If* he comes, give him this."

Of all English verbs, only *to be* uses more than two forms in the simple present and more than one form in the simple past. *Be* has four forms for the present: I *am;* he, she, it *is;* we, you, they *are;* and, for commands, the form *be*. In the simple past it utilizes the forms *was* and *were*. For the subjunctive mood it uses the forms *be* for the present, *were* for the past.

We speak of tense, mood, person, and number as though these concepts were all expressed by the forms of the verb, but in English they seldom are. In Spanish, for example, we have nine simple tenses (ten, if we count the imperative); of these, three tenses have six forms each to indicate person, number, tense, and mood; six of the tenses have five forms (the first and third person singulars are the same); and the imperative has two forms. We can perhaps see this better if we contrast the way forms are used with the Spanish and the English verbs. The Spanish verb *hablar* and its English equivalent *to speak* are conjugated in the present indicative as follows:

	Singular	Plural
First person	hablo (I speak)	hablamos (We speak)
Second person	hablas (You speak)	habláis (You speak)
Third person	habla (He/she/it speaks)	hablan (They speak)

As can be seen, the form of the Spanish verb contains, in itself, the indicator of both person and number; the subject may be omitted unless gender has to be indicated. (Similar formal contrasts express tense and mood. For example, if we run through the forms for the first person singular of the various simple tenses, we have hab*lo*, hab*laba*, hab*lé*, hab*laré*, hab*laría*, hab*le*, hab*lase*, hab*lara*, hab*lare*.) In the present indicative of English, the form of the verb varies in only one place, consequently we must use the subject to indicate person and number; in the second person we have no means of indicating number except by adding a word such as *both* or *all* to indicate plurality. The past tense tells us even less, for, except in our verb *to be,* the form for the past will be identical for all persons, numbers, and moods.

In addition to the simple present tense, we have a tense form called the *present progressive.* It consists of the simple present form of the auxiliary *to be* plus the present participle of the main verb. The present participles of all English verbs are formed by adding *-ing* to the common or infinitive form of the verbs (*being, play*ing, *run*ning, *think*ing, and so forth). The modal auxiliaries have no present participles.

One of the uses of the present tense not directly related to present time is that of expressing a continuing or habitual action. "I eat two eggs for breakfast." Such sentences suggest that this action is something which I have done for an indefinite period in the past and which I will continue to do for an indefinite period in the future; they say nothing whatsoever about my actions at the moment of speaking or writing. The simple present may express action taking place at the moment of speaking or writing, but it is used infrequently for this purpose in modern English. Some examples of this usage are:

> There *goes* Harry.
> Here *comes* the parade.
> Now I *see* it.

More commonly, we use the present progressive tense to express such ideas.

> Harry *is going.*
> The parade *is coming.*
> We *are looking* at it.

The very immediate future is often expressed, peculiarly enough, by these present tenses and the time word *now.*

> *Now comes* the denouement.
> We *are going now.*

Actually, the present is but a period of indefinite length that serves as a dividing line between the past and the future. Just as the point occupies no space in geometric thought, the present occupies no time. For purposes of thought, however, we can conceive of it as occupying any desired length of time, from a fraction of a second to a millennium. It is probably because of this variation in our concept of the length of present time that we have developed such varied uses for the present tenses and also those which express customary action over an indefinite period stretching from the past into the future.

The present tenses may also be used to express completed past actions. Children seem to be fond of using them to express some action they have seen or in which they have participated. (Sam *steps* up to the plate and *fans* like a windmill.) This use of the present is frequently frowned upon; nevertheless, serious writers often use it to provide a sense of immediacy to the events they are describing.

> While the unspeakable confusion *is* everywhere *weltering* within, and through so many cracks in the surface sulphur smoke *is issuing,* the question *arises:* Through what crevice will the main explosion carry itself?
>
> —Carlyle, *The French Revolution*

As was earlier mentioned, the present tenses are often used to express an indefinite time period which may be either past or present or possibly both. This is, however, not habitual action.

> They *say* she was divorced.
> They *are betting* he will be elected.

We use the auxiliary *do* to form an emphatic form of the present tense. As it must be followed by the common or infinitive form of the main verb, we cannot use it with the present progressive tense forms.

> I/you/we/they *do go.*
> He/she/it *does run.*

The foregoing uses of the present tenses are by no means exhaustive. It is hoped that you will find more uses for these tenses (and also various specific uses for the other tense forms) through working the following exercises.

Exercise 6-1   Verb Forms and Uses

1. Using the verbs in the lists provided below and the pronouns *I, you, he, we, they* as subjects, make oral statements about something that is occurring at this moment. What differences do you find in the forms of the verbs listed in group A and those listed in group B? Where do these differences occur?

A. do	B. can
have	could
hear	may
jump	might
keep	must
need	ought
play	shall
read	should
run	used
see	will
write	would

2. Is *will* in "I will go" the same verb as *will* in "I will it to you"? Is *can* in "I can do it" the same verb as *can* in "We can fruit"? What occurs when we use *he* as a subject in these sentences? Can the words in group B really be said to be verbs in themselves? Do we ever use them without also using some other verb? If so, under what circumstances? When we use group B words with other verbs, which verb carries the lexical meaning?

3. Are there any verbs in group A which may be used in the same manner as those in group B? Do they express the same meaning as full verbs that they do when used in connection with other verbs? Is this true of all of them, or only of some? Are there any verbs not listed in either group which are used as those in group B are? List as many as you can.

4. How many different written forms are there for the verb *to be*? How many different oral forms are there? How many written and oral forms are there for each of the verbs in group B? What is the smallest number of forms a verb may have? The greatest number?

5. Place a proper form of the verb *to play* in the blank in each of the following sentences.

I _____ tennis every day.
I _____ tennis yesterday.
I _____ tennis tomorrow.

Is it possible to use more than one tense form in any of these sentences? Can the same tense form be used in more than one of the sentences? Is the tense form of the verb the true indicator of time in all these situations? In any of them?

6. What time period is represented in the sentence "Men were deceivers ever"? What ideas other than time are expressed by the different forms of the verb that can be placed in each of the blanks in question 5? Can you use all of the group *B* verbs in each sentence? Can you use any of the group *A* words with some form of the verb *to play* in these sentences? If you use words from group *A*, what form or forms of *play* can you use with them? What do you conclude about tense (the varying forms and combinations of the verb) and time? Are tense and time identical?

7. Consider the following groups of sentences.

a. I have to eat.
   I have to go.
b. I must eat.
   I must go.
c. I ought to eat.
   I ought to go.
d. I should eat.
   I should go.
e. I may eat.
   I may go.
f. I might eat.
   I might go.
g. I can eat.
   I can go.
h. I could eat.
   I could go.

What do you find when you compare the concepts expressed by *a* and *b*, or *c* and *d*? What occurs when you add such words as *today*, *yesterday*, and *tomorrow* to the sentences? What happens to *have* in *a*? Can you use *must* with all three of these time words? Are *may* and *might*, *will* and *would*, *shall* and *should*, *can* and *could* related to one another in the same way that *have* and *had* are?

Exercise 6-2   Verb Forms and Uses

1. When you use the pronouns *I*, *you*, and *he* as subjects for the present tense of the verb *to go*, what occurs in the form of the verb? What change, if any, takes place if we use *John and I* instead of *I*? *John and Mary* instead of *you*? *John and Mary* instead of *he*?

2. What is meant by the terms *first person*, *second person*, and *third person*? Does the plural simply express more than one of the singular?

3. Is the change in verb form in the third person singular present indicative consistent for most English verbs? What phonetic differences do you note in the verbs of the following sentences?

    a. The boy tacks the rugs.
       John takes a cab to work.
       The girl caps the bottles.
    b. The boy tags the luggage.
       The crowd mobs the celebrity.
       Mother bids them welcome.
    c. The junior college bridges the gap.
       The mother kisses her baby.
       The pilot buzzes his girl friend's house.

4. Is the pattern the same as that we found in the formation of noun plurals? Some of the verbs in *c* add *s* and some add *es*. Does the pronunciation vary in these two types? What sounds would you add to the verbs *laugh* and *tat* if you used them in the third person singular? Why?

5. In the simple past tense, what forms do we use for the following verbs—that is, how is each spelled and pronounced: *tap, tab, pick, bag, mat, pad?* Think of some other verbs that would fit into each of these classes and try to develop a generalization which accurately describes both the spelling and the pronunciation of these verb forms. Do you find anything comparable here to the /iz, əz/ form of the third person singular? Under what conditions is it used?

6. In what ways do the present tense forms for the verb *to be* differ from the present tense forms of other verbs? What differences do you note in the past tense forms of *to be?* In what way is this different from the normal pattern for forming past tenses?

7. We have said that the allomorphs of a morpheme should have two characteristics: they should convey the same basic idea (be semantically similar), and they should not be freely substitutable for one another. List the allomorphs for noun plurals that would end in the *-s, -es* spellings, those for noun genitives, and those for the third person singular of the present indicative of verbs other than *to be*. Can phonetically or orthographically identical morphs appear in allomorphs of different morphemes? Can semantically different morphs appear in allomorphs of the same morpheme? Are there any possible exceptions to the definition provided for the allomorph? Consider borrowed and native plurals for the same word

—for example, cherub (cherubim, cherubs). What meaning does *do* have in the question "How do you know?" Must a morpheme have meaning, or do some morphemes merely signal structure?

We have already noted the manner of forming the simple past for a large number of verbs in English, and found it to be the addition of the *-ed* inflection in writing and the /t/, /d/, or /əd, id/ in speech. When we studied the inflections for the noun, we discovered that some nouns may form their plurals in more than one way and that, in the case of some of these nouns, the difference in form for the plural was nondistinctive (e.g., cherub*s*, cherub*im*), but in others, the different plurals represented different concepts (hose_, hose*s*). In our study of the verb, we will find a similar situation. In a verb such as *dream*, we have alternate forms for the simple past (*dreamed*, *dreamt*) which convey the same meaning; but we also have verbs such as *fly*, which have alternate forms for the past tense (*flew*, *flied*), and we find that one of these has a specialized meaning (*flied* in baseball terminology).

While the number of irregular verbs in English is quite large, the number of irregularities in the past tense inflection is much smaller. The materials in Exercise 6-3 are designed to help you recognize and pull together the different groups of irregular past tense forms. When you have discovered all the possible changes in the form of the verb used to indicate past tense, you will have the various allomorphs of the *-ed* past tense morpheme.

Exercise 6-3   Past Tense Forms

1. How do we form the simple past tense of the verbs provided in the list below? Does the form vary for person or number? Can you add other verbs to this list? What phonetic characteristics do these verbs have in common?

cast	bid	spread
cost	let	shed

2. Does any verb in the above list have more than one way of forming its simple past? If so, does the meaning differ for the

variant forms? Are both forms in current use, or does one of them tend to be archaic?

3. How do we form the simple past tense of *spend, build,* and *gird?* Do any of these have more than one form for the simple past? If so, is one form more commonly used than the other?

4. What do the verbs in each of the groups provided below have in common? Wherein does each verb differ from each of the others in its group?

A. lie	B. eat	C. fall	D. awake	E. sit
bite	read	draw	take	give
write	speak		slay	stick
strike	see			
fly				
fight				
find				

F. stand	G. hold	H. run	I. tear	J. shoot
hang	blow	come	get	choose

5. Do any of the verbs in the above groups have more than one way of forming the past tense? If they have more than one form, does the meaning differ? Are there other English verbs which could be grouped under any of the above?

6. Do the verbs *buy, creep, say, hear, tell,* or *do* belong in any of the groups in question 4? How does the past tense of these verbs differ from that of the verbs provided in the groups?

7. What phonetic changes take place in the formation of the simple past tense of the verb *lose?*

8. What phonetic changes take place in the formation of the simple past tense of the verbs *have* and *make?*

9. What phonetic changes take place in the formation of the simple past tense of the verbs *teach, catch,* and *bring?*

10. List all the different ways we have noted of forming the simple past tense of verbs in English.

11. Is there any evidence to indicate that some of these irregular verbs are showing a tendency to become regular in the formation of their past tenses? To how many of the verbs in this exercise can we now add the *-ed* inflection?

As you have undoubtedly noted, the form for the past tense and that for the past participle of regular verbs in English are identical.

With such verbs it is the presence or absence of an auxiliary which enables us to distinguish the past tense from the past participle. In standard English the past tense is never used following an auxiliary, and the past participle is never used as part of the verb without having one or more auxiliaries preceding it. The auxiliary immediately preceding the past participle will be either *have* or one of the linking verbs, such as *be, seem, appear, get,* and so on. Any form of the auxiliaries may precede the past participle. When a form of one of the linking verbs is used, the subject of the verb will be either a word or unit that would stand in object relationship to the verb in active voice (The girl was struck by the car), or it will be described by the past participle. In the latter case, the past participle is functioning as an adjective and is subject to the tests of the adjective. It may be changed to attributive position (The girl was tired. The tired girl), and it may be modified by an intensifier (The girl was *very* tired). The distinction between this adjectival use of the past participle and the verbal use of it in the passive voice will be discussed in greater detail when we consider voice in transitive verbs.

Some irregular verbs have identical forms for the past tense and the past participle (teach, *taught,* have *taught*), but the majority of irregular verbs will have differing forms for them. The use of the past tense for the past participle (She has *went*), the past participle for the past tense (I *seen* her do it), and the substitution of a regular for an irregular form of either (He *knowed* him immediately. This corn was *growed* by my son) are very noticeable characteristics of substandard English.

If we use the naming form of the verb as a base, we can divide past participles into a number of different classes or groups on the basis of the different types of phonetic changes from the base they exhibit. As you should have learned in working with similar groupings of past tense forms in Exercise 6-3 above, such groupings aid us neither in the identification of the forms when we see or hear them nor in the use of the forms when we speak or write. The knowledge of the kind of changes that occur in one such verb does not enable us to predict what changes will occur in another. We cannot use these patterns of change for analogical creation as we can use those found in regular or weak verbs. To do so would produce analogies such as *fight: fought :: sight: sought.* Each of us must learn to identify and use irregular forms individually. Most of us have already done so. If we did not already know these forms, we could not make such an analysis without consulting a dictionary.

Most of the auxiliaries that may be followed by the past participle may also be followed by the infinitive. The infinitive itself can serve either as the final or full verb or as an auxiliary, and it may have auxiliaries as part of its tense form (*to go, to be gone, to have been gone,* and so forth); it may also be used as a modifier or as a noun. The word *to* is sometimes called the sign of the infinitive. *And* also appears at times as a sign of the infinitive, particulary after *try* and *go.* (Try *and* stop me. Go *and* see him.) The sign of the infinitive is not used after any of the modal auxiliaries except *ought;* it is always present after any form of *have* or any form of the linking verbs when these appear as auxiliaries before the common or naming form of the verb. The sign of the infinitive never appears immediately before a past participle, though it may occur as part of the preceding auxiliary (see the examples above). We occasionally find it in an idiomatic construction before an *-ing* form. (We got *to* talk*ing* and forgot what time it was.) In a few verbs, the naming form of the verb and the form of the past participle are identical (to *run,* have *run*).

If we except the modal auxiliaries and some few verbs which are used only as passives, practically all verbs in English have a present participle form. The method of forming the present participle is invariable: we simply add the inflection *-ing* to the common or naming form of the verb. In those instances in which the common written form ends in one consonant letter (except *x* or *w*), preceded by one vowel letter, we double the consonant letter before adding the inflection. In spoken English, we frequently hear /n/ substituted for /ŋ/ in the inflection.

The infinitive, the present participle, and the past participle are sometimes called the *nonfinite* forms of the verb. As verbs, these forms appear only in the analytical tenses. All three of these forms may appear as modifiers, and the infinitive and *-ing* forms may appear as nouns, even without determiners. When the *-ing* form is used as a noun, it is generally called a gerund instead of a participle.

Exercise 6-4   Verb Forms

1. When we speak of a particular verb in English, we generally designate it by using the common form of the verb with or without

to—for example, the verb *to be* or the verb *have.* Is the word *to* a necessary adjunct to the infinitive? When you give a command, what relationship exists between the form of the verb you use and this naming form? When you use the verb in the present tense, what relationships exist between the forms of that tense and the form of the infinitive? Is this true of all verbs? When you construct the past tense of regular verbs, what relationship exists between its form and the form of the infinitive?

2. Certain auxiliaries, particularly *have, be,* and *get* are frequently used in combination with a form of the verb called the *past participle.* What form of the verb *play* would we use in the following sentences? What relationship exists between this past participle form and the form for the simple past tense?

> The music was _____ by the orchestra.
> John has _____ baseball for many years.

3. Supply the simple past tense form and the past participle form for each of the following verbs: *bid, jump, spend, have, fight, tell, leave.* Is identity of form for the past tense and the past participle a quality only of regular verbs in English?

4. Supply the past tense and the past participle for each of the following verbs: *come, awake, lie* (recline), *choose, blow, give, begin, fly, ride.* Analyze the phonetic changes that occur in changing the infinitive to each of these forms.

5. Are there many verbs in English for which the form of the infinitive is identical with the form of the past participle? List as many as you can.

6. Are there many verbs in English for which the form of the past participle is "regular" and the form of the past tense is "irregular"? List as many examples of these as you can.

7. Of the two verbs *to lie* (to recline, to prevaricate), which has the irregular form for the past participle? Is the form for the past tense of this verb also irregular? Which is the base form for the past participle of the irregular verb, the common form or the past tense form? What phonetic changes occur in forming the past participle?

8. In what way is the formation of the past participle for the verb *choose* different from that of the irregular verb *lie?* Does the phonetic structure of the verbs account for this difference in any way? Do these two verbs belong to the same subgroup in

terms of their manner of forming the past tense and past participle forms?

9. In what way is the formation of the past participle of *blow* similar to that of *come?* In what way does it differ? Compare *blow* and *give* as you did *lie* and *choose.* What do you find?

10. What occurs in the formation of the past tense and the past participle of *begin?*

11. Compare the forms of *fly* and *ride* to those of *begin,* and then compare the forms of *fly* and *ride* to one another. What do you find? What are the past tense and past participle forms for *fly* when we use the verb in the situational context of baseball?

12. Find at least one other verb which fits the past tense and the past participle patterning of each of the verbs listed in questions 3 and 4.

13. Look up the past tense and past participle forms of each of the following verbs in your dictionary. What do these verbs have in common? How many of these verbs may form either their past tense or their past participle in the regular manner? Does this suggest anything about what is happening to irregular verbs in English? What forms are marked *archaic* or *obsolete?* Are these most frequently regular or irregular?

abide	burn	get	slide	stink
be	chide	hide	slink	strike
bear	clothe	hold	smite	swear
beat	curse	leap	sow	swing
bet	dig	light	speak	thrive
bid	dive	show	speed	tread
bite	dream	shrink	spin	wake
break	drink	sing	spring	wind
build	dwell	sink	sting	wring

14. In what way does the past tense of the verb *to be* differ markedly from the past tense forms of the other irregular verbs?

15. Supply the form of *play* that would be used in each of the following sentences. What do we call this?

He is _____ the organ at this moment.
She was _____ the organ when I arrived.

16. List as many verbs as you can for which there is no present participle form. Do any of these have a form for the past tense or for the past participle? Do any of them have a special form

for the third person singular present indicative? What variations, if any, do you find for the present participle inflection?

Exercise 6-5   The Combination of Verb Forms

1. Look up the word *analytical* in your dictionary. What is its meaning when it is used grammatically?

2. When we use any of the modal auxiliaries (*will, would, shall, should, may, might, can, could, must, ought*) with another verb in a sentence, what form or forms of the other verb word will follow it? How does *ought* differ from the other auxiliaries?

3. When we use the auxiliaries *be, do, have, get, need, dare, keep,* or *used* with another verb in a verbal unit, what form or forms of the second verb may we use with each of them?

4. When we use *must*, or *have* + the common form of some other verb, what differences do you find in the modal and nonmodal usages? Consider the following examples.

We _____ go tomorrow.
We _____ go now.
We _____ go yesterday.

5. What difference in meaning can you observe in the following sentences? In which of them is the past participle as much an adjective as it is a verb?

He is tired.
He has tired.

6. After which of the nonmodal auxiliaries can we use the *-ing* form of the verb? Does it ever appear to be a noun in these constructions?

7. After which of the auxiliaries can we use the past participle forms? Does there appear to be any variation of our usage in these combinations? Can you account for it?

8. What differences in meaning are expressed by the verbs *be* and *have* when they are used as auxiliaries and when they are used as full verbs? Is there a similar difference in meaning expressed by the verbs *dare, need, plan, keep, wish,* and *hope?* Should the former group be considered as full verbs or as function words? In all cases? Are the verbs in the latter group full verbs or func-

tion words? What functions does the auxiliary *do* serve? Is *do* ever used as a full verb? If so, what meaning does it convey?

9. When we use a modal auxiliary, such as *shall* or *can*, in the same unit with a full verb, does the auxiliary precede or follow the full verb? Can any other words appear between it and the full verb? If so, to what class or classes do these words belong? Are there any parallels between the uses of the modal auxiliaries with verbs and the uses of the determiners with nouns?

10. When we have used one infinitive or common form of the verb after a modal auxiliary, do we ever make use of a second infinitive form after the first form? What other forms of the verb may follow directly after the modal auxiliary + infinitive combination?

11. What form or forms of the verb may follow a present participle? Are these forms part of the verb?

12. What form or forms of the verb may follow a past participle? Are these forms part of the verb?

13. What types of verbs do you find between the modal auxiliary and the form of the verb that carries lexical meaning? What types of meaning are supplied by the auxiliaries? Are we justified in calling these verb-auxiliary combinations *analytical* tenses? Why?

14. What kind of meaning is supplied by *have* in "I have to go"? In "I have ordered it"? What meaning is supplied by *do* in "I do believe you"? What function is served by *do* in "Do you think so?" In "I do not know"? In "How many of you know the answer? I do"?

15. In which of the following sentences is the action of the verb completed? In which is it still to take place? Is this concept of *completion* as important an aspect of tense as *time* is? Why?

He goes today.	He goes tomorrow.
He will go today.	He will go tomorrow.
He is going today.	He is going tomorrow.
He is going to go today.	He is going to go tomorrow.
He went today.	He went yesterday.
He has gone today.	He had gone yesterday.
He could have gone today.	He could have gone yesterday or tomorrow.

16. Review the modal auxiliaries, and list as many of the concepts as you can that may be expressed by each of them. If you find any overlapping, make note of it.

In our study of the noun we discovered that nouns are frequently composed of more than one word, and that we sometimes write these combinations as though they were one word, as in *longshoreman;* sometimes we hyphenate them, as in *sister-in-law;* sometimes we write them as separate words, as in *army worm.* We also found that such words could be made up of elements which, taken alone, would normally function as some part of speech other than the noun.

We will find similar and equally widespread phenomena operating in the formation of words used as verbs. We have already encountered the verb phrase composed of one or more auxiliaries plus a full verb, and we observed that the full verb appears as the last member of the phrase and provides lexical meaning.

In addition to the nouns formed by combining full words, we found that many nouns are formed by adding derivational suffixes to root bases or to word stem bases. Similarly, we find many verbs formed by adding derivational prefixes and/or suffixes to root bases and to word stem bases (*be+head, be+little, en+dear, en+liv+en, isol+ate, renov+ate, energ+ize, short+en, length+en*). We also find verbs constructed of full word bases, but in this case one of the unit words is generally clearly recognizable as a verb in itself, whereas in the construction of nouns we often find componds composed of units which are not nouns (*ever+green*). Some of these compound verb forms are written solid (*offset, outgrow, overlook*) and some are separated in writing (*turn in, hand out*).

With the noun we found that the methods of adding inflections to such units varied. For most simple compounds the head word or head unit was the final one, and it was this word or unit that took the inflection whether it chanced to be the plural or the genitive inflection (table lamps, longshoreman's). With the so-called group noun the head word or head unit usually appeared first; we added the plural inflection to the head word, but placed the genitive inflection at the end of the unit (men-at-arms, brothers-in-law, but Governor of Maine's office). There were a few situations in which there was apparently no universal agreement whether the partial unit or the complete unit was the true head; with these, we found variation in usage (two cupsful of sugar, two cupfuls of sugar).

There is rarely any doubt as to which is the head unit in a two-word verb, for one of the two words would normally serve as a verb outside the combination, and it is to this word that we add the verbal inflections. (The tree over*hangs* the house. The merchant is under*cutting* his competitors. The auditor *looked* over the books. The news has *shaken* up the country.) Inflections may be present on any auxiliary or on the main verb, but they will not be added to the combining word (*is* undercutt*ing*, *has* be*en* look*ed* up to, *has* shak*en* up).

Our real problem with the verb is often that of determining which word or words actually compose it. We can see just how complicated this problem is by carefully examining some dictionary definitions. As one meaning for the verb *endorse*, *Webster's New World Dictionary* has "to give support or approval to." To show that this is an adequate definition for one aspect of *endorse*, we substitute one for the other in a sentence: "The union *endorsed* the school bond issue," "The union *gave approval to* the school bond issue." In one sentence the verb is expressed by a single word; in the other, the identical verbal idea is expressed by what would normally be construed as a verb, its object, and a preposition.

Such situations may also present some very different complications. In requesting that you give me your papers, I could use a verb such as *submit* or a combined form such as *hand in,* but in using this latter form I may separate the two parts. I may say "*Hand in* the papers that you prepared for today," or "*Hand* the papers *in* that you prepared for today," or even "*Hand* the papers that you prepared for today *in.*" Though I may move the *in* around quite freely, I may not omit it. It is definitely a part of the unit that provides the verbal meaning of the sentence.

This indispensability is not, however, a characteristic of all such combinations. We have the verb *pick,* one of whose meanings is *to choose.* We also have the verb *pick out* which also conveys the idea of choosing, and, although it is probably more common to use this form than the other, the *out* is by no means essential. As if this were not complicated enough, we find also that some of these words which are added to the verb may not be separated from the main verb. For example, I may use *to come with* as a synonym for *to accompany,* and so say "Come with me"; but I cannot say * "Come me with."

It should not surprise us to learn that one word may often do

1. The asterisk indicates atypical English.

the work, or carry the meaning of two or more other words, for we encountered situations of this nature at the very beginning of our study. What we need to be concerned with here is the question "What kind of words are we using in these combinations?"

The verb may have a number of different types of complements: adverbs in their various forms, such as simple adverbs, phrasal adverbs, and clausal adverbs; objects of various types, such as direct, indirect, reflexive, phrasal, and clausal; and objects which are themselves complemented by complements of adjectival, adverbial, or nominal types. In some structures the verbal idea may be expressed by the verb alone, but in other structures it is expressed by the verb plus its complement. If I say "He kicked me," for example, I express the verbal idea by the word *kicked*. If, instead, I say "He gave me a kick," I express the same idea by using the verb plus its complement—in this structure, an object—*gave a kick*.

One of the most troublesome distinctions we must make is that between the adverb which helps convey the verbal meaning and the preposition (with or without an expressed object). In writing, the same form may often represent either a preposition or an adverb. For the native speaker of English, stress patterning will help to distinguish between these two. In such sentences as "This is the drive we turn in," "It is time to turn in" (go to bed), and "These are the papers to turn in," we find a stress pattern used in the first sentence which is different from that used in the other two. In the first sentence we will normally stress the word *turn;* in the second and third sentences, we will normally place our strongest stress on the word *in*. When the stress is placed upon *in*, we have an adverb; when it is on the verb, we have a preposition. It makes little difference whether we define the verb as being the verb word plus an adverb, the verb plus a preposition, or whether we simply say that this is a verb and an adverb or a verb and a preposition— two words are required to provide the meaning which would be provided in other structures by either fewer or more words. Any inflections which are to be added will be placed on the main verb (He turn*ed* in the driveway. They are turn*ing* in for the night. She turn*s* in her papers on time. The papers were proofread before they were turn*ed* in), and our stress patterning will be strong on the adverb and weak on the preposition.

Both the preposition and the adverb may be found in various positions: "To whom shall I give this," "Who shall I give this tŏ"; Dówn he went," "He went dówn"; "Look óver these accounts," "Look these accounts óver"; "Turn ĭn this driveway," "This is the driveway to turn ĭn." However, there are some positions which both cannot occupy: "The driveway he turned ĭn," "The driveway ĭn which he turnéd"; "The spy he turned ín," but *not* * "The spy ín which he turned."

Fortunately, although such grammatical patterns *do* present real difficulties for some of us in terms of analysis, they present little difficulty in terms of natural usage for the native speaker. We have learned to use them freely just as we have learned to use all other patterns of English—by hearing them and imitating what we have heard.

Exercise 6-6   Combining Verb Forms

In the previous exercise we noted some of the ways in which auxiliaries are combined with other verb forms to provide analytical tenses. In this exercise we will concern ourselves with quite a different type of verb form combination.

1. What are the various meanings of the verb *pick?* Consider the following structures: *pick up a room, pick on him, pick off an enemy, pick at your food, pick out a dress.* Does the verb appear to consist of more than one word in any of these expressions? Can you note any difference in the stress you use in pronouncing the words following *pick?* Which of these would you stress strongly and which weakly? Does the verb appear to consist of a single word in any of these expressions? Is there any correspondence between those situations in which the verb appears to be one word and those in which one of the basic meanings of *pick* is preserved? Is there any correspondence between those situations in which the verb appears to be one word and those in which the word following the main verb is strongly stressed? Those in which it is weakly stressed? Are any of the combinations capable of expressing more than one idea? Provide examples.

2. Earlier we decided that *lie* (to prevaricate) was a different verb than *lie* (to recline). If a verb has identical forms but expresses

more than one meaning, should we regard it as one verb or more than one verb? What meanings are expressed by the verb *get* in the following structures: *get a job, get a letter, get on well, get better, get a headache, get hurt, get off on the wrong foot.* Is the verb simply *get* in all these? How many verbs do we have here? Are there other forms with *get?* Consult your dictionary.

3. Provide a single-word verb to express the verbal idea found in each of the following sentences. Underline the word or words which express the verbal idea in each sentence. Indicate the stress you would use on each of these words.

    a. The policeman ran in the suspect.
    b. The driver ran down the pedestrian.
    c. The wife ran out on her husband.
    d. We ran off an election.
    e. She ran a bill up down at the grocery.
    f. We ran up the flag.
    g. He ran through a fortune.
    h. The gossip ran down her own mother.
    i. One student ran off with every prize.

4. Do we have anything similar to the combinations in question 3 in the verbs found in the following sentences? If so, wherein does the similarity lie? Where do we place the stress on such words?

    a. The weeds overran the garden.
    b. The contractor underbid his competitors.
    c. His gains offset his losses.
    d. We overlooked his deficiencies.

5. When a verbal idea is expressed by a verb plus a word which appears to belong to a different form-class or part of speech, where do the changes in the verb form occur? Is this equally true when the nonverb word comes at the end of the unit as well as when it is added to the beginning of the verb?

6. Can the nonverb word which is combined with the basic verb be separated from it by an intervening word or words? Is this true of all situations in which the nonverb word follows the basic verb? Is it true when the nonverb word precedes the basic verb?

7. Do we ever combine more than one word with the basic verb? Do we ever make combinations consisting of a nonverb word before the basic verb and another nonverb word following it? Provide examples.

Suggested Readings

SECTION 6

Brown, Dona Worrall, Wallace C. Brown, and Dudley Bailey, *Form in Modern English*, Chap. IV. New York: Oxford University Press, Inc., 1958.

Hill, Archibald A., *Introduction to Linguistic Structures*, Chaps. XII and XIII. New York: Harcourt, Brace & World, Inc., 1958.

Whitehall, Harold, *Structural Essentials of English*, Chap. VI. New York: Harcourt, Brace & World, Inc., 1951.

Function Shifts

One of the reasons why structure is of such great importance in English is that we have many words that do double, triple, or even quadruple duty. Without changing the form of a word, we can cause it to function differently by placing it in a different position in the sentence. (The officer will *arrest* you. The officer will make an *arrest*.) In the pure function shift, except for the addition of the normal inflections, there is no change in the word form when it shifts from one part of speech to another. Thus many words, such as *walk, seal, value, joke, kiss,* and so forth, can be used either as nouns or as verbs: as nouns they may take the *-s* plural inflections or the *-'s* genitive inflection; as verbs they may take the *-s* third person singular present indicative inflections, the *-ed* past tense inflections, the *-ed* past participle inflections, and the *-ing* present participle inflections.

We have other words which make no change in their written form, but which *do* change their spoken form to indicate their shift in function. In the sentence "I am content, and you will have to content yourself with this content, too," we have no change in *content* when it is used as adjective and verb, but when it is used as a noun, we find that it has undergone a number of changes in spoken English despite the lack of change in its written form. One noticeable change is the shift in stress, with the strongest stress falling on the first syllable of the noun, but on the second syllable of the adjective and verb. Accompanying this shift in stress is a change in vowel from the /a/ in the first syllable of the noun to the /ə/ in the first syllable of the adjective and verb. Other pairs of words, such as pérvĕrt (noun) and pĕrvért (verb), differ only in stress in spoken English. Still others, such as object (noun) and object (verb), may have the stress shift accompanied by changes in vowels in both syllables (/ábjĭkt/, /əbjékt/).

Many other words make use of derivational prefixes or suffixes to indicate shifts in function. The verb makes use of fewer of these than does the noun or the adjective. En- and be- are commonly used as prefixes, and -ate, -en, ify, and -ize are commonly used as suffixes in forming verbs.

Like most partial truths, the commonly held notion that verbs express action and time often leads us astray in our thinking about the verb. From the point of view of the student it would be nice if the verb were that simple, but any careful study of the verb (particularly of the modal auxiliaries and the combined tense forms, such as we made in Section 6) will show that the verb is used to express a very wide variety of concepts. The materials in Exercise 7-1 will introduce you to a few means of forming verbs and of using them to express additional concepts.

Exercise 7-1

1. Consider the following sentences.

The motor was burnt out.
We will motor to Detroit.

How is the word *motor* used in each sentence?

2. Can every noun be made into a verb simply by putting it in the position of a verb? What is your feeling about the following usages?

   a. I'll banana you.
   b. They have governmented us.
   c. He is diffusioning it.

3. Do we ever make verbs from derived nouns? If so, provide examples.

4. What changes occur in the pronunciation of the italicized words in the following sentences? What, in addition to position and function words, indicates the noun and the verb? Is it merely stress?

 a. The *subject* was thoroughly discussed.
  They will *subject* you to an inquiry.
 b. The *contract* was a fair one.
  Don't *contract* to do more than you can.
 c. The *object* is to observe the language.
  Do you *object* to doing that?

5. What methods have been used to form the verbs in the examples provided below?

A. hyphenate	B. Christianize	C. deify	D. blacken
renovate	energize	purify	shorten
E. envision	F. engineer	G. prejudge	H. enliven
endow	volunteer	postpone	enlighten

6. Is each of the verbs in the above groups formed in the same way? Are there derivational suffixes other than those illustrated which are commonly used to form verbs in English? Are there other prefixes which are commonly used to form verbs? List as many of each as you can. Does there appear to be any relationship between the use of a particular prefix or suffix and the type of base to which it is attached?

7. Is there any relationship between the use of a particular prefix or suffix and the expression of a particular type of verbal idea? For example, do any of the verbs in the above groups express the concept of causation? If so, does this appear to be a quality provided by the use of particular prefix or suffix? Can it be expressed by verbs which do not use this prefix or suffix?

8. When we looked at verb tenses, we found them associated with the terms *past, present,* and *future.* What tense is used in the sentences provided below? What time relationship is implied? Is this time relationship the result of choice of tense or choice of verb?

I anticipate having a visit with you.
I recall my last visit with you.

9. What kind of conceptual relationships are implicit in the verbs of the following sentences? Is tense a factor?

He began to fight.
He continued to fight.
He stopped fighting.

Make lists of other verbs which imply or suggest initiation, continuation, and cessation.

10. What difference do you note in the ideas expressed by the verbs in the two sentences provided below? List as many verbs as you can that express repetitive actions. Do these verbs appear to have any formal quality in common? Do we have any other means of expressing this concept of repetitive action?

He hit the boy.
He hammered the boy.

11. What type of idea is expresed by such words as *hope, wish, desire?* When these words are used as verbs, is the action represented an action which has been completed? What time relationships are implied? Is there any implication of negation in the following sentences? If so, does this stem from choice of the tense or from choice of the verb? Is it a quality of the second verb used, or of something else?

I hope to go.
I hoped to go.
I hope he will come.
I hoped he would come.

12. Consider the following question and some of the possible responses that might be made to it. For what does each of these auxiliaries substitute? Under what conditions may they be used as substitute verbs?

Do you plan to go to the meeting?
I *do.*
I *may.*
I *can't.*
I *could,* but I don't think I *will.*

Suggested Readings

SECTION 7

Brown, Dona Worrall, Wallace C. Brown, and Dudley Bailey, *Form in Modern English*, Chap. III. New York: Oxford University Press, Inc., 1958.

Jespersen, Otto, *Growth and Structure of the English Language*, 9th ed., pp. 175-82. Garden City, New York: Doubleday & Company, Inc., 1955.

SECTION 8

Speech Pattern Units

To deal adequately with each of the possible variations in the patterning of English speech would require a much larger book than this one. We shall attempt here, therefore, to consider only the general areas in which these variations take place. Some of these we have already mentioned. Those that we will concern ourselves with at this point are stress, pitch, terminals, and juncture.

In the previous exercises we learned that shift of stress, sometimes alone and sometimes accompanied by phonetic changes, was used to distinguish some nouns from verbs and/or adjectives. When stress is used in this way to distinguish one word from another, we will have to recognize it as a type of phonemic contrast. Hence we can say that we have stress phonemes and stress morphemes.

Because stress is relative (that is, we could apply any degree of stress to a particular syllable or word) we could probably set up any number of stress categories that we might wish to observe. These could be assigned scientifically in terms of the actual number of decibels of sound used in pronouncing a particular word or syllable, the actual duration of sound, and/or the actual pitch that the sound has, all of which are related to stress. If we were to try this, we would soon find that this kind of distinction is of no real importance to us. We are rather concerned with the comparison of stress placed upon one word or syllable with that placed upon other words or syllables in the same speech unit. We have already noted (p. 58) that for practical purposes it is sufficient for us to recognize four degrees of stress: primary (´), secondary (ˆ), tertiary (ˋ), and weak or unstressed (˘). And, we have already seen in our study of the noun how stress patterning enables us to distinguish a compound noun such as *White House* from a modified noun such as *white house*. Stress also works in our larger units of speech. We find, for example, that we normally use strong stress on only one word or syllable of each phrase in English. Stress, therefore, is of great importance in providing the rhythm of normal English speech. But by shifting our stress, we can express different concepts—for example, in the prepositional phrase, the noun head would normally receive the strongest stress (in our hóuse), but if we wish to contrast the location represented by *in* with such locations as might be represented by *at, outside, from,* or *toward,* we would put the strong stress on the preposition (ín our house). If we desired to contrast this particular house with all others, we would place the strong stress on the determiner *our* (in óur house). Such variations in stress are not mere caprice; they are used as a means of contrasting one specific linguistic situation with all others of a similar nature.

Patterning of this type is one of the most difficult skills for foreigners to acquire. Many learn the grammatical forms, the vocabulary, and even the idioms of the language long before they learn the natural use of these speech patterns. The native speaker of English generally absorbs them by imitation before he enters school.

Pitch, like stress, is another variable which could be divided into infinitely small units. But, as in the case of stress, we are not concerned with this type of division in our speech; we are concerned only with the relationship of the pitch used in one section of a linguistic unit as contrasted with the pitch used in its other parts. The exact pitches used by two different native speakers of a particular English dialect might vary considerably as they produced the same sentence, but the patterns of relative pitch would approximate one another very closely. In other words, each speaker would begin his or her sentence at a particular pitch level but having begun on that level, would follow the same general *pattern* of rises and drops in pitch that any other native speaker would use. However, although the pitch would rise or drop according to the same pattern, it would not necessarily rise or drop to the same *degree*.

We shall limit ourselves to distinguishing four pitch levels. These are customarily designated by using as superscriptions the numbers *1* to *4*, with *1* indicating the lowest pitch a speaker normally uses and *4* the highest (or at least a pitch higher than normal). In normal English sentences we rarely make use of more than three levels; the fourth or highest level is used only in emotional situations. A simple statement, such as "He is a man," will normally start on *2* and maintain that level through the first three words, rise to *3* at the beginning of the final word, and then glide down to *1* as that word is pronounced. This dropping of pitch level will also be accompanied by a diminution of stress.

Most straightforward simple English sentences, be they statements, questions, or commands, end on or near the *1* level. When they do not, of course, the pitch patterning expresses a difference of meaning; hence, pitch constitutes another type of phoneme. Let us take a simple question as an example: "Are you from Detroit or Ann Arbor?" If, in asking this question, I assume that my listener is from one of these two cities, I will make use of the normal pattern and drop to the *1* level at the end of the sentence. If, on the other hand, I expect a negative answer—that is, I assume my listener is from a city other than Detroit or Ann Arbor—I will keep the pitch on or near the *3* level at the end of the question. This introduces another aspect of pitch—that of terminal pitch. Actually, the direction of the terminal pitch movement is of equal importance to the pitch level. We can drop from, rise from, or sustain any pitch level. In the normal prosaic question or statement such as, "What's the dog's name?" "His name is Bounce," we would have a pattern such as the following:

^{2}What's the dog's ^{3}name^1↘
^{2}His name is ^{3}Bounce^1↘

If we want to make the statement into a question, we would use a different pattern:

^{2}His name is ^{3}Bounce^3↗

Sustained pitch terminals are most commonly found after introductory dependent clauses and between absolute constructions and the main clause:

^{2}If I were ^{3}you^2→^{2}I wouldn't ^{3}do that^1↘
^{2}George^2→^{2}Will you open the ^{3}window^1↘

Terminals can also be phonemic, as is well illustrated by the often used examples:

^{2}What are we having for ^{3}dinner^1→^{1}Mother^1↗
^{2}What are we having for ^{3}dinner^1↘^{2}Mother^2↗
^{2}What are you ^{3}reading^1→^{1}Ma^{1}cauley^1↗
^{2}What are you ^{3}reading^1↘^{1}Ma^{2}cauley^2↗

In the first example of each pair, the words *Mother* and *Macauley* represent the person addressed. The pattern used for *Mother* in the second sentence suggests that she is to be eaten, and the pattern used for *Macauley* in the second sentence of that pair indicates that we are speaking of the author. Though most of us have never analyzed such refinements of English speech, we need only to have them called to our attention to find that we use them automatically.[1]

When we note the difference in speech between the constructions "I can't ache" and "I can take," we find that it consists of the way we join the /t/ to the sound preceding it or to the sound following it. Juncture is a two-way phenomenon. Not only is it a matter of joining the /t/ to /kæn/ or to /eyk/, it is also a matter of separating the /t/ from /kæn/ or from /eyk/. But whether we consider it to be a matter of joining or a matter of separating sounds, we find that it can be phonemic.

We shall observe but two types of juncture—*close* juncture and *open* or *plus* juncture. Close juncture represents the way the phones are tied together to form a syllable in which the various parts are not in themselves meaningful. Open juncture represents the way we separate meaningful combinations of phones from one another. For example, between the various phones that make up the word *oxide*, we would have close junctures. In *ox-eyed*, in which the same phones should appear, we would have an open juncture between the /ks/ and the /ay/. It is also this combination of close and open junctures that helps us to distinguish between groups of words, such as *car tracks* and *cart racks* or a

---

[1] Those of you who may wish to study this in greater detail will find a very clear presentation of it in Charles Hockett, *A Course in Modern Linguistics* (New York: The Macmillan Company, 1958), pp. 33-46.

good-looking glass and a *good looking glass*. Here again, we find another type of phoneme.[2] Thus, in addition to the phonemes we first observed, which were based upon contrasts of sounds, we also have discovered phonemes whose contrasts occur in stress, in terminal pitch, and in juncture.

Turn now to Exercise 8-1 for reinforcement of the concepts which have just been discussed.

Exercise 8-1   Speech Pattern Units

1. On what sound or sound group does the strongest stress fall in each of the following structures? Is stress the means we use for distinguishing one sound from another which is similar to it? Are these pairs distinguished by some phonetic differences, or by differences in the order of their sounds? If not, what does appear to be the distinguishing factor?

a nice box	an ice box
that's tough	that stuff
a vise	of ice
a vale	of ale
append	up end

2. Look up the words *adder* and *newt* in your dictionary. What does the history of these words show? Are new words ever created by the process of shifting points of juncture?

3. Is the juncture between *a* and *nice* in *a nice box* the same kind of juncture we have between *back* and *of* in *the back of the house?* In which is the juncture more pronounced? How many strong stresses do we have in each of these structures? Is the juncture in either of these identical with that found after *comes* in "If he comes, tell him I have left." What kind of pitch terminal would be used after *comes?*

4. Suppose the sentence "If he comes, tell him I have left," is followed by another: "I could wait no longer." Is the juncture

---

[2] This particular type of phoneme is open to question in that it consists of the absence or presence of a particular sound in a word or syllabic sound group. What we observe is the removal of a sound from one sound group and the addition of that sound to another sound group. Essentially, it is the same type of contrast that we find in such pairs of words as /kar/ and /kart/ or /art/ and /kart/.

between these two sentences similar to that we have observed in any other situations? What kind of pitch terminals would we use after *left?* Is there more than one way in which these sentences could be punctuated?

5. The statement is sometimes made that we raise our voices to indicate a question in English speech. There are two ways in which we can raise our voices: one is by increasing the volume or stress, and the other is by changing the tone or pitch of our voices. Which of these two is referred to in the above statement? Is this an accurate statement? Where does the highest pitch level occur in each of the following questions? What type of terminal pitch is used in each of these questions? Is it possible to vary the pitch pattern? How would you say *Who is he* when you intend to follow it with "that he should give us orders?"

Who is he?
What do you mean?
Why did you do that?
Do you mean John?

6. What is our pitch pattern like in the normal short statement: Do we start on a high pitch and gradually move to a lower one? Do we make use of a middle pitch for the beginning of the statement and then have a rise in pitch just before we drop our pitch at the end? Is the pitch at the end of the statement normally lower or higher than the initial pitch? Describe your pitch pattern in making the statement "I feel sick." On which word do you use the highest pitch? On which do you use the lowest? Would it be possible to recognize more than three degrees of pitch? What would your pitch pattern be if you were using "I feel sick" to express surprise that someone should have asked you if you felt sick?

7. What occurs when primary stress is moved from one word to another in questions such as those provided in question 5? Is this true of statements also? If you are just leaving a party and your host comes out with an armload of coats, how would you say, "That's mine"? Have you ever heard a small child say the same sentence when someone is trying to take something from him? What differences are observable in the total patterning of the sentences in these differing circumstances?

8. Does the prolongation of a sound ever cause a distinction between two word meanings in your dialect? Does the prolongation of a word ever change the basic meaning of a sentence in modern English? Does the shifting of strong stress from one word to another ever change the basic meaning of a sentence? Does a shift in pitch ever change the meaning? In the sentences below, are the meanings of the repeated sections identical? How would you say each of them? What uses would you make of stress, pitch, and juncture?

    a. John is a hero.
       John is a hero? John! A hero?
    b. That can't be John. He came in earlier.
       That can't be John! He wouldn't do such a thing.
    c. Was it he who came, or was it Elsie?
       Was it he? How can you ask such a question?

9. From your work on questions 1-8, would you say it is simple to develop hard and fast rules for the use of intonation patterns? Can you develop any generalization to which there are no exceptions?

10. The passage provided below is made up of nonsense syllables, inflections, derivational suffixes, prefixes, and function words. Indicate the syllables on which you would put primary or strong stress. Do you find that you are also making use of pitch and juncture in reading this aloud? Do you also use terminals in reading this nonsense? Are these elements as much a part of speech as sound itself?

If a gumer in guming would gume a gume, with three gumes of his gumer, he gumes the gume. If, in guming the gume, he ungumes one gume, the gume that's ungumed ungumes the whole gume.

11. Can you identify the nouns and verbs in the passage provided above? What clues do you have to their identification?

Suggested Readings

SECTION 8

Hill, Archibald A., *Introduction to Linguistic Structures*, pp. 13-29. New York: Harcourt, Brace & World, Inc., 1958.

Hockett, Charles F., *A Course in Modern Linguistics,* pp. 33-61. New York: The Macmillan Company, 1958.

Trager, George L., and Henry Lee Smith, *An Outline of English Structure,* pp. 35-52. Washington, D.C.: American Council of Learned Societies, 1951.

The Concepts
of Modification

One of the big problems in language is that of distinguishing between the general and the specific. One of the means we have in English of indicating specific meaning is modification; another is word selection. When we use either, we limit the meaning by making it more specific.

We saw the *foal*.	We saw the *baby horse*.
John is coming.	*The boy who was here before* is coming.
He received a *tremendous ovation*.	He received a *very great ovation*.
We *pounded* the door.	We *hit* the door *again and again*.

Modifiers tend to do their limiting in a number of different ways, the chief of which are through describing, quantifying, indicating or pointing out, relating the word modified to some other concept, and locating. (These categories are not mutually discrete. We often find a particular modifier serving more than one of these functions.)

Describing modifiers: The *big* boy is John.
The *warm* toast tastes *good*.
The boy runs *swiftly*.
The car moved *backwards*.

Locating modifiers:	The *Chicago* fire was a bad one.
	Boys *here* are busy.
	He works *Wednesdays.*
Quantifying modifiers:	*Few* people know this.
	We do not have *much* sugar.
	They visit us *frequently.*
	That is *hardly* enough.
Indicating modifiers:	*That* book is mine.
	The third inning was rough.
	The boy *talking* is my brother.
Relating modifiers:	*Your* hat is too large.
	The *Marshall* plan works well.
	They developed a *working* agreement.

Descriptive modifiers may be divided into two subgroups: those which are logically absolute—that is, from a strictly logical basis, they should not be further modified—and those which indicate a concept which is in itself relative, and hence is subject to further modification. By strict logic we should add no further qualifications to such adjectives as *perfect, pure, round,* or *yellow,* for the item being described is either perfect or imperfect, pure or impure, round or not round, yellow or not yellow. But in actual usage we frequently deny logic by speaking of a *more* perfect understanding, an *almost* pure substance, a *nearly* round ball, or a yellow*er* shade. When we make use of the comparative form of such words or use a comparative function word with them, we are indicating a degree of the quality somewhat less than would be indicated by the unqualified modifier. Thus, a *rounder* ball is less round than a round ball, but in most situations in which we would use such a modifier, we would be comparing the object or concept modified to another object or concept of like type rather than to the perfect concept represented by the modifier. In this type of comparison, there can be degrees of perfection.

Most descriptive modifiers represent concepts which are relative—that is, they have meaning in terms of comparison and in terms of situational context. Thus, if the temperature is twenty degrees today but was ten below zero yesterday, we say that today is *warmer* than yesterday. A temperature of ninety-eight degrees would lead us to speak of a *hot* day, but the temperature would have to be more than double that in a car motor before we would speak of it as being *hot.* In other words, whenever we apply some modification to a descriptive modifier, whether it be in the form of a degree indicating inflection or of a modifying word, we are indicating a quantifying relationship which is relative to some understood or indicated standard.

When nouns or verbs are used as modifiers of other words, they cannot be quantified in this manner. Thus we cannot use *very* or any word that might be substituted for it before such noun or verb modifiers as *brick* house, *north* wind, *pruning* shears, *John's* hat, he went *home*, they came *running*, they remained *seated*.

Modifiers that represent relative qualities or quantities may take inflections to indicate degree. We normally recognize three degrees: the positive (the uninflected form), the comparative, and the superlative. The comparative degree is indicated either by the inflection *-er*, which may be used on words of one or two syllables, or by the function words *more* and *less*, which are used with words of two or more syllables. The superlative degree is indicated either by the inflection *-est* or by the function words *most* and *least*. The usage with regard to the number of syllables in the base word parallels that of the comparative degree.

Like the qualifiers, some quantifying modifiers express exact quantities of countable concepts (*two* books), and others are used to indicate indefinite quantities of countable concepts (*few* days, *many* actions); some, but not all, of the latter may be used to indicate relative degree (*fewer* people, but *not* *several*er houses).

Certain quantifying modifiers are used only with words representing abstractions, masses, or noncountables (*love, truth, sugar, salt, water*). When we speak of *much* truth, we are concerned with the abstract idea of truth; when we speak of *many* truths, we are concerned with individual statements. *Much* salad indicates a mass concept; *many* salads indicates different individual salads or different types of salad.

A few modifiers may be descriptive in some situations and quantifying in others. (The *little* child has *little* consideration for others.) A few modifiers expressing indefinite quantities may be used with either countables or noncountables (*some* men, *some* salt; *any* boys, *any* traffic). Most of the modifiers we have been discussing also function as noun determiners and as substitutes for the noun.

Roughly related to these quantifying modifiers are some noun adjunct modifiers that express measures: *foot, pound, quart, bushel,* and so forth. When these are preceded by a numeral, the numeral and the adjunct fuse or combine to make a single modifier. Even when the numeral represents more than one, we continue to use the singular form of the noun with it in these situations (a *three mile* run, a *ten degree* rise in temperature). Some of these compounds appear frequently in genitive form (a *two day's* trip). Possibly because there is some confusion between the genitive and the plural inflections, which happen to be identical in speech, we find such expressions written in a variety of forms: two-day's vacation, two days' vacation, and two days vacation.

The concepts expressed by indefinite quantifying modifiers may be intensified by the addition of other modifiers (*more* boys, *many more* boys, *very many more* boys).

The function of indicating or pointing out is normally expressed by noun determiner modifiers. Some of these, such as *this* and *that*, have plural forms that must be used with plural nouns. Such modifiers are often accompanied by modifiers of other types which assist in the identification of the object or concept modified (that *green* car, a *second* boy, the *next* hour).

The types of concepts that may be expressed by relating modifiers are many and varied. Only a few of the more commonly used ones will be discussed here. Ownership, for example, may be expressed by the pronominal adjective or noun genitive type of determiner or by some of the noun adjuncts (*her* skirt, *John's* tie, the *Smith* house). Such relating modifiers are frequently used to express use or purpose (*pruning* shears, *bath* tub, he studies *to learn*). The manner of doing things is another common concept expressed by modification (an *Indian* giver, a *Dutch* treat, he came *running*, she went *by plane*, they gave *grudgingly*).

One of our most commonly felt needs is that of expressing negation. We can express negation through modification of the noun or its substitute, through modification of the verb, or through modification of a modifier. (*No* child was hit by the car. The boys did *not* work. The girls were *not* happy. This was *not* often the situation.) In addition to our form *not* and the phonetic variations of it used with verbal contractions, we make use of a number of prefixes and suffixes to express negation and related privative concepts, such as the absence of a quality. The more common prefixes are *un-*, *non-*, *in-*, *im-*, *il-*, *ir-*, *ig-*, and *a-*; *-less* is commonly used as a suffix to express such concepts. Any of these prefixes or suffixes may be used in the same construction with *not* (The action was *not* worth*less*, *il*legal, *un*popular), but there are some other privative words, such as *never, hardly, scarcely, rarely,* and *seldom,* which in standard usage we do not combine in the same construction with *not.*

Oftentimes the relationship expressed by a modifier is one that involves an action of one type or another (a *drilling* machine, a *worried* man); in some constructions, the action is indicated by the word modified rather than by the modifier (a dog *trainer*), and occasionally both the modifier and the word modified involve actions (a *practice teacher*).

Because we frequently wish to locate objects or actions in time and/or space, we have modifiers to indicate these relationships. Such modifiers may locate exactly or only approximately. We do not use degree inflections or degree function words with those which provide exact location (the *county* courthouse, the *noon* train). Those which provide only approximate location may, of course, be further modified to express the degree of approximation (a *more distant* view, the *most recent* issue of *Time*). Related to the time modifiers are some that indicate definite or indefinite frequency (He came *twice*. We saw him *very often*). Related to the space modifiers are those that indicate direction and distance (He went *north*. His course was *very northerly*.) (We drove *two miles*. We could see *very far*). Some descriptive modifiers also tend to be locative (a *nasal* infection).

Like other words, modifiers normally are capable of expressing more than one meaning (a *sharp* pencil, a *sharp* knife, a *sharp* rebuke, a *sharp* necktie). In such situations the exact meaning of the modifier is usually determined by the word modified, but occasionally we need a larger context before we can determine the exact meaning (a *retired* taxi).

Exercise 9-1   Modification

1. Which represents the greatest number of animals—*horses* or *mares, rams* or *sheep?* What is the effect of using a modifier, such as *female* or *male,* before an animal-naming noun? Do we do a similar thing when we use modifiers such as *large, brown,* and *old?* Which represents the larger class, *horses* or *old horses?*

2. What happens when we place one noun before another in English? Can we use more than two nouns in such a series? Is it the position which determines that one noun is the modifier of the

other? Consider the units: *piano player* and *player piano*. Do we ever place a modifying noun after the noun that it modifies? What do we have in units such as *attorney general, Knight Templar,* and *Operation Bootstrap*? Look up the first two of these units in your dictionary. What is their history? Where did the third have its origin? Are there others like it?

3. How do we form the genitives of such combined words? How, for example, would you speak of a chair belonging to the attorney general, or of a stool on which the piano player sits? What forms do we use for the plurals of such nouns? Would we be justified in thinking of these units as single words which custom has decreed we must write as two words? Is the formation of these words different from the formation of such words as *football* and *housewife*?

4. Are words belonging to the *old-large-brown* class ever used in the same way that these noun modifiers of other nouns are? What is the difference between *hot cakes* that you might eat for breakfast and *hot cakes* that you should allow to cool before you frost them? Is your oral patterning different for these two phrases? Describe it.

5. What difference do you observe between words such as *hot* and *stone*, both of which may be used to modify nouns? Does either of them express a quality which might be termed relative? When the motor of your car is running hot, what is the minimum temperature of the water in your radiator? When you yourself feel hot, what is the temperature likely to be? If your deep freeze unit were maintaining a temperature of thirty-eight degrees, what word would you use to describe it? Does the word *hot* have an antonym? Does the word *stone* have an antonym?

6. What kind of concept is represented by the noun adjuncts in each of the following groups? Are these the only types of concepts which may be expressed by noun adjuncts? If not, make up and label some additional groups illustrating conceptual areas expressed by noun adjuncts.

A. a quart jar	C. a glass jar
a mile run	a straw hat
a foot rule	a brick house
a two-ton truck	an iron bar
B. the Monroe Doctrine	D. the Eisenhower cabinet
a Bogen amplifier	the train tracks
a Ford car	the China Sea
the college policy	the apartment agency

7. What function do modifiers serve in each of the sentences provided below in group *B*? Consider them in relation to the corresponding sentences in the *A* group.

A. We saw the calf.

Mary is pretty.

He inherited an immense fortune.

He kept repeating the verses.

B. We saw the baby cow.

That girl in the front seat is pretty.

He inherited a very large fortune.

He repeated the verses over and over.

8. Which modifier expresses the idea of an angle of exactly ninety degrees—a *square* corner or a *squarer* corner? Does either of these suggest something which is not square? When we describe something as being *more* perfect, do we mean something that is beyond perfection or something that is actually less than perfect? Why do purists object to such constructions?

Exercise 9-2   Modifiers

1. What effect does the noun have upon the meaning of the modifier in the following phrases?

a flat tire   a flat denial   a flat taste
a flat color   a flat price   a flat (musical) note

2. What function is performed by the words *few, two, some,* and *much* in the following phrases? Where have we encountered these words before?

few people   some friends
two girls   much sugar

3. What function is performed by the words *this, those, yonder,* and *third* in the following phrases? Are all of these words noun determiners? Do those that are do anything in addition to acting as determiners?

this boy   yonder tree
those books   the third inning

4. What is the function of *my, your, its,* and *John's* in the following phrases? How does their function or functions differ from the function or functions of the words noted in questions 2 and 3?

my hat	its tail
your book	John's brother

5. What function is performed by the present and past participles in the phrases noted below? Study these situations carefully. What relationship exists between the modifier and the word modified in each? Is the relationship the same for all of them? Are all of the -*ing* forms present participles? Are all of the -*ed* forms past participles?

a working agreement	a retired minister
some dancing training	a two-toned car
a flowering almond	a tired boy
a looking glass	a baked ham

6. Are all the adjectives that look like past participles verb-based? Consider a blue-*eyed* girl, a *wooded* lot, an *oaken* bucket, a three-*drawered* desk. Are any verb forms other than participles used as modifiers? If so, what position do they take in the phrase or sentence?

7. Indicate what is modified in each of the phrases and sentences below. Indicate the type of meaning each modifier provides. Do these all belong to the same form-class? In what ways do they differ from one another?

the Chicago stockyards	He came twice.
the 7 P.M. train	We saw him often.
a distant view	Go away.
a recent issue	She will go far.
a buccal infection	They went South.

8. What concepts are represented by the modifiers in the following phrases and sentences?

an Indian giver	Drive slow.
a Dutch treat	She danced gracefully.
a boyish smile	He came running.

9. What type of relationship exists between each of the modifiers and the words modified in the following phrases?

a hole-boring machine
a very boring afternoon
a dog trainer
a welder trainee

10. Review what you have previously been taught about the

questions answered by adjectival and adverbial modifiers. Do these generalizations appear to be valid? Why or why not?

11. Make a list of as many functions of modification as you can recognize at the present time. Provide an example of each. Do not overlook such differences as those of exact and relative location. As you work on other problems in future exercises, keep your mind open to discover new functions of modifiers and, as you find them, add them and examples of them to your list.

More About Modification

Most grammars attempt to set up two classes of modifiers, adjectives and adverbs. In some books, these classes are described in terms of their head words—the adjective being a word that modifies a noun, the adverb being a word that modifies a verb, an adjective, or another adverb. In other books, they are described semantically —the adjective answers the questions *Which one*, *What kind*, and *How much* or *How many*, and the adverb answers the questions *When, Where, How, Why, How often, How far, In what direction, For what purpose*, and so forth.

A few examples will suffice to show the inadequacy of these definitions. In the first place, nouns may be modified by words that are not adjectives. They may be modified by other nouns (the *sound* equipment, the *boy's* father); they may be modified by verb forms (the *dancing* boy, the *opened* door, the show *to see*); they may be modified by words customarily classed as adverbs (the *above* decision, the *down* movement). Second, many modifiers of nouns answer the questions supposed to be answered by adverbs. Location, or the answer to *where*, is indicated by such modifiers as the *Detroit* depot, a *laryngeal* infection; *for what purpose* is answered by a *cook* stove, a *reading* lamp; *last* week and *Wednesday's* paper supply an answer to *when*. Similarly, we find nouns modifying adjectives (an *ice* cold drink, a *coal* black night), nouns modifying verbs (a *hole*-boring machine), and verbs modifying verbs (he studied *to learn*). We obviously cannot accept either of these bases for distinguishing the adjective from the adverb.

Fries, in his *Structure of English*,[1] sets up two classes of modifying

---

[1] Charles C. Fries, *The Structure of English* (New York: Harcourt, Brace & World, Inc., 1952), pp. 82-86.

words which closely parallel (but are not identical to) the classes normally labeled adjectives and adverbs. He defines his classes in terms of the positions the words may occupy within the sentence. His Class 3 words appear before nouns and after linking verbs. The numbers and letters above the words in the following examples identify the Fries classes.

    D   1   2   3
The boys are good.

    D   3   1   2 D   1
The good boy told his mother.

Sledd, in *A Short Introduction to English Grammar*,[2] distinguishes four parts of speech by position (nominals, verbals, adjectivals, and adverbials) and four other parts (nouns, verbs, adjectives, and adverbs) by word forms and stress patterning. The noun, verb, and adjective are distinguished by their inflections, the adverb by the presence of the derivational suffix *-ly* added to the positive form of the adjective. Sledd's rigid classification leads him to omit words of more than two syllables, such as *beautiful,* from the adjective class because they do not have forms in *-er* and *-est,* but both *dead* and *deadly* would be adjectives because they may take the forms *deader* and *deadlier. Quick* would be an adjective and *quickly* an adverb because we have the form *quicker* but not the form *°quicklier.*

Stress patterning, as was noted earlier, is also a definite part of Sledd's system of classification. The adverb and adverbial normally receive primary stress. The adjective and adjectival normally receive secondary stress, but in one situation (when it appears after a noun object) the adjectival receives primary stress. This leads to the necessity of making an arbitrary decision about the classification of a few words.

Earlier, using basically the Fries classification, we defined the adjective as being a word which would fit in both slots of the frame sentence "The very _____ boy is very _____." Although this test will serve as a rule of thumb, it by no means enables us to recognize every word which would normally be classified as an adjective. Some will not take the intensification provided by *very,* and some

² James Sledd, *A Short Introduction to English Grammar* (Chicago: Scott, Foresman & Company, 1959), pp. 69-111.

cannot be used in predicate position. In addition to this, all modifiers are not relatable to all nouns. We can have a *wooded lot,* but not a **wooded house.* Also, when a particular modifier can be used with two different nouns, it is not always used in the same manner with both. We may say, "His accent was *very* British," but not * "His nationality was *very* British." And, when nonlinking verbs are used, we may get sentences such as "The very *fast* train disappeared very *fast,*" or "The very *hard* blow made the horse run very *hard.*" In such sentences the modifier is a modifier of the noun in one position and of the verb in the other. We will find, however, a difference in stress patterning. The modifier of the noun will have a stress not stronger than secondary, whereas the modifier of the verb will receive primary stress. The function word *very* or a substitute for it is useful in distinguishing the noun modifying another noun from the adjective. We do not speak of **a very stone house* or of **a quiet John's book.* Words that belong to the adjective class normally do not appear in the position after the noun they modify. The title of the magazine *House Beautiful* seems to be an exception to this generalization, but this is hardly a normal usage. Certain nouns, particularly those whose chief function is that of indicating *which one,* may appear after the noun they modify (Lake *Erie, attorney general,* Henry the VIIIth, Operation Bootstrap); most of these represent either single units borrowed from other languages at an earlier period or analogies to these older forms which have recently been developed, particularly in military jargon. As can be noted from the stress pattern of such word groups, the effect of placing the modifying noun after the noun modified is to emphasize the modifier. It should be recalled that when we have a word-group unit such as *White House* or *hot dog,* we recognize the unity of the group by the fact that the modifying word receives primary stress.[3] Closely related to such situations are our identifying appositive usages, such as *the word dog* or *George, the baker;* but here we have two possibilities in stress patterning. In so-called close apposition (the type normally written with no punctuation between the units) the first unit receives lighter stress than the second, but when the units are separated by terminal juncture (the type normally

---

[3] There are a few exceptions to this—for example, *best man.*

punctuated by setting the second unit off with commas) both units normally receive strong stress.

Some words normally classified as adverbs may appear either before or after the noun they modify (the abóve discússion, the discussion abóve). In prenoun position they normally receive secondary stress, in postnoun position, primary. The noun preceded by the modifier receives primary stress in such a phrase, but when the modifier follows it the noun may have either primary or secondary stress. Other words normally classified as adverbs appear only after the noun they modify (the boy *here* is my brother). When participial verb forms are used as modifiers of nouns, they may appear either before or after the noun (the *giggling* girl, the girl *giggling;* the *chosen* road, the road *chosen*); when the infinitive is used as a noun modifier, it is accompanied by its sign and appears only after the noun (the road *to choose*).

Through such tests we can recognize the varying classes of words used as modifiers, even though the words be identical in written form. For example, we have words ending in *-ing* which may be nouns, verbs, or adjectives. When such words are used as descriptive adjectives, we use intensifiers, degree-determining function words, and sometimes even inflections for degree with them. (She is a *very charming* girl. We had a *most boring* afternoon. I never spent a *more trying* hour. That is the growing*est* plant.) When *-ing* words are used as gerunds (nouns) they cannot be so qualified (a *dancing* lesson, a *rowing* machine), nor can they be placed after the noun they modify. When they are verbs modifying nouns, they cannot be qualified by an intensifier or a degree determiner, but they may appear either before or after the noun they modify (the *running* boy, the boy *running;* the *dancing* girl, the girl *dancing*). When they appear before the noun, any modifiers that they themselves might take cannot intrude between them and the noun (*softly* glowing light, but not *glowing *softly* light). When their position is following the noun, their modifiers may appear either before or after them (light, *softly* glowing; light, glowing *softly*), or they may take an object (the water softly lapping *the pier*). It is possible to combine more than one *-ing* word as modifiers of a single noun head (the *very charming living* room *glowing* with soft light).

In our study of the verb, we noted a group of direction-indicating words which are frequently used as separable parts of the verb.

Many grammarians prefer to call these adverbs and speak of verb-adverb combinations. One of their characteristics is that some of them may appear either before or after the object of the verb; another characteristic is that they receive primary stress. (We took alóng the dog. We took the dog alóng. He put ón his shirt. He put his shirt ón.) Direction- or position-indicating words which do not combine with the verb cannot be placed between the verb and its object. (He moved the piece *backwards*. She held the book *upside down*. We keep the dog *there*. I want the bookcase *here*.) However, we *can* use locative noun adjunct modifiers or genitive modifiers of the object in this position. (We took the *Chicago* train. We met *Denver's* mayor.)

Time and frequency modifiers which modify the entire construction do not appear between a verb and its object. Temporal modifiers appear frequently at the beginning of the sentence as well as at the end. (We will cut the cake *tomorrow*. *Tomorrow* we will cut the cake.) But we may place temporal and frequency modifiers of the object between the verb and the object. (He made *frequent* digressions.) Modifiers of the verb indicating frequency also appear before the verb or within the verb unit. (*Often*, he studies the teacher. He studies the teacher *often*. He *often* studies the teacher. He will *often* study the teacher.) Not infrequently, we find these in objectionable examples of split infinitives (He tries to *often* study the teacher), but we never find them between the verb and the object in standard speech *(He studies *often* the teacher).

Qualifying modifiers of the verb may assume the same positions as the frequency modifiers. (*Unhesitatingly*, I believe her. I *unhesitatingly* believe her. I believe her *unhesitatingly*. I will *unhesitatingly* believe her. I want to *unhesitatingly* believe her.) Again these normally produce the objectionable type of split infinitive.

When the object is a word group instead of a single word, the modifiers of all these classes except the direction indicators may appear between the verb and the object. (I assume *here* that he will come. I said *yesterday* that it would fail. He admitted *afterwards* that it was the truth. I want *here* to make plain my position. We tried *often* to eliminate the difficulty. I believe *unhesitatingly* that all will be well.)

We frequently make use of more than one modifier for a single head word. If we have a series of place-locative attributive modifiers of a noun, our normal procedure is to begin with the least exact or largest area and work down to the most exact or smallest area. Exceptions to this are the names of states or nations (The East Lansing (Michigan) High School Auditorium). With temporal locations our formula is generally hour, month, day, year (10:00 P.M., August 16, 1960). In passing, we should note that when one noun is the modifier of another, it may itself be modified. Thus, in the examples provided above, we have *East* Lansing, *High* School, and 10:00 *P.M.* It is possible to mix all the various types of modifiers in a single series such as "Michigan State University's large well-known marching band." It is also possible to pile up postpositional modifiers. (The boy *working here Wednesday* was my brother. They gulped their food *down eagerly often then.*) Generally, however, the speaker or writer will take advantage of the mobility of such modifiers to spread them through the sentence (*Then* they *often* gulped *down* their food *eagerly*). And, of course, the careful speaker or writer will refrain from using such a sentence.

We have a large group of words which may be used as modifiers of either the noun or the verb. One subgroup of these is made up of the so-called *flat* or suffixless adverbs. Many others have the *-ly* suffix attached to them. (A *slow* mind; drive *slow*. A *hard* decision; hit it *hard*. He left *early* on an *early* train.) In such situations, the adverb will not only appear in a different position, but it will also receive stronger stress than does the adjective. This stress contrast cannot be used alone as a test for distinguishing adjectives from adverbs. The predicate adjective and the adverb in sentence final position both normally receive primary stress. (The sky is blue. The boy is here.)

In our brief glance at speech pattern units, we learned that two words such as *white* and *house,* if uttered in a particular stress-juncture pattern, become in effect one word designating a specialized meaning quite different from the meaning that these two words would produce if they were uttered as separate words. This same process operates for modifiers as well as for nouns and verbs. Within the combination, however, it is always possible to distinguish the characteristics of the original word-classes of the elements making up the unit. Thus we have, for example, a *clear mind* and a *clear-minded* decision (it should be noted here that the *-ed* suffix is the derivational suffix added to the noun, not the inflection added to the verb), but *clearly worded* and a *clearly worded* message (here we have the verbal inflection). Further, we can ascertain that while we cannot use *very* as an intensifier of either *minded* or *worded*, we can use it before either *clear* or *clearly*, and hence we can have either a *very clear-minded* decision or a *very clearly worded* message. Also, we can observe that while **a decision clear minded* makes no sense for us, we can have either *a message clearly worded* or *a message worded clearly*. Actually, what we have is a series of layers of modification, with each modifier retaining the characteristics of its original word-class. Thus the verb modifying the noun may be placed either before or after it, and the modifier of the verb may be placed either before or after *it*. The intensifier moves with its head word (a message *very clearly* worded, a message worded *very clearly*, a *very clearly* worded message), and the adjectival modifier must remain before its noun head, but may be intensified.

	Noun Head	Verb Head	Modifier of Noun as Head	Modifier of Verb as Head
Noun as Modifier	*horse* race *dog's* tail Postmaster *General* a *dining* room *Verbal Noun Head* *pole* vaulting	arrived *Tuesday* *machine* made *Verbal Noun Head* *pole* vaulting	*pitch* dark room	
Verb as Modifier	house *to rent* a *running* brook a brook *running* the *opened* door	They came *to look.* He came *running.*		
Modifier normally classed as Adjective	a *happy* adolescent *Noun-Adjective Modifiers* *white* snow *British* subject *French* student	He arrived *happy.*		
Modifier normally classed as Adverb	the problem *here* the *up* movement the movement *up* *quite* a lot	He came *here.* They went *up.* Take *along* a book. He *almost* died.	*quite* happy boys *most* unlikely place The girl was *almost* ready.	He moved *quite* slowly.

To sum up, we have discovered that both the noun and the verb frequently function as modifiers. In addition to them, we have another class of words which serve primarily as modifiers. Within this class is a large group of words whose primary function is that

of modifying the noun, a smaller group of words used only as modifiers of the verb, a third group of words used to modify either verbs
or other modifiers, and still another group of words which may function as modifiers of the noun, the verb, or of other modifiers. In
terms of expressing or understanding English, the exact classification of these words is of little importance. What is important is that
we be able to recognize the head word for each modifier and the
type of modification provided by each modifier. Whenever words
are placed in a structure that does not permit us to recognize modification, we have ambiguity as a result.

In addition to single-word modifiers, we have group modifiers of
three major types: the phrasal, the coordinate, and the clausal.

There are three subtypes of phrasal modifiers: One, which we
have already looked at, consists of a series of modifiers representing
different levels of modification (a *very well-mannered hostess*); a
second consists of a verb and its complements used as a modifying
unit (The boy, *having been thoroughly indoctrinated,* knew what to
reply); the third consists of a preposition, its head word, and the
modifiers of the head word (The boy *in the big armchair* is my
brother).

Coordinate units consist of two or more modifiers of the same
level modifying the same word or unit. They may or may not be
connected by a conjunction, and they may appear either before or
after the head word. Normally the conjunction will *not* be used
when they appear before the head word, but *will* be used when they
appear after the head word (the *skinny old grey* horse; the horse,
skinny, old, and *grey*). Within this group are a number of idiomatic
adverbial formulas consisting of words of opposite meanings connected by a conjunction (*here and there, now and then, near and
far, off and on*); in addition to these, we have other formula units
that are used primarily for modification, such as *by-and-by, by and
large,* and *here and now.*

Clausal units are those containing within themselves a subject and
a verb. These are of two classes: those in which the verb is composed of nonfinite forms (John, his license *having expired,* was
given a ticket) and those in which the verb has a finite form (John,
whose license *had expired,* was given a ticket). The normal position
for all word-group modifiers of the noun, except those of the series
or coordinate type, is after the noun that they modify. Word-group
modifiers of other word classes have more freedom of mobility,

although not as much freedom of mobility as their comparable single-word modifiers. When modifiers are placed at the beginning of a sentence or clause, they tend to modify the entire clausal idea rather than any single unit within it. This is illustrated by the sentence you have just read and also by the sentence which begins the next paragraph.

Like many nouns, single-word modifiers are frequently formed through the addition of derivational suffixes. The principle of the derivational suffix has already been discussed, so at this point we will merely note some of the more commonly used suffixes found on modifiers. The following words contain most of these:

work*able*	north*ern*	help*less*
fat*al*	Chin*ese*	child*like*
Rom*an*	Roman*esque*	week*ly*
relev*ant*	mani*fold*	illus*ory*
consul*ar*	Egypt*ian*	adventur*ous*
revolution*ary*	inde*lible*	fool*proof*
inveter*ate*	bas*ic*	seven*teen*
restor*ative*	vert*ical*	nine*ty*
hyperbor*ean*	boor*ish*	back*ward*
wood*ed*	illic*it*	back*wards*
oak*en*	care*ful*	cross*wise*
abhorr*ent*	act*ive*	cheer*y*

We have already noted the morphs -*ed* and -*en* as inflections of the verb. It should be noted here that in such words as *wooded* and *oaken*, the -*ed* and -*en* suffixes are derivational and not attached to verb roots. Many of these -*ed* noun root modifiers are commonly joined to a preceding modifier of the root noun (a *blue-eyed* girl, a *three-drawered* desk). At times we may have identical forms from the noun root and the verb root—a high-*minded* individual (noun); a well-*minded* store, a store well-*minded*, a store *minded* well (verbs).

Exercise 9-3   Forming Modifiers

Answer the following questions about each of the modifying words provided in the phrases below.

1. Does the modifying word contain a derivational suffix?

2. Does the modifying word contain an inflection?

3. Can the modifier be used as a noun or as a verb without further change in form?

4. Can the modifier be used to modify a noun, a verb, or another modifier? Both a noun and a verb? All three?

5. If the modifier contains a derivationl suffix,
   a. Is the suffix attached to a free morph or to a bound morph? May it be attached to either? If so, provide examples. If it is attached to a free morph, what part of speech is the base word?
   b. Is the suffix discrete, or is it a variant form of another suffix? (For example, *-ible* is a variant spelling of *-able*. The *-ible* form is generally attached to roots from Latin verbs which ended in *-ire* or *-ere*.)

a comfortable house	a consular decision
a workable plan	an insular attitude
a capable worker	a revolutionary doctrine
a national scandal	a literary club
a tropical storm	an inveterate liar
a local affair	a moderate proposal
a Roman holiday	an invertebrate animal
a Herculean effort	restorative measures
a relevant detail	the Mediterranean sea
a verdant prairie	a hyperborean idyll

Exercise 9-4   Forming Modifiers

Answer the same questions as in Exercise 9-3 for each of the modifying words in the following phrases:

a wooded slope	a western horse
a baked ham	the postern gate
a blue-eyed girl	the Japanese people
an oaken bucket	an obese woman
a sunken boat	Romanesque architecture
a broken toy	a picturesque view
an abhorrent notion	the smallest incident
a pertinent observation	the best solution
a bigger slice	manifold duties
a handier tool	a threefold increase

Exercise 9-5   Forming Modifiers

Answer the questions provided in Exercise 9-3 for each of the modifying words in these phrases:

an indelible pencil	a merrier Christmas
an indefeasible position	an illicit act
an Egyptian patriot	implicit instructions
Italian spaghetti	a girlish smile
the basic motive	a boorish individual
a romantic novel	a British subject
an egotistical attitude	active participation
a vertical line	relative humidity
a practical solution	a pensive look
a working program	a helpless girl
a walking delegate	worthless money

Exercise 9-6   Forming Modifiers

Answer the same questions as in Exercise 9-3 for each of the modifying words provided in the phrases below.

a childlike solution	an illusory smile
a godlike figure	fourteen boys
solely responsible	the umteenth suggestion
the daily paper	twenty men
a weekly occupation	the ninetieth man
rapidly developing	a backward look
a porous substance	a forward girl
an adventurous boy	lying crosswise
an advantageous position	doing likewise
a windproof jacket	a funny boy
a foolproof lock	a cheery smile

Exercise 9-7   Forming Modifiers

1. Summarize in table form what you have learned from the preceding exercises about the formation of modifiers. Some of the derivational suffixes and inflections found on modifiers are also used as derivational suffixes or inflections for other parts of speech. Does this suggest anything to you? How important is position in de-

termining whether a word is a modifier or some other part of speech? How important is stress and juncture patterning? What has happened in the following examples?

coal-black   snow-white
diamond-hard   knee-high

2. What is determined by position in the following sentences?

We got the daily paper.   Was there an earlier one?
We got the paper daily.   We saw him earlier.

Did you see the Monday paper?   He used a crabwise motion.
Did you see the paper Monday?   He moved crabwise.

3. Are the concepts of place location, time location, manner, and purpose ever expressed by modifiers of nouns? What is expressed by each of the modifiers in the following examples?

yesterday's decision   the corner house
the April session   an Indian giver
the Lansing schools   a well-drilling machine

4. What is our criterion for choosing either the *-er, -est* inflection for modifiers or the corresponding function words *more* and *most?* What problem is presented by situations such as the following?

We need more beautiful books.

5. Is *more* in the phrase *more books* the same *more* we have in the phrase *more beautiful?* Are both function words? Do they have the same or different functions? Does the same problem occur in our use of *most?* If so, provide examples.

6. What types of modifiers take the *-er, -est* inflection or use the *more, most* function words? Would you use either of these with a noun adjunct? Would you use either with the following: *North, third, nasal, rational?* Is the distinction one of form? Can we speak of a *more oral cavity?* Can we speak of a *more oral approach to the study of language?* What is the difference? Why do some people object to the use of forms such as *more perfect?*

7. Check the modifiers provided in the lists of Exercises 9-3 through 9-6 to see with which you would use degree words and with which you would not. Do you find that this is a question which can always be answered in terms of the modifier itself, or must you take the entire construction of modifier and head into consideration?

Suggested Readings

SECTION 9

Francis, W. Nelson, *The Structure of American English*, pp. 297-325. New York: The Ronald Press Company, 1954.

Fries, Charles C., *The Structure of English*, pp. 202-39. New York: Harcourt, Brace & World, Inc., 1952.

Hill, Archibald A., *Introduction to Linguistic Structures*, pp. 171-90. New York: Harcourt, Brace & World, Inc., 1958.

Sledd, James, *A Short Introduction to English Grammar*, pp. 114-20. Chicago: Scott, Foresman & Company, 1959.

Whitehall, Harold, *Structural Essentials of English*, Chaps. II and IV. New York: Harcourt, Brace & World, Inc., 1951.

Syntactic Functions
—The Subject

Modification, we have learned, consists of two elements: the head and the modifier. The function of the modifier is to limit, narrow, or make more exact the concept conveyed by the head. Thus, the class of *pretty girls* is smaller or more limited than the class of *girls,* and the concept expressed by *running slowly* is narrower or more exact than the concept expressed by *running.*

Predication also consists of two elements: the subject and the verb. Most English sentences contain these two elements. A few types do not. The command normally contains no subject (Go away). Answers to certain questions may be expressed by single words, such as *yes, no, certainly;* when used in this manner, these words constitute a sentence. We also have certain formula types of verbless sentences, such as "The more the merrier." Exclamations of pain, surprise, horror, and so forth, may be expressed without the elements of predication. (*Ouch! Oh! Heavens! My God!*)

With the exception of the command, all of these sentences are either sequence sentences or situational context sentences. A sequence sentence is one which must be preceded by some other sentence or sentences. It is, in other words, never used to start a conversation or a piece of writing. A situational context sentence is one whose meaning is made clear by the context of the situation in which it is uttered. *"Fire!"* has one meaning when we hear a siren and quite a different meaning when it is given as a command to soldiers. *"They are pulling the float"* has a different meaning at a parade than it has at a lake. *"My God!"* has a different meaning in prayer than it has when uttered beside a bloody corpse near a wrecked automobile. Most sequence sentences and most situational context sentences contain the two elements of predication.

In most English sentences, the subject precedes the verb. The subject of the sentence is always either a noun or something that is substituted for a noun. When a verb is substituted for the noun, it may retain some of its characteristics as a verb and also acquire some of the normal characteristics of the noun. (*Running slowly* is good exercise. *Slow running* is good exercise.) As we see, it can be modified by a modifier of the verb or by a modifier of the noun. When a noun modifier is used as a noun, it may be modified by the intensifiers or by the normal modifiers of the noun. (The *aged* are poorly cared for. The *very aged* are poorly cared for. The *male aged* are more poorly cared for than the *female aged*.)

Verb forms are normally divided into two types: those that are limited by inflections for person, number, mood, and/or tense, and those that are not. The first are called *finite* forms, and the others (participles and infinitives) are the *nonfinite* forms. Nonfinite forms appear as part of the finite verb only when auxiliaries are used. Finite forms are used as the full verb without the aid of auxiliaries. (I *walk*. He *walks*. They *walked*.) Analytical combinations of auxiliaries and nonfinite forms are considered as finite. (I *will go*. He *is going*. They *have gone*. This *will have been accomplished*.)

The subject plus the finite form of the verb may provide the English hearer or reader with a sense of completion (*John works*), but this is not true of all such combinations. Before we experience a sense of completion from some predications, we must add a third element—complementation. One common type of complementation is modification. With certain verbs which we will call *links*, this will be modification of the subject. (*John is good*. *Mary seems better*. The objection appeared *trivial*.) With nonlinking intransitive verbs, the modification, if any, will be of the verb rather than of the subject (*John arrived early*. *Mary dressed beautifully*), but it will most often not be essential to the completion of the sentence.[1] (*John arrived. Mary dressed.*)

---

[1] In a few structures, chiefly those in which *be* is used as a nonlink, the modification cannot be omitted. (The boy was *there*. * The boy was. The boy is

A second type of complementation utilizes nouns rather than modifiers. With linking verbs, these nouns perform one of two functions: they identify by naming the same individual or thing as does the subject word (George is *the secretary*), or they classify by naming a class to which the concept represented by the subject word belongs. (The flower is *a rose*.) One characteristic of the identifying complement is that the position of the subject and the complement may be interchanged without in any way changing the meaning of the sentence or the function of identification. (George is the secretary. The secretary is George. George is my brother. My brother is George. The price is a dollar. A dollar is the price.) In such sentences we determine which is subject and which is complement by position.

We also make use of sentences which involve inversion. In these sentences we determine which word is the subject by the concord of the two elements of predication. (Who *am I?* Who *were they?*) The form of the verb will agree with the person-number indication of the subject.

With nonlinking verbs, the noun complement may be of the type which is sometimes called the adverbial noun or the adverbial objective. This type of noun will be locative semantically, that is, it will name a location in space or time. (He went *home*. He arrived *today*.) Such nouns are generally found after verbs expressing motion toward or away from some point. They are also used with the verb *to be* to express location. (He is *home*. The game is *tonight*.) Locative words can also be used as noun identifiers with linking verbs. (The time is *now*. *There* is the place.) As is the case with the other identifying sentences, the position of subject and complement in such sentences may be interchanged. (*Now* is the time. The place is *there*.) When *to be* is used as a nonlinking verb, we may sometimes find the complement preceding the subject. (*There* the books are.) This pattern is common with the nonnoun locative words. (*Here* the boys come. *Now* the play begins.) Locative noun complements of nonlinking verbs frequently require a preposition between them and the verb. (He remains *in* school. She goes *to* church.)

---

lying *on the bed*.) In this last structure, "The boy is lying" would produce the meaning of prevaricating if there were no modification. But *to be* may also be used without complementation:

> What entered into thee,
> That *was, is,* and *shall be:*
> BROWNING, "Rabbi Ben Ezra"

Nonlinking verbs are of two types, transitive and intransitive. (Linking verbs are intransitive, but not all intransitive verbs are links.) Nonlinking intransitive verbs frequently express concepts of existence, of condition, or of movement toward or from a stated or implied location. (The idea persists. My head aches. She arrived (in Chicago).) The type of concept expressed is of less importance than our feeling that with such verbs predication may be complete without complementation of any kind. Transitive verbs are normally said to express concepts of action or possession, but again the conceptual relationship expressed by the verb, whether it can or cannot be assigned to one of these two classes, is of little real help in recognizing this structure. For a verb to be used transitively, the sentence must contain one or more complements of the verb that will take the form of a pronoun or of pronouns (or for which we could substitute a pronoun or pronouns). Such complements are termed *objects*. Objects are of various types; these will be discussed when we concern ourselves with complements in detail. Before leaving this topic, we should note that a verb may satisfy the criteria listed above for intransitive usage, but still be found in a structure in which an object is present or implied. (He ate. He ate his dinner.) The concept of transitivity is based upon the presence or absence of the sentence element we call an object. If an object is present, the verb is used transitively; if no object is present, it is used intransitively. But certain nouns or noun substitutes may appear in the same positions as objects without serving as objects. It is with these that we must now deal.

All three types of verb usage may appear in the simple sentence pattern in which we find a noun or a noun substitute, a verb, and a second noun or noun substitute. In such patterns the link can be distinguished from the others by the fact that, with few exceptions (It is they. It is the Smiths), the two nouns or their substitutes will require number concord. When one of the two nouns is a group naming collective, the concord may be ideational rather than formal, but if a pronoun is substituted for the collective noun in such a structure, the formal concord will appear. (That is a man. Those are men. The class are seniors. They are seniors. Two dollars was the price. That was the price. The poems were a lyric and an ode.) Verbal nouns may appear in either position in such structures and may be accompanied by complements. When they have no complements, pronouns can be substituted for them. (His recreations were fishing and hunting. Those were his recreations.) Finally, non-noun words expressing location in time or space may appear in either of the noun positions. When they do, the words in both positions will represent either a temporal or a spatial concept. (Now is the time. The place is there.) Again, pronouns may be substituted for these. (This is the time. That is the place.)

When the intransitive verb is used as a nonlink, the number of either the preverbal or postverbal noun or substitute may be changed without affecting the other. (He works Fridays. They will work Friday.) In most instances this postverbal noun may appear as the object of a preposition. (He works on Friday. They work at night.) When a noun is used postverbally in this structure, it will express a temporal or a spatial concept and it may take a singular or a plural form. In most such sentences the predication would be complete if the noun were removed. If a word is substituted for the noun, it will be of the *now-then* or of the *here-there* class.

Verb forms may appear in the position of the postverbal noun. When they do, they will be marked with the *-ing* inflection or with the sign of the infinitive *to*, and it will be impossible to substitute a pronoun for them. In other words, this verb form found following an intransitive nonlink is *not* being used as a noun. Occasionally, for rhetorical effect, such a verb form may be placed at the beginning of the word group; in that case it will be followed by the noun and the intransitive verb in that order, and it will normally be set off from the main structure of noun + verb by a terminal juncture. (Smiling, they agreed.)

When the verb is used transitively in the noun + verb + noun structure, the two nouns or their substitutes again are not required to express number concord. (Men drink it. A woman took them.) A pronoun may be substituted for the noun, regardless of its type or the meaning expressed by it, in either position. (I like to dance. I like it. Dancing tired the man. It tired him. He hates October. He hates it. She chose Chicago. She chose it.) Words of the *here-there*, *now-then* classes will not serve as substitutes for these nouns. Where the pronouns have case-distinctive forms, the *I, he, she, we, they, who* forms will normally appear in preverbal position and the *me, him, her, us, them, whom* forms in postverbal position. The *you, it, mine, yours, his, hers, ours, theirs* forms may appear in either position.

There is still another situation in which the identification of verb-type usage may be confusing. We have sentences such as "John is himself," "John came himself," and "John drove himself." In all of these, the postverbal pronoun shows person and number concord with the preverbal noun, and this is required so long as the *-self* form is used, for in all of these structures the same entity is represented by both forms. So long as these structures are maintained in the simple three-word form, the pronoun may be used as an intensifier; as such, it may be moved to the position between the noun and the verb. If we so move it, the first sentence becomes one that would normally require complementation of the subject. Without complementation, such a sentence is possible if we accept the meaning of *to exist* for *to be* (John himself is), but it would be most improbable that we would ever hear such a sentence or have occasion to use it. If complementation were provided in the form of a noun for which a pronoun might be substituted or in the form of an adjective, we would have a linking verb by our other criteria. If the complement provided is a word such as *home*, for which we would have to substitute a word of the *here-there* class rather than a pronoun, the verb usage can be classified as nonlinking intransitive.

Many verbs can be used in structures such as "He himself came," in which no further complementation is necessary. When they are so used, they are intransitive nonlinks. There are also many verbs which might appear both in this structure and in a transitive usage structure. Our third example, John drove himself, is one of them. If we add another noun to the end of our basic sentence, we will find that when the *-self* form is being used as an intensifier, it cannot appear between the verb and the complement, but may appear after the complement. (*He drove himself the car. He drove the car himself.) We also find that the noun which is added is one for which we could substitute a pronoun. If the additional complement is one for which we could substitute a word of the *here-there, now-then* classes, the *-self* form may appear between the verb and it. (He drove himself yesterday.) In the first of these situations the *-self* form is an intensive and the verb is used transitively. In the second, the *-self* form may be either an intensive or an object, and the verb may be either intransitive or transitive. The *here-there, now-then* words do not provide a test; the possibility of substituting a pronoun does. There are other constructions in which the *-self* form can take the position between the verb and an additional noun complement, and the complement may be one for which we can substitute a pronoun. (He bought himself a car. He taught himself Spanish.) In such structures the other complement may appear between the verb and the *-self* form, but when it does, the *-self* form will appear in a prepositional phrase. (He bought a car for himself. He taught Spanish to himself.) Some of these verbs will require two complements; others will not.

Finally, let us return to the simple three-element structure "He drove himself." If the verb is used transitively in such a structure we will say the sentence with no terminal before *himself*, and in writing it we will never separate *himself* from the rest of the sentence by punctuation. Also, we could fill the position of *himself* with many nouns and with any objective case form pronoun. (He drove a truck. He drove it. He drove her. He drove them.) If our verb is used intransitively we normally will use a terminal juncture between the verb and *himself*, and we may separate *himself* from the rest of the sentence by a comma. Neither structure can be confused with the link structure, for we would not use a terminal juncture between the linking verb and *himself*, and the substitutions we might make in the position of *himself* would be limited by the requirement of number concord.

Types of Concepts Expressed by the Subject

We have already noted that the subject may be the person or thing described, the person or thing identified, or the person or thing classified. All three of these situations require linking verbs and complementation.

The subject of nonlinking intransitive verbs normally names that which exists or moves. (The *girls* were there. The *boy* stopped here. *Snow* falls.) In some situations, however, it may represent the receiver of an action. In sentences such as "The game began" we recognize that the concept expressed by the word *game* is in itself incapable of being a mover or actor. Someone must begin the game. This construction is generally described as the *notional passive*. A few verbs involving reciprocal movement or action on the part of more than one person may be used intransitively only with plural subjects. (*They* met.)

The subjects of transitive verbs are usually words representing an actor (a person or object that does something rather than one that merely moves or refrains from moving) or a possessor. It is possible to divide the actor group into several different categories. In one of these the actor is a provider. (The *school* gave John a book. The *experience* taught her caution.) In another type, the actor might be described as the performer. (The *police* conducted an investigation. *John* runs a store.) In a third type, the actor subject and the receiver object represent the same individual or thing. (*She* hurt *herself*. The *drawer* closed *itself*.) Where more than one actor and more than one receiver is concerned, we may have a reciprocal type of action in which both the subject and the object represent both the actor and the receiver of the action. (*They* hated *one another*.) The subject and object in such structures are necessarily plural in concept. Certain verbs are lexically associated with the idea of reception. With such verbs, the subject becomes the receiver not of the action of the verb, but of the object. (John drew a blank. Mary received a book.) Some verbs express the concept of causation. With such verbs the object may be complemented by a modifier describing a state or condition or by a noun identifying or classifying the object; in such structures the subject normally represents the person or things causing the condition, identification, or classification. (That made me sick. We proved John the culprit. They elected George secretary.) Some verbs lexically express ideas of incipience or conclusion. Such verbs do not express action in themselves, but they are commonly followed by a verbal object designating the action. (They began *sandblasting* the capitol.) When, however, the meaning is reasonably clear without such a verbal noun, the verbal noun is frequently omitted. (We began [reading] the book. He finished [writing] the article.) As can be seen, such structures are frequently ambiguous unless they appear in a larger context. (We began the book as part of our literature assignment. He finished the article in time to meet the deadline for publication.)

With such verbs as *have, own, possess*, and so forth, the subject normally represents that which possesses the object. (We own a car.) *Have*, however, is frequently used with an object noun formed from the two elements of a structure of predication. In such sentences the subject is that in which a particular condition exists. (I have a *backache*.)

Earlier we looked at some reciprocal action verbs that require a plural subject when used intransitively. These verbs may be used transitively with either a singular or a plural subject. (*She* met him. *We* met her.)

The objects of most transitive verbs may be shifted to subject position. When this occurs, the verb will be analytical and will consist of some form of a linking verb used as an auxiliary (most commonly *be, get,* or *become*) plus the past participle form of the full verb; the action expressed by the verb will be directed toward the subject.[2] The agent or actor may or may not be expressed in such a sentence. This structure we term the *passive voice.* When a transitive verb has two objects, either of these may be shifted to subject position; the one remaining in the object position is then referred to as the *retained object.* When the inner or personal object is retained, it frequently is preceded by a preposition. (*Active voice:* John gave Helen a book. John gave a book to Helen. *Passive voice:* Helen was given a book. A book was given [to] Helen [by John].)

There are, however, some verb-object structures which cannot be put into the passive voice. In sentences such as "This hat cost ten dollars" or "The package weighs three pounds," we have objects (*ten dollars* and *three pounds*), but we do not use these as subjects for a passive construction. Reflexive objects (She hurt *herself*) are rarely found as subjects of a passive construction, nor are objects of the verb *have* (I have a *cold*).

A few verbs, such as *to be engaged,* are used almost exclusively in the passive voice. Occasionally, however, we find such verbs used in the active voice with a reflexive object. (She engaged *herself* to him.)

Substitutes for the Noun Subject

The most common substitutes for the noun are the pronouns, but, as has already been noted, the adjective and the verb frequently appear in subject position as substitutes for the noun. (The *poor* are always with us. *To be elected* was his ambition. *Walking* is good

[2] Two types of action are involved in many sentences. In sentences such as "She hears the band" or "The band was heard by her" we have an action of *hearing* expressed by the verb and a movement or action of sound waves without which there can be no hearing. It is the action expressed by the verb with which we are concerned. The action of hearing in the sentences above is directed toward *the band,* regardless of whether *the band* stands in subject or object position.

exercise.) We may also find the prepositional phrase or the clause standing as subject. (*Over the fence* is out. *That he was dishonest* is now certain.)

Exercise 10-1   Syntactic Functions—The Subject

In each of the sentences below you will find that a noun precedes the verb. For each group of sentences, describe the relationship that exists between the noun subjects and the rest of the sentence. For example, in the sentence "John has a dog," the noun subject *John* is the possessor of an animal represented by the noun *dog*.

1. John is a man.
   The boy is a scout.
   The girl is a counselor.
2. Mr. Eisenhower was the President.
   The President was Mr. Eisenhower.
   That boy is the secretary.
   The secretary is that boy.
   The dog is the culprit.
   The culprit is the dog.
3. Mary is beautiful.
   The children are happy.
   The house is white.
4. Helen smokes.
   The band played.
   The girls arrived.
5. George hit the ball.
   The oxen pulled the cart.
   The ringmaster directed the circus.
6. The toy was broken.
   The children were tired.
   The boy got hurt.
7. The war was started by the Japanese.
   The audience became tired by sitting so long on the hard seats.
   The girls were reprimanded by the teacher.
8. The game began at 2:00 P.M.
   This book reads well.
   Your play opens tonight, doesn't it?
9. John has plenty of self-assurance.
   The Smiths have a house now.
   Mary owns a horse.

10. Mary has a cold.
    George had the measles.
    Helen is running a temperature.
11. George is a dog in the manger.
    Henry is an amateur wolf.
    Louise is another Gloria Swanson.
12. The sun marched across the sky.
    The boat shuddered and sank.
    Memories of a similar experience galloped madly through her mind.

Exercise 10-2

1. Consider the following sentences. Do any of the italicized subjects represent the person speaking? Do any of them represent the person spoken to? What is represented by these noun subjects? Can you think of a situation in which a noun subject is used to represent the speaker or writer, the listener or reader? How do we normally represent the speaker? How do we normally represent the person or persons to whom we are speaking? What term is commonly used for this class of words? Do they really substitute for nouns? All of them?

   a. The *boy* ran.
   b. *John* is a man.
   c. The *crowd* was anxious.
   d. The *house* was painted white.
   e. The *truck* demolished the bicycle.

2. We normally use the term *first person* to represent the speaker or writer, the term *second person* to represent the listener or reader, and the term *third person* to represent anything or anyone other than the speaker or the person, animal, or thing addressed. Do we have logical plurals for subjects in all three persons? What is the plural form normally associated with *I*? What person or persons does this plural represent? In the sentences below, is it a logical plural for the first person?

   John and I are going.   We are going.
   You and I could do it.   We could do it.

3. Are the grammatical plurals found in the second and third persons logical plurals? What is the plural form normally associated

with *you*, with *she*, with *he*, and with *it?* What is represented by these plurals in the following sentences?

> John and Mary, can *you* go?
> You and he can go, can't *you?*
> John and Mary are happier since *they* parted.

4. Do common nouns, such as *dog* and *man*, represent a specific individual or a class? What is represented by a proper noun, such as *George* or *Lansing?* Is this in any way related to the number problem we encounter with the personal pronouns? What person or persons can be represented by the first person plural pronouns, by the second person plural pronouns, and by the third person plural pronouns?

5. What forms would you substitute for the subject nouns in the sentences provided below?

John's is the larger.	_____ is larger.
Mary's is the larger.	_____ is larger.
The book belonging to me is larger.	_____ is larger.
The heads of John and Mary are larger.	_____ are larger.

6. In what ways are the uses of these genitive pronouns similar to the uses of the genitive nouns? In what ways do their uses differ? Are there any which are used in exactly the same manner as genitive nouns?

7. There is a form corresponding to each of these genitive pronouns which may be used before nouns rather than as substitutes for nouns. What are these forms? Where have we encountered them before? Can any of these forms also serve as noun substitutes? For what kind of nouns do they substitute?

Exercise 10-3

1. What present tense forms of *to be* do we use with the first, second, and third persons singular? What person is represented formally in each of the sentences below? What person is represented notionally?

> a. Your Majesty is right.
> b. Is Your Eminence really serious?
> c. Is Your Honor ready to give the decision?

2. What person is represented when a ruler or an editor uses *we* in formal writing or speaking?

3. What person is represented by *you* in the sentence provided below? Does this represent desirable usage?

You never know about such things.

What is the difference between this usage and the use of *one* in "One never knows about such things"?

4. For what noun does *it* substitute in the sentence "It is raining"? For what noun does *you* or *one* substitute in the sentences in question 3? Is *I* ever a substitute for a noun?

5. For what purpose do we use *myself* and *yourself* in the following sentences? Are these words a part of the subject?

    a. I myself did it.
    b. You yourself should know better.

Do these words serve the same purpose when their position is shifted ("I did it myself")? Does the meaning provided by this last sentence differ in any way from that of the sentences "I did it by myself" or "I did it alone"? Are these constructions grammatically identical? Can we also say "I alone did it"?

6. Are the *-self* forms ever used alone as subjects in American English? Have you encountered this usage in your reading of literature? What does your dictionary say of such usage?

7. In creating the *-self* forms, do we combine *-self* with pronouns or with adjectives in the first and second persons? With what do we combine it in the third person? Does this suggest any explanation for the appearance of such forms as *hisself*? How do we form the plurals of the *-self* forms? What differences exist between the standard and the substandard usages of this group of pronouns?

8. Do the *-self* form pronouns serve any function other than that of intensifier?

9. What function do words such as *good, old, second,* and *three* normally perform? In the sentences provided below, what function do they perform? Can any of these words be used as a subject without having a noun determiner before it?

    a. The good die young.
    b. The old have many memories.
    c. The second was the best inning.
    d. Those three are fighting again.

10. What differences do you observe in the use of *good* in the sentences "The good die young" and "Good will conquer evil"? With which would you use *much* and with which would you use *many* as determiner or modifier? Which of the two is a noun and which is a noun substitute? Is *goods* a plural form of the noun *good* as it is used here? Do we have a singular form for the word *goods?* Is there any word formed by adding a derivational suffix to *good* that could be substituted for *good* in "Good will conquer evil"?

Exercise 10-4

1. To what word class does *beautiful* belong in the sentence "Beautiful is as beautiful does"? Does it belong to the same word class in the sentence "The beautiful always appealed to him"? Must the adjective have a noun determiner before it in order to function as a subject? Is *beautiful* a noun in the first sentence?

2. In the sentence "Over the fence is out," can the phrase *over the fence* be considered a noun? What would be the function of this phrase in the sentence "He threw it over the fence"? What is the function of *out* in our original sentence? Can modifiers of parts of speech other than the noun ever serve as subjects of the verb? If so, under what conditions?

3. What part of speech is serving as subject in each of the sentences below? Is there a type of verbal subject with which we must use determiners? Can we use a determiner with all three types (gerunds, infinitives, and past participles)? Would you consider all of these to be normal English?

   a. To travel was his ambition.
   b. Swimming is good exercise.
   c. The retired suffer from inflation.
   d. Gone is gone.

4. What is the subject of each of the following sentences? How do these differ from the subjects of the sentences provided as examples in question 3?

   a. For him to go was unthinkable.
   b. To know him was to dislike him.
   c. To drive so fast troubled him.
   d. His driving disturbed her.

e. Going home is pleasant.
f. Fast driving is hazardous.

5. What kinds of subjects do we have in the sentences provided below? Can any of these subjects stand alone as sentences?

a. That he was responsible is now certain.
b. What he meant is clear.
c. Which ones he invited is not known.
d. How many more he had invited is a moot question.

6. What is the grammatical subject of each of the sentences below? What is being talked about? Does the grammatical subject have any referent in the sentence? What verb do you find used in sentences of this type? Can you use any other verb or verbs in such constructions? Rewrite each of these sentences, omitting the *it*.

a. It is well to remember this.
b. It is true that he came early.
c. It was necessary to recall the troops.
d. It was essential that he study.
e. It was fun running the boat.
f. It was difficult drinking that water.

7. In what way, if any, do the constructions illustrated in question 6 relate to such constructions as "It is raining"? What verb do you find used in his construction? Can you use any other verb or verbs in it? Does the subject have a referent within the sentence? Would there normally be a referent for it in some earlier sentence?

8. List the various kinds of substitutes for the noun that can be used as subjects. Which of these refer directly to some noun? Which have no noun referents?

Suggested Readings

SECTION 10

Fries, Charles, C., *The Structure of English,* pp. 173-201. New York: Harcourt, Brace & World, Inc., 1952.

Jespersen, Otto, *The Philosophy of Grammar,* pp. 144-56. London: George Allen & Unwin, Ltd., 1924.

Whitehall, Harold, *Structural Essentials of English,* Chap. IX. New York: Harcourt, Brace & World, Inc., 1951.

Some Functions
of the Verb

In our last discussion, we noted three distinctions in the verb: the linking verb, the intransitive nonlinking verb, and the transitive verb. Actually, these are not three different types of verbs, but rather three functions that the verb may serve. Some verbs may be used in all three ways. (The soup smells good. The dog smells well. I smell a rat.)

When we look closely at linking verbs, we find that we can divide them into several groups. The first we will consider is that of the pure link, and it contains but a single verb, *to be*. When *to be* is used as a link it has no meaning of its own; it merely performs the function of linking subject and complement. One characteristic of it in this usage is the freedom to invert the sentence. (He was the man. The man was he. Old King Cole was a merry old soul; a merry old soul was he. The days are gone. Gone are the days.)

A second group contains a few verbs, such as *appear* and *seem,* which suggest that the complementation is comparative rather than absolute. With such verbs it is always possible to insert the infinitive *to be* without in any way changing the function of the verb or the meaning of the sentence. (She appears happy. She appears to be happy. He seems honest. He seems to be honest.)

A few verbs expressing sensory perception make up a third group of linking verbs. When such verbs are used as links, the subject is the receiver of the action of the verb. The actor is left unnamed, but it is, of course, the speaker or writer or, in some, the person addressed. The complement in such structures is always of the adjective type. (This soup *smells* good. The table *felt* sticky. The ice cream *will taste* sweet.) When the subject of a sensory-perception verb is the actor, the verb ceases to function as a link. (He sounds the gong. She felt the table. He tasted the ice cream. We could smell the soup.)

A fourth group of linking verbs are those that express concepts of inception or continuation of a state or condition. These verbs may take either adjective or noun complements. (The dog became furious. They became the owners. She remained disconsolate. He remained a widower.) A few verbs related to these will take only adjective complements when used as links. (He went crazy. She gets angry.)

Quite a large number of verbs (sixty or more) appear occasionally as links, but by far the great majority of links in actual usage are made with the verbs *be, seem, become, appear, smell, taste, feel,* and *sound.*

Because the past participle of many verbs functions as a descriptive adjective, and because the passive voice of transitive verbs is constructed by using as an auxiliary a verb which may frequently be used as a link, and adding to it a past participle, we sometimes have difficulty in deciding whether we have a linking verb construction or a passive voice construction. In a sentence such as "The boy was tired" we normally would consider the verb to be a link and the participle to be an adjective. We can test this, of course, by using an intensifier such as *very* before *tired.* But if we have an agent expressed, we would normally consider the structure to be passive voice. (The boy was tired by the exercise.) When the agent is present, we normally would not use the intensifier before *tired.*

A similar situation exists when the present participle is used after *to be* or some few of the other linking verbs. In some of these constructions the adjectival nature of the participle is clearly dominant (His speech was boring); in others the verbal nature of the participle is clear, and we have a progressive tense form (His speech was boring the audience). It should be noted that the stress patterns differ, but this difference results from *boring* being used in final or medial position in the sentence.

Intransitive nonlinking verbs often express some kind of movement or some kind of static condition. Their intransitivity is determined by the absence of a word that we would term an object. Their nonlinking function is determined by the absence of a predicate adjective or a classifying or identifying predicate noun. The subject of such verbs will be the mover or the one undergoing the static condition. In most sentences of this type the subject and the verb will in themselves constitute a structure of predication without any necessity for complementation of any kind. In other words, the subject and the verb will make a complete sentence. The verb may, however, be complemented by an adverb or by any word or word group functioning as an adverb. Some few sentences will seem to require such complementation. (*The baby lay.) Not infrequently, intransitive verbs will, by the nature of their lexical meanings, imply an object; if the object is not expressed, the verb is still considered as intransitive. For example, in the sentence "The girl sang," we know that a girl cannot sing without singing something—a song, an aria, a ballad, or what-have-you. Such a verb implies an object, but because the object is not actually designated, we consider the verb to be used intransitively.

The verb in the notional passive construction is sometimes confused with the intransitive verb. In this structure, as has already been noted, the subject is the receiver of the action of the verb, and the actor is generally left unnamed. (The class began. This book reads well.) Such a structure presents a meaning which is a denial of our experience: a class cannot begin itself, nor can a book read. The actor in such a structure may be indicated in a prepositional phrase following it, or by a genitive-adjective type of noun determiner preceding the subject. (This book reads well *to me*. The day began *for us* with a light breakfast. *Our* day began with a light breakfast. The *team's* practice ended at four.)

A transitive verb appears in a structure in which the action of the verb is received by some person or object, or both. Some transitive verbs express a mental rather than a physical action, or even what might be considered a state or condition. (I *believe* him. We *miss* the children.) With such verbs the object cannot really be said to be a receiver of the action. Often the object of such a verb is an abstraction, such as a clause, which would be incapable of receiving anything. (I know *what you mean*.) A transitive verb in the active voice may take one object or two.

When there are two objects, one will usually represent a person and the other a thing or an action. (He took the *girl* a *drink*. He gave the *boy* a *shove*.) However, it is possible for both objects to be personal or for both to be impersonal. (He got his *daughter* a *boy friend*. He gave the *table* a *kick*. We gave the *house* a *coat of paint*.) The inner object—the one next to the verb in such constructions—may be placed after the outer object, but when it is so placed, it takes the form of a prepositional phrase. (He got a boy friend *for his daughter*. He gave a kick *to the table*. We gave a coat of paint *to the house*.)

Most objects of transitive verbs may become the subjects of those verbs when the voice of the verbs is changed from active to passive, but (as was noted on page 139) a few transitives, for which Lees uses the term *middle verbs*,[1] do not use a passive form. This is not, however, a quality of the verb itself, but rather of the construction, for some of these verbs may be used with objects which serve as passive subjects. (The doctor weighed the baby. The baby was weighed by the doctor.) In addition to their lack of passive form, a further characteristic of verbs used in the middle voice construction is that they will not take modifiers indicating manner after their objects. Thus, we may have structures such as "He weighs babies *efficiently*" or "The baby was weighed *efficiently*," but *not* * "The baby weighs ten pounds *efficiently*." [2]

The formal characteristics of the passive voice are these: (1) Some form of a linking verb will appear as the auxiliary or as one of the auxiliaries. (2) The lexical or meaning-carrying verb will be the final verb word in the verb-word sequence, and it will be in the form of a past participle. (3) The subject will be the receiver of the action of the verb. (4) If there were two objects in the active voice construction, the object which has not been moved to subject position will be retained in its object position; if it was the inner object, it will generally be retained in the form of a

---

[1] Robert B. Lees, *The Grammar of English Nominalizations,* Publication 12 of the Indiana University Research Center in Anthropology, Folklore, and Linguistics, as a supplement to *International Journal of American Linguistics,* XXVI, 3 (1960), 8.

[2] In some of these situations, it might be possible to construe the postverbal unit as a modifier of the subject. If the baby weighs *ten pounds,* it is a *ten-pound* baby. The hat that holds *ten gallons* is a *ten-gallon* hat. In any case, these cannot be used to form passive voice constructions.

prepositional phrase. (5) The subject of the active voice sentence may or may not appear; if it does appear, it also will appear in the form of a prepositional phrase. The following examples should clarify the nature of these structures:

Active voice transitive verb with single object
John drove the car.
George struck Mary.
Passive voice transitive verb
The car was driven.
Mary was struck.
Passive voice with agent expressed
The car was driven by John.
Mary was struck by George.
Active voice transitive verb with two objects
He offered me a drink.
She bought Mary a coat.
We gave the car a push.
Passive voice variants with retained object
I was offered a drink.
A drink was offered to me.
Mary was bought a coat.
A coat was bought for Mary.
The car was given a push.
A push was given to the car.
Passive voice variants with retained object and agent
I was offered a drink by him.
A drink was offered to me by him.
Mary was bought a coat by her.
A coat was bought for Mary by her.
The car was given a push by us.
A push was given to the car by us.
Active voice transitive with analytical tense forms
He has damaged the car.
The lawyer will have pleaded the case by this time.
We have offered the Russians a compromise.
Passive voice equivalents with analytical tense forms
The car has been damaged.
The case will have been pleaded by this time.
The Russians have been offered a compromise.
A compromise has been offered to the Russians.
Middle Voice
She resembles her mother.
Such actions mean trouble.

It may be well now to look at two special types of transitivity that we recognize in verbs. One of these may be noted in verbs expressing the concept of possession. Verbs such as *have, own,* and *possess* denote a condition rather than an action; yet we consider them to be transitive verbs, and the noun or noun substitute which normally follows them in the sentence is called the object of the verb. Most of these verbs will form natural passives. ("The car was owned by John." "She was possessed by the idea." But *not* * "The pencil was had by me.") The verb *have* does occasionally appear in the passive construction (We have been had), but in such idiomatic expressions it is no longer expressing the concept of possession. As a verb expressing possession, it is in middle voice.

The second special type of transitivity consists of those verbs which semantically express a passive concept. Verbs such as *receive, acquire,* and *obtain* belong to this class. The meaning inherent in such verbs makes the subject both the actor and the receiver of the action named by the verb. The transitivity of such verbs can be noted by the fact that they do require objects and that they have a passive voice form in which the object becomes the subject.

Active Voice:	Passive Voice:
She acquired an accent.	An accent was acquired.
We obtained a permit.	A permit was obtained.
They received the package.	The package was received.

Exercise 11-1   Verb Functions

1. In an earlier exercise (Exercise 10-1) we looked at certain sentences which were built on the pattern: *noun + to be + noun.* We learned that a slight variation in the choice of the noun determiner placed before the noun which follows the verb will create two subpatterns; in one the noun at the end of the sentence will name a class to which the subject belongs, and in the other it will serve to identify the subject. Can the positions of the two nouns in either pattern be interchanged without changing the meaning of the sentence? The term *subjective complement* is sometimes given to nouns following verbs in these patterns. From what noun is the word *subjective* derived? From what verb or adjective is the word *complement* derived? Is this word in any way related to the word *compliment?*

2. A third type of related structure that we studied had the pattern: *noun + to be + adjective.* What is modified by the adjec-

tive in such a sentence? Is this also a form of the subjective complement? Is there a difference between the structures "Mary is beautiful" and "The toy is broken"? If so, how do they differ?

3. What other verbs could be substituted for the verb to be in such structures? List as many as you can.

4. Structurally, the sentences we have just been discussing appear to be the same as "Louise is another Florence Nightingale" and "Harry is high." Is the basic difference in meaning provided by the sentence *types* represented by the examples in question 2 and those represented in this question, or does it stem from something else? On what basis do we decide whether we are to accept a literal or a figurative meaning in such structures?

5. What difference in meaning do you observe in the sentences "The dog smells good" and "The dog smells well"? To what word is the modifier related in each sentence? In which sentence is the modifier a subjective complement? Does the verb perform identical functions in both sentences?

6. What function is performed by the verb in the following sentences? Could the verb to be be substituted for any of the verbs used in these sentences? Do any of these sentences represent figurative usage?

    a. She remains a widow.
    b. This coffee tastes sweet.
    c. He became a lawyer.
    d. They appear happy.
    e. She looks a fright.

7. In the sentences below, what function does the modifier perform? Could you substitute to be for any of the verbs in these sentences?

    a. Helen smokes too much.
    b. The band played badly.
    c. The girls arrived early.

8. In what way are sentences such as "The coffee tastes sweet" and "The dog smells good" related to sentences such as "The game began" and "The book reads well"? Do the verbs in such sentences imply some action? If so, is the actor indicated? Are the relationships expressed by these two types of sentences identical?

9. What difference in the meaning of the verb *appear* do you find in the following examples? Is it used in the same way in both

sentences? Is the difference in the functioning of *appear* the same difference you find in the uses of *become?*

a. They appear happy.
They appear together.
b. She becomes the new secretary next week.
That dress becomes her.

Exercise 11-2   Verb Functions

1. Can you note any differences in the kinds of ideas expressed by the verbs in the different lists provided below? Are the verbs in group *A* normally used in simple sentences consisting only of subject and verb? If some other word is used with the subject and verb in such sentences, what is the relationship of that word or word group to the other parts of the sentence? To which part is it related?

A. come	*B.* hit	*C.* sing
go	chase	eat
arrive	lead	run
depart	shorten	leave
rise	lay	set

2. Are the verbs in group *B* normally used in a simple sentence consisting only of a subject and a verb? If some other word is used with the subject and verb, what is the relationship of that word to the other parts of the sentence? Always? Consider the sentences "He hit to second" and "The hen lays badly."

3. What grammatical difference exists between the sentences paired in the examples provided below? What does this suggest about the verbs in group *C* above? Does the meaning of the verbs in the paired sentences remain constant?

a. He left his hat.
He left the room.
b. He ate eggs.
He ate hurriedly.
c. The hen set a record.
The hen set badly.

4. Check the grammatical meaning of the word *transitive* in your dictionary. Which of the verbs in question 3 are transitive? Which are intransitive? Are verbs followed by a predicate noun or a predi-

cate adjective (subjective complements) transitive or intransitive? Are verbs that may be followed by an object transitive or intransitive? Is transitivity a quality of the verb itself or of the structure in which the verb appears? Are verbs transitive or intransitive when followed by a modifier of some part of speech other than the noun? When a verb is complemented by both an object and a modifier of the verb, is the verb transitive or intransitive?

5. In what ways are the adjective subjective complement and the verb-modifier complement different? In what ways are the noun subjective complements and the objects complementing the verb different? Are the adverb and the adjective subjective complement parallel? What do you feel about the completeness of the following units?

John is	John runs
Mary seems	Mary drives
Louise appears	Louise knits

6. In Exercises 11-1 and 11-2 we have identified three types of verbal functions: that of linking a subjective complement to the subject, that of expressing a complete thought with the aid of the subject, and that of expressing an action done by the subject and received by the object. We also have verbs which express a concept of possession rather than one of action, and which require a noun or a noun-substitute object that represents the thing possessed. Can a single verb satisfy the requirements of more than one of these classes? Basically, when we have a verb that may satisfy the requirements of more than one of these classes, do we have one verb or two? On what do you base your decision?

7. Should the quality of transitivity or intransitivity be considered as a quality of the verb alone, or is it a quality of the construction in which the verb appears? What is our basis for determining whether a verb is being used transitively or intransitively? Is the passive voice form an infallible test for transitivity?

8. In which of the sentences below is the verb intransitive linking, in which is it intransitive nonlinking, and in which is it transitive? Are there any examples of middle verbs?

a. He hates Chicago.
b. He left Chicago.
c. He arrived Monday.
d. He hit safely.
e. He hit the pole.

f. She became his friend.
g. They went home.
h. They swam the river.
i. The runner broke quickly.
j. The girl broke her watch.

Suggested Readings

SECTION 11

Francis, W. Nelson, *The Structure of American English*, pp. 342-55. New York: The Ronald Press Company, 1954.

Lees, Robert B., *The Grammar of English Nominalizations*, pp. 53-80. Bloomington, Indiana: Indiana University Research Center in Anthropology, Folklore, and Linguistics, 1960.

See also the readings suggested for Section 6.

Syntactic Functions
—The Object

Object Types

A common definition for the object is "the person or thing that receives the action of the verb." As we have already seen when we studied the passive voice, the notional passive, and the type of verb in which the subject is at once the doer and the receiver of the action, this definition is inadequate. We shall define the object as being a noun or a substitute for a noun which, in normal word order, is found in the position immediately after the verb or after another object of the verb, which is needed to complete or clarify the meaning of the verb, and which does not express a time or space locative concept, identify another noun or pronoun, or name a class to which another noun or pronoun belongs.

The concept of the object may be subdivided in a number of different ways. One type of subdivision may be made on the basis of meaning. Some objects represent animate beings and others represent inanimate things or abstract concepts; the first group is sometimes designated as *personal* objects and the second as *impersonal* objects. Thus in the sentence "I gave her a book," *her* is a personal object and *book* is an impersonal object. Another type of subdivision is based upon the relationship of the two objects to the verb and to each other. In our above illustration, *book* is the object which receives the action of the verb *give,* and *her* receives the object *book,* not the action of the verb. The names *indirect* and *dative* are often used to describe the object illustrated by *her,* and *direct* and *accusative* are frequently used to describe or indicate the type of object illustrated by *book.*

But the personal object is not necessarily the indirect object, nor is the indirect object necessarily personal. In a sentence such as "Miss Brown taught me French," *me* is as much the receiver of the action of teaching as *French* is. We might conclude, therefore, that in this sentence we have two direct objects. We could note that the indirect object, in itself, fails to complete the verb. A word group such as "He gave me" or "She offered me" leaves us with a feeling of frustrated incompleteness; we demand to know what was given or offered. This is not true when we have a word group such as "She taught me"; here we have a feeling of completeness, and hence we are willing to recognize this as a sentence.

The indirect object is frequently impersonal. In the sentence "He gave the writing his attention," *writing* is an impersonal indirect object. If the word group stops with the word *writing,* the thought will be incomplete. It is equally possible, though not so usual, to have personal direct objects. In the sentence "The father gave the suitor his daughter," both objects are personal.

The position of the two objects may be interchanged, but when this occurs, the object which was originally the inner object will appear after a preposition. (She gave *me* a book. She gave a book *to me.* He provided *her* an escort. He provided an escort *for her.* She taught *me* French. She taught French *to me.*) Verbs that involve the general concept of giving or conveying will normally use the preposition *to* before the inner object in final position. Those involving other concepts will frequently use the preposition *for.* (She cooked *him* a dinner. She cooked a dinner *for him.* He bought *the girl* a coat. He bought a coat *for the girl.*) This prepositional phrase object is sometimes called the *periphrastic* object.

When we have a sentence with two objects, as we have already seen on pages 149-50, only one of them at a time may appear as the subject of the verb in the passive voice. The one which is not so used must therefore be kept in the object position, and in this situation it is called the *retained object.* As either of the two objects may serve as the subject of the passive voice verb, either of them may also be the retained object. The passive forms of the sentence "She gave him a book" would be "He was given a book" and "A book was given to him." In the first of these we have a retained direct object; in the second, a retained indirect object.

In certain situations the object of the verb and the subject of the verb represent the same individual or thing. When this occurs, we have what is known as a *reflexive object*. In normal English, reflexive objects are always pronouns. The pronoun most commonly used will be one of the group that ends in -*self* or -*selves*, but other object-form pronouns quite frequently appear in this construction. Some examples of the reflexive object are:

> The meteor buried *itself* in the earth.
> He taught *himself* Greek.
> I want to get *me* a new hat.
> Georgie hurt *Georgie*. (Young child's language)

The -*self* form pronouns are also used as noun intensifiers. Note the difference between "He taught himself Greek" and "He himself taught Greek."

In certain types of constructions the object of the verb appears to represent something which is the result of the action of the verb rather than something which receives the action. If you burn a hole in a suit or a dress, the *hole* is not the thing that was burned, but is rather the result of the burning. Such objects are sometimes given the name *object of result*.

Another specialized object is one we call the *cognate object*. The word *cognate*, as it is used here, means "related in origin." When a verb and its object come from the same linguistic root, we speak of the object as being a cognate object. An example of the cognate object is "He dreamed a *dream*." We normally avoid the use of cognate objects by using substitute verbs. Instead of saying "He dreamed a dream" or "He prescribed a prescription," our tendency is to say "He had a dream" or "He gave a prescription." In some situations, however, it is impossible to find such substitutes.

When we have a plural subject and either *each other* or *one another* is in object position, we have what is known as a *reciprocal object*. In the sentence "John and Mary teased one another," *John* and *Mary* individually represent both the doer and the receiver of the common action expressed by the verb. It would be unnatural

English to make a reciprocal object the subject of a passive voice construction, but we can use the passive voice with the same subjects. (John and Mary were teased by one another.)

The semantic content of certain verbs makes it possible to interchange the position of subject and object without in any way changing the meaning of the sentence. In such cases the noun or noun substitute which appears in subject position is considered the subject, and that which appears in object position is considered the object. Where necessary, the form of the verb will change to provide subject-verb concord. (Mary meets the girls every afternoon. The girls meet Mary every afternoon.) Either of the two forms of such a construction may be put into the passive voice.

Earlier we learned that predicate nominatives and predicate adjectives served as complements of the subject and were given the name *subjective complements*. Objects may also have complements, and three of the four types of objective complements parallel the types we found used as subjective complements. When we looked at the noun subjective complements, we found that they could serve either as classifiers or identifiers. We find noun objective complements serving identical purposes.

> They made John *a sergeant*. (Classifying)
> We elected Smith (*the*) *Senator*. (Identifying)

Before we go on to the other types of objective complements, it may be well to note that the noun objective complement cannot serve as the subject of a passive voice construction. When the object becomes the subject of a passive voice construction, the objective complement is retained in object position in the sentence and is called a *retained objective* complement. From our examples given above, we could derive the following passive voice constructions:

> John was made a sergeant.
> Smith was elected Senator.

But to place the objective complement in subject position would result in impossible English.

> * A sergeant was made John.
> * The Senator was elected Smith.

The third type of subjective complement was the predicate adjective which modified the subject. The objective complement may also take the form of the adjective, but when it does, of course, it is an adjective which modifies the object. (They made the girl *unhappy*. We found the boy *tired*.)

In constructions where we have an object of result, the objective complement frequently seems to modify the verb quite as much as it does the object, and it also receives primary stress, which we previously noted was characteristic of the adverb. (We dug the basement *deep*. We built the house *crooked*.)

Earlier we noted that we have more than one meaning for most words in English. The verb is no exception. In fact, some verbs may express forty or more meanings. We must, of course, have some way of deciding which of these varied meanings we are to accept for a verb. In some cases, as we have seen, the verb appears to consist of the verb form itself plus an adverb which may appear immediately following the verb or, in some instances, after the object of the verb. (*Look after* the baby. *Turn in* your papers. *Turn* your papers *in*.)

With some constructions it is the object which helps us to determine which meaning we are to select for the verb; in others, the subject may be the determiner of meaning.

Object Determiners	*Subject Determiners*
He ran a race.	The clock struck.
He ran a store.	The union struck.

Just as we sometimes have difficulty determining in the written form whether we have a verb-adverb combination followed by an object or a verb followed by a prepositional phrasal adverb, we also have difficulty at times in determining whether certain nouns following verbs in writing are being used adverbially or as objects. In the sentence "He climbed the mountain," for example, we have such a problem. The verb *to climb* may be used either transitively or intransitively, and *mountain* tells us not only what he climbed, but also where he climbed. In such situations we may use voice as a criterion for classification. If the sentence can be put into the passive voice, we will consider the noun following the verb to be an object; if not, we will consider it to be an example of the adverbial object or noun used as an adverb.

At times a verb which is normally used intransitively will be used transitively when combined with an adverb. In such cases the passive construction may help us to determine that the adverb is an essential part of the verb. A clear example of this is the differentiation between the verb *laugh* and the verb *laugh at*. The latter is transitive, as can be seen from the passive voice construction "I was laughed at."

Exercise 12-1   Types of Objects

1. What is the relationship between the verb and the noun which follows it in each of the sentences provided below?

   a. John hit Mary.
   b. Harry told a story.
   c. The boy broke a window.
   d. We have a Volkswagen.

2. Transform the sentences in question 1 by using the noun which follows the verb as the subject of a new sentence expressing the same idea. Which of the four results in unnatural English? Is this unnaturalness a result of the construction, of the idea expressed by the verb, or of the choice of verb? Substitute the verb *own* for the verb *have* in the fourth sentence, and then try the transformation. What do you find? Did you use one verb word or more than one in these revised sentences? What verb or verbs could you use as the first verb of the revised unit? What form of the second or main verb do you use? What relationship exists between the verb and the subject in these revised sentences? What does the subject of the original sentence become in the revised sentences? Can it be omitted?

3. In what situations is a noun that receives the action of a verb considered an object, and in what situations is it a subject? Is this always true? Consider the following situations.

   Mary met a friend.   A friend was met by Mary.
   A friend met Mary.   Mary was met by a friend.

4. What kind of action is involved in the sentences for question 3? What kind of nouns are used? Could you interchange the positions of the nouns in the sentence below in the same manner? Why

not? Could you change the pattern of the sentence by using a form of *to be* and a past participle instead of the presently used verb form?

Mary encountered an obstacle.

5. Are the situations considered in questions 3 and 4 identical? Is either of them identical with that of the third sentence provided below? If not, how do they differ?

   a. Mary hurt John.
   b. John hurt Mary.
   c. They hurt each other.

6. Some sentences contain more than one object. What difference can you observe between the first and second objects in the sentences provided below? Can you omit either of the objects and still have a complete sentence? Can you omit both of them? Can you express the same idea by interchanging the positions of the objects? What occurs when you do this?

   a. John gave Mary a book.
   b. George offered me a drink.
   c. Harry told her a lie.

7. When we have a sentence containing two objects, can either of these objects be made the subject of a different sentence expressing the same idea? Is the relationship between the verb and the first object the same in all three sentences in question 6? Is the relationship between the verb and the second object identical in all three sentences? Does the relationship between the two objects appear to be the same in all three sentences?

8. In the sentences for question 1 the verbs were used in the active voice. In those you were asked to write for question 2 the verbs should have been in the passive voice. The sentences for question 3 illustrate both the active and the passive voice. What are the characteristics of the passive voice subject? What are the characteristics of the passive voice verb? Is the first verb used an auxiliary or a full verb? What inflectional form does the main verb take? Could the auxiliaries which are used in forming the passive voice be labeled linking, intransitive nonlinking, or transitive?

9. Look up the grammatical meanings of the terms *dative, accusative,* and *instrumental.* Do we have any word forms expressing

these cases in modern English? Do we use any function words in modern English to express these relationships? Are there any indirect objects in the sentences for question 6? When we have two objects in a sentence, must one of them be an indirect and the other a direct object? Is a sentence that contains only an indirect object a complete sentence?

Exercise 12-2   Types of Objects

1. What relationship exists between the object and the subject in the sentences below? Where have we encountered these -self form pronouns before? Can any other form of the pronoun be used in this structural pattern? Is the structure of this pattern identical with that of the sentences "They belittle one another" and "They love each other"? In what way does the meaning expressed by this structural pattern differ from that expressed by the pattern of "I hurt myself"? What names could be given to such objects?

    a. I hurt myself.
    b. We consider ourselves first.
    c. They must blame themselves.

2. What relationship exists between the object and the verb in the following examples? Look up the word *cognate* in your dictionary. Why are these objects called cognate objects? Are the objects and the verbs in these sentences true cognates? All of them? What relationship must there be between verb and object before we apply the term *cognate* to the object?

    a. She sang a song.
    b. He dreamed a dream.
    c. They rode on a raid.
    d. We ran a race.

3. What relationship exists between the verb and the object in the following sentences? Why are such objects called *objects of result?*

    a. They built a house.
    b. We dug a hole.
    c. She knitted a sweater.

4. You will recall that we were able to identify three types of subjective complements: a noun naming a class to which the subject belonged, a noun representing the same person or thing that was named by the subject, and an adjective modifying the subject. Keep these distinctions in mind as you consider the sentences provided below. What parallels do you find between subjective complements and the final words in each of these sentences? Do these words appear to "complete" any element in the sentence? If so, which element? What type of stress do they receive in speech?

    a. They made Jane a secretary.
    b. We chose George captain.
    c. He painted the fence green.

5. In the sentence "We dug the well deep," what does the word *deep* complement? Is it merely a modifier of the verb, or does it also tell us something about *well?*
6. Is it possible to have an objective complement to only one of two objects? What do we have in the sentence "They served me the soup hot"? Which object is complemented? Does the indirect object ever have a complement?
7. Which of the following may serve as the subject of the passive voice verbs: indirect object, direct object, reflexive object, cognate object, object of result, noun objective complement?
8. In an earlier exercise we observed that a verb plus a directional word such as *in, off, up, down, through,* sometimes supplies an idea quite distinct from those provided by the verb alone; for example, *look over* provides us with the concept *inspect.* Are there any unusual meanings for the verb in each of the examples given below? Can the object have any function as a determiner of verb meaning? Do all the verbs in these sentences have objects?

He hit the boy.	He threw a stone.	He walked.
He hit the bottle.	He threw a party.	He walked the dog.
He hit the road.	He threw the game.	He walked the plank.
He hit the hay.	He threw a fit.	He walked the floor.

9. If we give the name *adverb* to a word or word group that modifies, changes, or clarifies the meaning of a verb, must we also say that some objects appear to be adverbial in their nature? What are our criteria for distinguishing the adverb from the object? Which do we have—objects or adverbs—in each of the following

examples? Try putting each of these into the passive voice construction. Is this a criterion? Try reading them aloud. Is stress a criterion?

He left there.	He arrives soon.	He swam the river.
He left Chicago.	He arrives Monday.	He swam in the river.
He left the city.		He swam across the river.
He left a book.		

Suggested Readings

SECTION 12

Jespersen, Otto, *The Philosophy of Grammar*, Chap. XII. London: George Allen & Unwin, Ltd., 1924.
See also the Fries reference in the bibliography for Section 10.

The Connectors

Prepositions

Prepositions are the most frequently used of all connectors. They have been given the name *preposition* because they are commonly found in the position before a noun or a noun substitute. Many of the prepositions are semantically locative—some primarily in terms of space, others primarily in terms of time. A few, such as *across from* or *during*, are restricted to one sphere, but most of the locative prepositions may be used with either temporal or spatial situations. (It lies *on* the desk. He arrived *on* the hour. He stood *before* the class. They left *before* noon.)

Closely related to the locative prepositions are a group that we might call *directional* prepositions, because that is the type of relationship they express. Once again, many of these will be found used as temporal position locators as well as spatial directional indicators. (He went *toward* home. He arrived *toward* dusk.)

Prepositions are also used to imply comparisons and to express contrasts. (I'll be there in *under* an hour. It is *over* a mile. I prefer tea *to* coffee. I like everything *except* the horseradish.) When constrast is expressed by a preposition, the contrast is generally between the whole and a part; if we are contrasting two complete or equal entities, we normally do so by using a conjunction rather than a preposition. The preposition is also used to express the partitive relationship in noncontrastive situations (the tail *of* the dog, the handle *from* the cup, the bearing *for* the motor). It should be noted that other relationships in addition to the partitive are simultaneously expressed by most of these. For the main part, these varying associational relationships are those that are also expressed by the genitive case forms (the dog's tail, the cup's handle, the motor's bearing).

We have seen also that the preposition is used as a part of certain grammatical objects. (I gave *her* the book. I gave the book *to her*. I bought *him* a shirt. I bought a shirt *for him*.)

Agency is also commonly expressed by the preposition. (He was hit *by* the ball. He gets a discount *through* the school.) In certain situations, chiefly with the verb *to take*, the preposition may serve as an alternative for the infinitive *to be*. (He takes me *to be* a fool. He takes me *for* a fool.)

Many prepositions and adverbs have identical written forms. As has been previously pointed out, these can be distinguished by oral stress. The adverb will receive strong stress in speech, the preposition will not.

Adverb: This copy is the one to turn ín.

Preposition: This driveway is the one to turn in.

The foregoing discussion has by no means exhausted the varying uses and meanings of prepositions; it is, in fact, but a slight introduction to this topic. If you are interested in delving deeper, check the entries for the various prepositions in the *Oxford English Dictionary*[1] or search out and read some of the articles on this topic listed in A. G. Kennedy's *A Bibliography of Writings on the English Language*,[2] or in bibliographies published in *American Speech*.[3]

Prepositions take numerous forms. Some of them, such as *at, by, to,* or *from,* are simple; others exhibit a combined form. Of the latter, some are constructed by combining two simple prepositions (*into, onto, upon*), and others combine a simple preposition with

[1] Sir James A. H. Murray, ed., *A New English Dictionary on Historical Principles* (Oxford: Clarendon Press, 1888-1933).

[2] Arthur Garfield Kennedy, *A Bibliography of Writings on the English Language from the Beginning of Printing to the End of 1922* (Cambridge and New Haven: Harvard University Press, Yale University Press, 1927).

[3] *American Speech: A Quarterly of Linguistic Usage* (New York: Columbia University Press, 1925-   ).

some other bound or free form (*inside, outside*); still others are used as single prepositions in speech, but are written as though they were separate words (*across from, except for*); others represent a combination of a prepositional phrase and an additional preposition. In some instances the noun object of the first preposition is written as a separate word, whereas in others it is combined with the preposition (in *place* of, in *lieu* of; in*side* of, in*stead* of).

The -*ing* form of certain verbs has come to be commonly used as a preposition. It is easy to see this verbal origin in such forms as *concerning* or *regarding*, but we are less likely to recognize it in a preposition such as *during*, which is a comparable form of a now obsolete verb.

Although the primary functions of prepositions are to connect parts of a sentence and to show the various relationships between them, words normally identified as prepositions may also serve as members of the major form-classes. Thus we have a fourth *down* in football, and we can *down* a drink, or coast *down* a *down*grade. In effect, what we have here are homonyms. And even though the prepositional phrase normally serves as a modifier, it too may occasionally be found functioning as a noun or verb; it is commonly the object of a verb or the object of a preposition. (Get up from *in under that table.*) Its use as a subject is relatively rare (*To the guns* echoed through the land). As a verb it is even more rare, if we exclude the infinitive (which, historically, was a prepositional phrase). We occasionally hear sentences such as "I'll *in a minute* you," but we rarely find these forms in standard speech or writing.

The preposition is regularly joined with other morphs to form English words. In some the preposition appears as the initial form in the compound (*in*come, *off*set, *over*grown, *under*done, *with*hold, *by*pass, *down*fall, *before*hand, *out*landish), and in others it appears as the final element (kick*off*, take*out*, drive-*in*, passer-*by*).

Idiomatic usage demands that particular prepositions be used in certain situations. Thus we can be *at* home, *at* church, or *at* school; but even though we go *to* church and *to* school, we do *not* go *to* home. We live *in* a particular geographical area or region. Our houses are *on* streets, and they are found *at* particular locations on those streets. Sometimes ambiguity results from such idiomatic usages. (Should South Viet-Nam be lost *to* the Communists, it will also be lost *to* us. At first, I fought *with* him and later I fought by his side. At first I fought *with* him, and then I fought against

him.) Native speakers have learned to use these prepositions automatically in the accepted manner, but the individual who has
learned English as a second language is frequently betrayed by
his use of preposition. (*I went *at* the store yesterday.)

Problems also develop from the use of case forms of pronouns
with prepositions. The noun, of course, shows no difference in form
for nominative or objective case, but six pronouns (eight, if we
count the combination forms of *who* and *whom* with -*ever* and
-*soever*) still have distinctive forms for these cases. The six in
the nominative and objective forms respectively are: *I, me; he, him;
she, her; we, us; they, them;* and *who, whom.* According to modern
standard usage, the object of a preposition should be in either the
objective or in the genitive case. Because the four written forms
of the noun (*boy, boys, boy's, boys'*) have but two spoken forms,
and the corresponding pronouns have the forms *he, his, him; they,
theirs, them,* this inevitably leads to confusion, and hence to mis-
usage in writing.

The second usage problem is likely to occur when pronouns are
found as compound objects of a preposition. When the pronoun
follows a conjunction it is removed from its usual position (which
is directly after the preposition). As a result, we frequently hear
such expressions as "between you and I." Rarely do we hear or see a
nominative form pronoun used between the preposition and the
conjunction.

A third usage problem occurs when the object of the preposition
is removed from its normal position and put at the beginning of
the sentence as an interrogative pronoun. (*Who* shall I give it to?)
Here we have a conflict between the position signal and the form
signal; as might be expected, because word position rather than
word form has become the dominant signaling device in modern
English, such usage has become standard. The same situation occurs when the pronoun is the object of the verb. (*Who* did you
see?)

Exercise 13-1   Prepositions

1. In our study of the double objects taken by some verbs, we
noted that the positions of the two objects were fixed. When an accusative and a dative object follow a verb, which comes first? When

a personal and a nonpersonal object appear after a verb, which is placed before the other? If we make no change in the subject or verb of the sentence "John gave me a book," in what other manner can we express this idea?

2. What are the words *to, in* and *on* usually called? In what position are they commonly found? Is the preposition ever followed by anything except a noun or a noun substitute? Is the *to* that we find in the infinitive forms a preposition? How can we distinguish prepositions from adverbs which have the same written form and which appear in the same position in the sentence?

3. When a preposition is followed by a noun, what syntactic function does the entire phrase usually serve? What function does the prepositional phrase have in each of the sentences below? Are any of these words adverbs rather than prepositions? Are any of these usages substandard?

    a. Over the fence is out.
    b. After the storm we had a beautiful sunset.
    c. John, as secretary, was very diligent.
    d. The man at the desk is my father.
    e. All but she had bought their tickets.
    f. The car was damaged by the truck.
    g. We went down the river.
    h. We went down to the river.
    i. For you to recognize this is important.
    j. They arrived from Cairo.
    k. They arrived in a new car.
    l. I want for him to go.

4. Consider the following possibilities of expressing particular relationships. Do they in any way suggest a reason for our extensive use of the prepositional phrase?

the *cup handle*	the *truck load*	the *egg shell*
the *cup's handle*	the *truck's load*	the *egg's shell*
the *handle on the cup*	the *load on the truck*	the *shell of the egg*
for the cup	*from the truck*	*around the egg*
from the cup	*in the truck*	*from the egg*
of the cup	*of the truck*	*for the egg*
	for the truck	*on the egg*
		in the egg

5. The preposition is sometimes defined as being a connector. In addition to connection, what may be expressed by each of the following prepositions? Can you add others to this list?

above	below
across from	beneath
against	beside
alongside of	between

6. What concept do the following prepositions express? Can you add others to this list? Could any of these be placed in the list for question 5? Could any items in the list for question 5 be added to this list?

after	since
before	throughout
during	until

7. What idea is expressed by the following prepositions? Can you add others to this list?

but	except for
except	instead of

8. Can prepositions be used to express more than one type of relationship? Look up one of the prepositions in the *Oxford (New) English Dictionary* and study the various meanings assigned to it. Are the meanings inherent in the preposition itself, or do they appear to stem from the context in which it is found? What meanings do you find in the following examples?

We sat by the boy.
The fish was caught by the boy.
We went to Chicago.
I prefer coffee to tea.
We took him for a ride.
We took him for a Dane.

9. Can words which are normally classed as prepositions serve as other parts of speech? To what word-class does each of the italicized words belong?

a. Because of the *outs'* out and out opposition, the *ins* have had their *ups* and *downs* this legislative session.
b. If you *up* the ante, he will *down* his drink.
c. The *up* grade was slippery, and the *off* wheels slid into the ditch.
d. We turned *off* at the corner.

10. A list of commonly used prepositions is provided on page 172. How many of these can also serve as some other part of speech? (Give examples.) How many express but a single meaning when used as prepositions? Which of them are commonly attached to verbs?

about	below	from	outside of
above	beneath	in	over
across	beside	in lieu of	over to
across from	between	in place of	regarding
after	betwixt	inside	round
against	beyond	inside of	since
along	but	instead of	through
alongside	by	into	throughout
alongside of	concerning	like	till
along with	considering	near	to
among	despite	of	toward
apart from	down	off	under
around	down from	off from	until
as	down off	off of	up
at	due to	on	upon
away from	during	onto	up to
back of	except	out	with
before	except for	out of	within
behind	for	outside	without

11. Are there any words in the above list which are used as prepositions only in substandard English? Which of the prepositions—*on, in* or *at*—would you use in each of the following sentences? What reason can you give for your choice?

    a. We live _____ Chicago.
    b. We live _____ State Street.
    c. We live _____ 540 S. State Street.
    d. We live _____ the corner of State and Sixth Streets.

12. As we learned in an earlier exercise, adverbs which have written forms identical to the written forms of prepositions are frequently added to verbs, sometimes without changing the basic verbal meanings and sometimes to provide new meanings. We have also seen (in this exercise) that prepositions can change their function and serve as other parts of speech. In which of the sentences below is the italicized word a part of a prepositional phrase? How do you determine when a particular word is being used as a preposition?

    a. Look *over* the fence and see if he is in the garden.
       Look *over* the fence and see if there are any flaws in it.
    b. We saw him *round* the corner on two wheels.
       We played a *round* of golf.
       The bakery is *round* the corner.
       The ball is not *round*.
       We went *round* and *round*.

c. He is always *concerning* himself with nonessentials.
He is always careful *concerning* himself.
Concerning himself about the cares of the world is his chief occupation.

Exercise 13-2

1. Does the form of a noun used as an object differ from its form when it is used as a subject? Is this true of genitive nouns as well as others? What is different from the ordinary genitive in the following sentence?

She is a friend of my father's.

2. Are different forms used for the pronoun as an object and the pronoun as a subject? Is this true of all pronouns? If not, of which is it true? How many pronouns have different forms when they are used as subjects and as objects? Do any of these combine with other words?

3. What sometimes happens to pronoun forms in our speech when a sentence presents a conflict between word-order patterning and grammatical function? Would you consider all of the situations in the examples below to be standard English? Why or why not? Is *but* a preposition in the third sentence?

a. Who shall we call?
b. Who shall I charge this to?
c. The boy stood on the burning deck/Whence all but he had fled.

4. What is the meaning of *whence* as used in the above example? Do we have any other words in English that can be substituted for prepositional phrases? Are these words in common usage?

5. Are genitive pronouns ever used as objects? Do we ever find verb forms serving as objects of other verbs or as objects of prepositions? Under what circumstances, if any, can we use modifiers as objects of prepositions? Provide examples.

6. Do we ever use a prepositional phrase as the object of a preposition? Can a clause be an object of a preposition? If your answer is *yes*, give an example.

7. What is the object of *for* in the sentence below? For what syntactic function is the prepositional phrase used in this sentence?

For me to do that would be wrong.

8. List all the different classes of words and grammatical units that can function as the object of a preposition. Compare each of these with the classes of words and grammatical units that can be used as objects of verbs. Do your lists differ at all? Compare each of them with the classes of words or grammatical units that can be used as subjects of the verb. Do these lists differ?

9. Which is of most help in identifying objects: the form of the noun or noun substitute, its meaning, or its position?

10. We may say either "She leaves on Monday" or "She leaves Monday." In such a construction we do not feel it necessary to include the preposition. In other structures, however, such as "She arrives in Chicago," we find that we must use the preposition. Under what conditions may the preposition be omitted, and in what situations must it be retained? Are there any situations in which it would be bad usage to use a preposition?

Conjunctions and Conjunctives

We have just discussed one type of connector—the preposition. In terms of frequency of use, the next most common type of connector is probably the conjunction. Conjunctions are commonly divided into two major groups: the coordinators and the subordinators. The coordinators appear in but one position—between the elements that they coordinate—and only join elements which are syntactically identical: subjects are joined to subjects, objects to objects, verbs to verbs, modifiers of nouns to modifiers of nouns, modifiers of verbs to modifiers of verbs, prepositional phrases to prepositional phrases, noun clauses to noun clauses, adjective clauses to adjective clauses, and so forth. In some situations we demand not only syntactical identity but also morphological identity before we coordinate elements. Thus we never coordinate a noun adjunct type of noun modifier with an adjective type of noun modifier, nor do we even coordinate an infinitive with a gerund or participle. In a few situations we even demand a sort of semantic identity for coordination, for with the exception of a few combinations, such as *here and now* or *then and there*, we rarely coordinate a place-indicating adverb with a time-indicating or a manner-indicating adverb, nor the latter two with one another.

Within the coordinating group we can identify a number of subgroups. First we have a number of conjunctions whose function it is to add the elements that appear before and after them. (*John and Mary* are going. We *played and sang.*) As a second subgroup we have some conjunctions whose function it is to tie together elements which contrast with one another. (*I like coffee but I don't like tea.*) A third group joins elements which are presented as alternatives. (*John or I* will be there.) A fourth joins elements which are being compared. (She is happier *than* he is.) A fifth joins a reason or a cause to an action or to the result of an action. (The people must have wanted Lincoln to be President, *for* they elected him.) A sixth group tends to reverse this process by connecting a conclusion to some action or premise. (We chose to be free, *so* we must accept the responsibilities concomitant with freedom.)

Occasionally, for stylistic purposes, elements which would normally be incongruous may be combined, but such usage is by no means normal. (*John* and *studying* appear to be incompatible. *John* and *the poor* have in common their ubiquity.)

Subordinating conjunctions are tied to one of the elements being connected and occupy the initial position in that element. As result, they may appear in two positions: at the beginning of the sentence or between the connected elements. (*If* he comes, tell him I had to leave. Tell him I had to leave, *if* he comes. *Though* ugly, she was attractive. She was attractive, *though* ugly.)

A third type of connector, called the *conjunctive adverb* (or, by some grammarians, the *sentence connector*), is used to link sentences or clauses. These sentences or clauses may be written as though they represented a single sentence or as two sentences. In speech, we always use a sentence-terminating pitch-juncture pattern before such a connector. The primary function of the conjunctive adverb is to provide transition. (He never studies. *Consequently*, he never passes a course.)

Connectors are frequently used in pairs called correlatives. The more commonly used of these correlatives are:

both . . . and
not only . . . but (also)
either . . . or
neither . . . nor
as . . . as
not so . . . as
rather . . . than
if . . . then
where . . . there

Like the prepositions, conjunctive connectors also make use of combined forms (*as long as, inasmuch as, in addition to,* and so forth). Prepositional phrases may also be used as transitional devices to connect independent sentences, paragraphs, or other such units; they may even be found at the beginning of units as large as chapters of a book (*on the other hand, as a consequence* [*of*], *as a matter of fact*). Quite as frequently this type of connection is achieved through the use of a different type of cliché, generally figurative in origin, which functions as a grammatical unit within the sentence. (*The other side of the coin* shows.)

When a phrase is used as a substitute for an additive conjunction, it tends to be parenthetical; hence the subject-verb concord is different in the two constructions, though the meaning is changed little if at all. (George *and* his sister are going to Europe. George, *as well as* his sister, is going to Europe. George, *in addition to* his sister, is going to Europe.)

We saw earlier that the *-ing* form of a few verbs is commonly used as a prepositional connector. As a matter of fact, whenever a word-group modifier stands in postpositional relationship to the element being modified, the initial word of the modifying word group normally serves as a connector. Frequently these words are participles or infinitives. (The girl *frying* the steak is my sister. The man *tried* by the court was a foreigner. The fellow *to see* about a loan is George.) Occasionally, particularly when a comparison is being expressed, the modifying adjective stands in the initial position in the modifying unit. (The day, *dark* as night, was depressing.)

Pronouns are commonly used as connectors. (The boy *who* was here is my brother. The book *which* we chose was not available.) When used in this manner, they perform a double job: (1) They connect two clauses, and (2) they have some syntactic function within the clause they introduce. Such pronouns are called *relative* pronouns. When the syntactic function of the relative pronoun is not one which is essential to predication, the relative may be omitted. Actually, this occurs only when the relative pronoun has a referent within the sentence. (He is the man [*whom*] I met.) Pronominal adjectives may also be used to introduce and connect clauses. (I will work *whichever* hours are convenient.)

And finally, the linking verb is also used as a connector. As these varying structures are discussed in greater detail elsewhere, they have been listed here merely as a synthesis.

Exercise 13-3   Connectors

We have learned that prepositions are most commonly used to connect the noun object with the unit modified by the prepositional phrase. We have also learned that the preposition frequently defines the particular type of relationship between the object of the preposition and the word or unit modified by the prepositional phrase. In this exercise our chief concern will be with connectors other than prepositions.

1. What meaning do we generally attach to the word *and?* How frequently do we use this word in English? What function does it perform in each of the sentences given below? Can you supply examples in which it performs other functions?

   a. John and Mary have gone.
   b. Try and stop me.
   c. Harry played and sang.
   d. Ruth is beautiful and good.
   e. He responded to the questions completely and truthfully.
   f. She is bad; she is good and bad.
   g. The truck hit the car and a telephone pole.
   h. Go and see if the paper has come.

2. When we use two singular nouns connected by *and* as the subject of the verb, will the verb be singular or plural? Is this simply a question of adding one to one? What differences do you discover in the usages in the sentences below?

   John and his mother are ready.
   John, as well as his mother, is ready.
   In addition to his mother, John is going.

3. Another of the more commonly used connectives is the word *but*. What type of concept is normally introduced by this word? Which word—*and* or *but*—is more frequently used with negations? Must we have a negative in every sentence in which we use *but?* If we do use a negating word with *but*, at what point or points in the sentence may this word appear? Consider each of the following sentences, then try to write an accurate description of our manner of using the word *but*.

   a. I like raw cheese, but not cooked cheese.
   b. I don't like Harry, but I do like his wife.
   c. John went to the store, but Mary remained at home.

 d. She was intelligent, but unprepared for this.
 e. She was ugly, but happy.
 f. They worked dejectedly, but swiftly.
 g. He had little desire to go, but he did go.
 h. Everyone but John had studied his lesson.
 i. I enjoyed everything but the shrimp.

4. Are any of the *but's* in the examples for question 3 used as prepositions? If we change the tense of the verb in the penultimate sentence from the past perfect to the present perfect, would we use a singular or a plural form for the auxiliary? If we changed the first word of that sentence from *everyone* to *all*, what form of the verb would we use with it? Do you find any parallel between this and the *as well as* situation of question 2?

5. In what way do the connectors we have just considered differ from the connectors which appear in the examples below? Consider both the position or positions that the connectors may take in these sentences and the function or functions of the connectors themselves. Do we have any other means of expressing this type of concept? Which of the modal auxiliaries can we use? What changes occur in the word order pattern when we use a modal auxiliary to express the concept of condition? Can we use such a pattern as a substitute for each of the three sentences?

 a. I will come if he comes.
 b. We can eat if the meal is ready.
 c. He did not win the game, though he was a skillful coach.

6. In what way does the word *or* differ from other connectors we have considered? When this word is used between two singular noun subjects, do we use a singular or a plural form of the verb with it? With what is the reader or listener presented when we use a sentence containing the connector *or*? Is the situation the same when we use the negative form *nor*? In speech, which would you use—a rising or a falling terminal—if you expected a *yes* or a *no* response to the question "Do you drink tea or coffee?" Which type of terminal would you use if you expected a *tea* or a *coffee* response? Which is the question offering an alternative?

7. For what purpose do we use connectives in pairs? Do we ever combine different types of connectors in such pairs? Describe the type of connection provided in each of the following sentences.

 a. Both John and his sister will be there.
 b. Not only John, but also Mary, is responsible.

    c. Either Mary or John will be there.
    d. Neither Mary nor John will be there.
    e. Whether he comes or not, we will eat at twelve.

8. Make a list of the connectives used to express the additive function, a second of those commonly used to express the contrastive function, a third of those used to express conditions, and a fourth of those used to present alternatives. Do any of the connecting words appear in more than one list?

Exercise 13-4   Connectors

In Exercise 13-3 we worked with words whose primary function is that of connecting. In this exercise we will work with some in which the connecting function might be considered secondary.

1. To what word-class do the connectors in each of the sentences provided belong? Do these words have any other syntactic function within the sentence? Can the connecting word be omitted from any of these sentences? Can it be omitted from all of them? Under what circumstances may it be omitted? Should *who* be used in place of *whom*, or *whom* in place of *who*, in any of these sentences? Does the use of *that* in the second sentence represent standard or substandard usage?

    a. The boy who was here before is back again.
    b. The man that I met is a soldier.
    c. A girl whom we knew won the prize.
    d. The man whom I referred to has since died.

2. To what word-class do the words belong that perform the function of connection in the following sentences?

    a. The man walking the dog is my friend.
    b. The boy injured by the car has been taken to the hospital.
    c. The dog barking his heart out is ours.
    d. The roast, done to a turn, was delicious.
    e. The sun, red as blood, sank below the horizon.
    f. The girl, sweet as saccharin, simpered abominably.

3. By what class of words is the connecting function performed in the sentences below? Can any of these be omitted?

    a. We must make hay while the sun shines.
    b. Though he is my friend, I must denounce him.

    c. Because he is my friend, I will defend him.
    d. I will go wherever I am needed.
    e. I know the place where he lives.
    f. Do you know how to do it?
    g. The dog came when he was called.

4. In addition to the function of connection, what function do the connecting words from the examples of questions 2 and 3 serve? Do any of these sentences contain more than one connecting word? Does the connecting word appear to be omitted from any of them?

5. Are the connecting words in the sentences provided below of the same type as those found in question 3? If not, in what way or ways do they differ?

    a. The evidence, when pertinent, must be admitted.
    b. The clothes, when usable, were saved.
    c. The curtains, though fading, were useful.
    d. The dog came when called.
    e. While driving, we were entertained by the radio.

6. What words serve as connectors in the sentences below? What other function or functions do they serve?

    a. This syrup is as sweet as sugar.
    b. I like him as well as I like her.
    c. This apple tastes good like a good apple should.
    d. John, like Mary, detests coffee.

7. In what way or ways are the following sentences related to those in question 6?

    a. She is good as gold.
    b. It was bitter as aloes.
    c. He stood firm as a rock.

8. Which are the connecting words in the sentences below? What is the normal position for the connecting word in such a structure? What is characteristic of the word that precedes the connector?

    a. He is bigger than I.
    b. I like him better than her.
    c. He ran swifter than lightning.
    d. She is more beautiful than talented.
    e. He acted more indignant than angry.
    f. Rather than saccharin, I will take sugar.

9. To what word-class do the connectors belong in the two sentences given below? Can we express comparison or contrast with a

connector of this type without using a verb that denotes the concept of preference?

I prefer saccharin to sugar.
The coach chose John over George.

10. To what word-class do the connectors in the examples belong? What relationship exists between the two words that are connected in each example?

a. He was the tallest in the lineup.
b. That is the best of the lot.
c. Among the Vietnamese, he was the strongest.

11. What relationship exists between the structure illustrated by the examples of question 10 and that of the following sentence?

He was the first to arrive in Sparta.

12. What relationship exists between the example sentences of questions 10 and 11 and those which follow?

a. There were three girls in the room; two of them were my sisters.
b. There were some twenty people at the party; several had been drinking.

13. How are the two clauses related in each of the sentences provided in the examples below? What syntactic function does the connecting word have in the clause to which it belongs? If you supply a connecting word where none is present, what syntactic function would it have in the clause to which it is attached?

a. I left before he arrived.
b. He remembered who was there.
c. She knew which boy took the money.
d. We know what you mean.
e. Did you see where he went?
f. They hope that he will come.
g. They expect he will come.
h. That he was there is certain.
i. It is certain he was there.

14. What types of concepts are connected by linking verbs? What is the connector and what is connected in each of the following sentences?

a. They trained him to be a lawyer.
b. They wanted him to be the secretary.
c. We expect her to be busy.

d. They took him for a peddler.
e. They mistook him for the radio repairman.
f. We considered him honest.

Suggested Readings

Section 13

Francis, W. Nelson, *The Structure of American English*, pp. 355-66. New York: The Ronald Press Company, 1954.

Roberts, Paul, *Understanding English*, pp. 191-92, 197-99, 217-36. New York: Harper & Row, Publishers, 1958.

Whitehall, Harold, *Structural Essentials of English*, Chap. V. New York: Harcourt, Brace & World, Inc., 1951.

Basic Sentence Patterns
—The Statement

A little thought should convince us that the sentence patterns of any language which are truly basic must necessarily be simple in their nature. Whether he be born in the United States, Brazil, or the Congo, the normal child will learn to speak the language of the area by the time he is three. If his parents speak one language and the servants, neighbors, and playmates with whom he also associates speak another, he will learn to speak both. In the process of learning any language, the child almost inevitably will confuse some of the patterns at first. A young friend of mine, for example, used to make his requests by using the question form which his mother had used in addressing him. He would say "Does David want a cookie?" when what he desired to say was "David wants a cookie." Although his mother made no attempt to teach him the conventional request form, in less than two months he had learned it from other children and had stopped using the question form. Most of us have learned the essential grammatical structures of our language just as David learned them—by hearing others use them and by changing our practices whenever we discovered that those practices differed from the practices of those with whom we conversed.

When we attempt to describe a language, however, we often find these practices so interwoven with one another and used together so naturally that we have difficulty in isolating them. Our automatic use of the language also interferes with our recognition of the fact that two or more sentences which may sound quite different from one another and which may express completely different meanings are in reality built upon the same basic sentence pattern. Thus, we may see no relationship between "The biscuit is hard" and "The child will be beautiful"; in fact, we may be inclined to think of them as having different patterns because we note variations such as tense and lexical differences.

As soon as we look at these sentences in terms of pattern, we discover that (1) in each of them some quality is being ascribed to a naming word or noun, (2) the position of the noun is before the verb, (3) the position of the qualifier is after the verb, and (4) the verb itself conveys little meaning other than a time relationship. When we have discovered these things, we have one of the basic sentence patterns of English: *Noun + Linking Verb + Adjective.* By using this pattern, we can construct literally thousands of different sentences.

> The sky is blue.
> The well became dry.
> The child looked sick.
> The decision would have been different.
> The old man gets tired.
> The story was true.
> The dinner was good.
> Mary is beautiful.
> The room is going to be large.
> The house had been square.

In the process of searching for sentences that fit this it is very likely that most of us would stumble upon another basic pattern: *Noun + Linking Verb + Noun.* The variation is slight. The noun which now appears in the position of the adjective—after the linking verb—tends also to describe the noun which stands before the verb. When we say, for example, "The baby is a boy," the word *boy* tells us something about the concept *baby,* just as *beautiful* tells us something about the concept *child* in the sentence "The child is beautiful." There is, however, some difference in the type of message conveyed by the two sentences. *Boy* names a class of beings; *beautiful* does not. The effect of our new sentence pattern is therefore that of placing the concept represented by the preverbal noun into the classification represented by the postverbal noun. Again, we have discovered a basic sentence pattern which can be used to create innumerable sentences.

The horse is a Percheron.
The dog was a poodle.
The gadget had been a cigarette lighter.
The school became a university.
The man was a mason.
The snow is a nuisance.
Thanksgiving is a holiday.
The ice cream will be a treat.
The automobile is a Ford.

One characteristic of these sentences is that each of them uses the word *a* before the classifying noun. If we substitute certain other noun determiners for the *a*, we find a quite different type of idea expressed. Instead of the postverbal noun naming a class to which the preverbal noun belongs, we now find that both the post- and the preverbal nouns represent the same individual or concept, and the verb has become practically the equivalent of an equals sign.

That boy is my brother.
John was your attorney.
This brick house will be our new home.
His home town had been New York.
Their mother was my sister.
The price was two dollars.
Nixon used to be the Vice President.
John appeared to be the winner.

We have already noted one difference between sentences of this type and those of the preceding type—the choice of determiner used before the noun which follows the verb. We should note another difference. Because the verb in such sentences is practically the equivalent of an equals sign, we should be able to interchange the positions of the two nouns in such sentences, and we find that in most of them we can do so. A little further inspection shows us that when a determiner is used before either noun, it will not be of the *a, an* class. When we try to substitute other determiners for *a* or *an*, we find relatively few that will serve.

It was *some* boy (at the door).
John was *no* gentleman.

More frequently we find the plural form of the noun used without a determiner to indicate the class.

Many boys were scouts.
Some girls will become nurses.
Few boys are gentlemen.

In such situations we also find plural nouns before the verb. These may or may not be preceded by a determiner; when they are not, we find that the class named by the preverbal noun is a subclass of the class named by the postverbal noun.

Roses are flowers.	The rose is a flower.
Dogs are quadrupeds.	The dog is a quadruped.
Chevrolets are automobiles.	The Chevrolet is an automobile.
Men are mammals.	Man is a mammal.
The flowers are roses.	The flower is a rose.

When the plural form of the noun is preceded by a determiner, we find that a subclass is being represented. When we say *the girls,* we are not speaking of *all girls,* but rather of a particular group of girls. In a sentence such as "The girls were some hikers," we find that we are no longer classifying one group as being part of another, but rather a part of one group or class as being identical with a part of another. We are still distinguishing between *all* and *some.* As soon as we say *these* girls, *those* girls, *some* girls, *many* girls, *few* girls, and so on, we cease to speak of *all* girls; however, if we use a plural form without a determiner, we must assume that we are speaking of *all* of the class named. (*Men* are mortal.)

Because we have these two types of sentences (those in which the preverbal or subject noun is classified, and those in which it is identified), we shall need to make some refinements in our basic sentence pattern of *Noun + Linking Verb + Noun.* For the classifying type of sentence our subject noun may appear without a determiner, or it may be preceded by any type of determiner—that is, one indicating *one, some,* or *all.* The postverbal noun, if it is in plural form, may appear without a determiner; if it is in singular form, it will be preceded by a determiner of the *a/an* type. In the identifying structure, the subject noun may appear without a determiner if it is a proper noun, a noncountable mass noun, or a plural; otherwise it will be preceded by a determiner of the *the/my* type. The noun following the verb will show the same characteristics. In the following examples, the parentheses indicate that we have the alternative of using the determiner or not using it.

John was the man.   The man was John.
(The) Flowers are my choice.   My choice is (the) flowers.
(This) Candy is the fattening food.   The fattening food is (the) candy.

Before going on, it may be well to point out that patterns such as these will not permit completely free substitution—we cannot put just any noun in the noun position or positions, nor can we use just any verb or adjective in the verb or adjective positions. If we do, we may create sentences expressing sheer nonsense.

The fish are long-legged.
The stone is a wolf.
The evening was my sweater.

Such nonsensical sentences *do* conform to the *basic* structural patterns of English, but they do not conform to more detailed patterns which necessarily take into consideration the nature of the formal and lexical meanings attached to individual words. For example, only living things eat and drink; hence the list of nouns that may appear as subjects of the active voice of such verbs is limited to those that name living things. In like manner, the list of nouns that may appear as the object of such a verb as *to drink* will be limited to those that name some liquid. When we vary from such usage we move into the realm of figurative language.

To return to our basic patterns, we have a third type which also consists of *Noun + Verb + Noun*. To distinguish it from the identifying or classifying types, it is sufficient to say that it serves neither of these functions. It may be descriptive of a condition. (I have a *headache.* John caught a *cold.*) Or it may, and most commonly does, represent someone or something capable either of being possessed or of receiving some type of action. Some examples of this type are:

Harry owns a Plymouth.
John hit Mary.
The wind broke the trees.
George built a birdhouse.

The thought of most sentences of this class may be expressed by an alternate pattern which utilizes the passive voice of the verb. In the example sentences above, the verbs are in the active voice. An object of the active voice verb becomes the subject in the passive voice construction. The passive tense form is analytical and must include some form of a linking verb used as an auxiliary plus the past participle of the original active voice verb. The subject of the active voice verb may or may not appear in the new pattern. If the original verb was one expressing the concept of possession, it normally does appear (as the object of a preposition).

> The Plymouth is owned by Harry.
> Mary was hit (by John).
> The trees were broken (by the wind).
> A birdhouse was built (by George).

When the active voice verb is in analytical form, the corresponding passive form will contain the same forms of the auxiliaries; the linking verb auxiliary will be added to them.

> The accusation *had* hurt the boy.
> The boy *had been* hurt by the accusation.
> That toss *should have* broken the record.
> The record *should have been* broken by that toss.

There is one situation in which the subject and object of the transitive verb represent the same individual or concept, and hence might be confused with the identifying subjective complement. All such objects are pronouns compounded of some other word plus -*self*, -*selves*, or -*other*. (He cursed him*self*. They helped them*selves*. They liked each *other*. They despised one an*other*.) Such objects do not serve as subjects of the passive voice, nor do we normally find an object which expresses or names a condition or a quantity used as a subject for the passive construction. (I have an *earache*. The hat cost *ten dollars*.)

The quality of transitivity is not something inherent in a particular verb; rather it is a manner of using that verb. Nor is the passive voice structure one forming a contrastive pair with the active voice structure; instead it should be described as being a series of analytical tense forms which we may use as alternatives to *some* active voice transitive verbs.

We have a fourth type of sentence which has the pattern *Noun* + *Verb* + *Noun*. This sentence utilizes its verb intransitively. One characteristic of it is that the postverbal noun may be omitted from verbs (except *to be*) without destroying the completion of its predication. The postverbal noun in such sentences is frequently a noun indicating a location in time or space. In certain instances English idiom demands that these nouns be preceded by a preposition; in others the use of a preposition is optional; and in a very few, the noun almost invariably appears without the preposition. Some examples of such structures are:

Preposition Demanded	Preposition Optional	Preposition Never Used
They go *to school*.	She works *Mondays*.	She went *home*.
She arrived *in Chicago*.	She works *on Mondays*.	
	He is *home*.	
	He is *at home*.	

Closely related to these and sometimes confused with them are structures in which the verb may be used either transitively or intransitively, the postverbal noun tends to be locative, and the use of the preposition before the noun is optional. When the preposition is present, the prepositional phrase is normally construed as being adverbial; when the preposition is not present, the noun is generally considered an object, and it may serve as the subject of a passive voice construction. Such postverbal nouns are sometimes called *adverbial objects*. These constructions are illustrated by the following sentences:

We climbed the mountain. (The mountain was climbed by us.)
We climbed on the mountain.

The boys ran one race. (One race was run by the boys.)
The boys ran in one race.

The identification of such structures is further complicated by the possible appearance of transitive verb-adverb combinations. As has been previously noted, the distinction between this structure and the prepositional phrase can be distinguished by the stress patterning of speech.

The boys climbed ĭn the spring. (Prepositional phrase)
The boys climbed ín the spring. (Verb-adverb combination)

We also have situations in which both appear.

(The boys climbed ín the spring in the spring.)

Certain English verbs—generally those expressing a concept such as offering, giving, or acquiring—will take two objects. In such sentences there are alternative positions for the two objects, and they may both appear as simple nouns or substitutes for nouns, or one of them may appear as the object in a prepositional phrase. When the latter is used without its preposition, it will appear between the verb and the other object (He told me to give *her* the book), unless the other object appears initially in the structure, as it may in transposed word order ("He told me *what* to give her" or "what to give *to her*"). In this position, either may appear. In the third example, we must use the prepositional phrase. If it is used in prepositional phrase form, the other object will appear between it and the verb (He told me to give the book *to her*).

When we have two objects, the object that may take the phrasal form will represent the receiver of the other object, and the other object will represent someone or something that receives the action of the verb. Also, the object which takes the phrasal form may normally be omitted without destroying the essential predication of the sentence. In a very few situations, either object—but not both —may be omitted without destroying essential predication.

I bought myself a hat.	⎫
I bought a hat for myself.	⎬ (I bought a hat.)
	⎭
She gave the boy a quarter.	(She gave a quarter.)
He taught the children Spanish.	(He taught Spanish.)
He taught Spanish to the children.	(He taught children.)

Sometimes, although we have two nouns or noun substitutes following a transitive verb, only one of them will be the object. In such situations, we might find the following types of variation: (1) The noun nearest the verb may serve as the modifier of the other noun, and the modified or compounded noun serves as the object. (We saw the *dog biscuit.*) (2) The two nouns may be in apposition. (She liked my *friend John.*) (3) In a few situations, the noun modifying the object noun may appear after it. (They drained *Lake Erie.*) (4) The noun following the object noun may be an objective complement. (We elected *Roosevelt President.*)

In each of these situations, we can recognize the object by our ability to use it as the subject of a passive construction. When the object is either modified or in apposition, the modifier or the appositive (as a part of the unit object or subject) will move with it. (The *dog biscuit* was seen. My *friend John* was liked. *Lake Erie* was drained.) When the word following the object is an objective complement, it does not move with the other noun, nor can it appear alone as the passive voice subject. (Roosevelt was elected *President*.)

At the beginning of this section we considered three types of subjective complements: the predicate adjective, the predicate noun classifier, and the predicate noun identifier. In addition to these, with certain sentences (particularly those having *to be* as the verb) we often find nouns or prepositional phrases serving adverbially to locate the subject or even describe it. (He is *home*. She is *at church*. He is *in good health*.) The noun object takes complements paralleling each of these.

Adjective:	The soup made the boy *sick*.
Noun Classifier:	She thought the man *a fool*.
Noun Identifier:	We made John *the captain*.
Adverb:	We dug the well *deep*.

The objective complement, whatever its form, never appears in subject position. When the active voice object becomes the subject in the passive voice structure, the objective complement will be retained in its position following the verb.

The boy was made *sick*.
The man was thought *a fool*.
John was made *the captain*.
The well was dug *deep*.

Although it is possible to have an objective complement in a construction with two objects (She told him her story *straight*), we normally avoid such constructions by placing the modifier of the object either in attributive position or in the prepositional phrase position.

She gave the baby *warm* milk.
Give me a Congress *of Democrats*.

Related to the passive voice structure is one that is known as the *notional passive*. In this structure the noun standing in subject position receives the action expressed by the verb, but the real actor is not named and the verb itself is *not* in the passive voice. Nor does the verb take an object.

> The depression began in 1932.
> The fire started in the basement.
> This car steers effortlessly.
> His book sold well.

Another fairly common structure presents a peculiar mixture of active and passive elements. It is characterized by the following conditions: (1) The subject need not appear at all in either the active or passive voice constructions, though it may appear in either in the form of a prepositional object. (2) The verb *have* is most commonly found as the main verb, and is used to express the general concept of causation. (3) The passive participle is retained. (4) As in the passive structure, the subject of the active structure may appear in the form of a passive agent. Compare the following example of this structure with its corresponding active and passive voice structures.

> He had the shoes mended (for him) (by the shoemaker).
> *Active:* The shoemaker mended the shoes (for him).
> *Passive:* The shoes were mended (for him) (by the shoemaker).

The words *there* and, less frequently, *here* may be used as sentence starters; when they are so used, the position of the subject and the verb may be inverted when the subject is a noun, but not when it is a pronoun. (There *comes John.* There *John goes.* Here *he comes.*) Some few words, generally those expressing concepts of infrequency or of indefinite number, require inversion when used at the beginning of a sentence. (*Never* have I heard of that. *Rarely* can he be seen. *Scarcely* had they arrived. *Few* were the opportunities. *Many* are the hearts.) Occasionally (particularly in older verse) we find descriptive adjectives used as sentence starters. Inversion is so common that it is practically mandatory in such structures. (*Happy* is he who loves his work. *Lucky* that man is whose vocation is his avocation.)

There are a few structures in which a complement appears before the subject. If the order is *Complement + Subject + Verb,* we call this *transposed* word order. If the verb appears between the complement and the subject, we use the term *inverted-transposed* to describe the order.

We find transposed word order commonly used in noun clauses which function as subject of the verb, object of the verb, or object of a preposition. We also occasionally find a subjective complement expressed in this word order. (*What* he will do now is uncertain. I don't know *whom* you mean. Most of *what* he makes is useless. *Who* they really are is still unknown. He is what *he wants to be*.)

Some Structures with It as Subject

Like any of the other personal pronouns, *it* may appear with a definite referent. (When the *cigarette* rolled off the ashtray, *it* burned a hole in the rug.) In certain constructions, however, this pronoun is used without any definite referent. (*It* is raining. *It* is snowing. *It* was dark last night.) A third usage for this pronoun is that of serving as a mere sentence starter. In this structure the sentence actually has two subjects: (1) the *it* and (2) the noun clause, infinitive, or gerund (these latter two with or without complements) that the pronoun anticipates, and to which it refers. These sentences may be recast by eliminating the *it* and placing the clause, infinitive, or gerund in the normal subject position before the verb. Some examples of this structure are provided below.

It is certain *that he will come.*
That he will come is certain.
It is well *to remember this.*
To remember this is well.
It was fun *to work there.*
To work there was fun.
It was tiresome *working there.*
Working there was tiresome.

At times this structure may be confused with one in which the *it* is followed by a predicate noun modified by an adjective clause. Such sentences may be recast, but when they are, the predicate noun becomes the subject of the new sentence.

It was *John who broke the vase.*
John broke the vase.

Somewhat similar to these sentences are those in which pronouns other than *it* may be used as subjects, and in which what superficially appears to be a predicate adjective modifying the subject is actually a modifier of the infinitive that follows it. In such sentences the subject of the original form will become the object of the infinitive subject in the recast or transformed form. (*They* were *pleasant to know. To know them* was *pleasant.*) When such an adjective is actually the modifier of the subject in the original form of the sentence, the sentence cannot undergo such a transformation. (They were happy to go.)

Exercise 14-1   Basic Statement Patterns

1. What two types of relationship can be expressed by using a linking verb to join two nouns? What is expressed by the subjective complement in each of the following sentences?

    a. John is a secretary.
    b. John is my secretary.

2. Can the subjective complement in either of the sentences for question 1 appear as the subject? Must we use the noun determiner with it? Why? May plural nouns be used in this manner? If so, what must we use with them? Is the subject being classified or identified in each of the sentences provided below?

    a. Roses are flowers.
    b. The flowers are roses.
    c. Those girls are the Rockettes.

3. What name do we give to a construction in which the predicate noun names a class or unit with which it is literally impossible to associate the subject noun?

4. Do linking verbs ever carry a lexical meaning in addition to performing their function of linking? Can *to be* be used as a nonlinking verb? Provide examples. Does *to be* perform a linking function when it is used in an imperative, such as "Be a man"? In one such as "Be there at noon"?

5. When an adjective is joined to a noun by a linking verb, what is its relationship to the noun? Is there any test by which we can distinguish the participial adjective from the participle as

a verb form? Do we have an adjective or a verb in each of the following sentences?

    a. John is tired.
    b. John is thinking.
    c. John is tiring.
    d. The child was born.

6. Can any adjective be connected to any noun? What problem do you find with such statements as "The man is national" or "The sewer is tall"? Why do we not have a similar problem with "The boy is three"? Does *three* modify *boy* in this sentence?

7. What occurs to the adjective in each of the pairs of sentences which are provided below? Is this related to the problem raised in question 3?

    a. The music was loud.   b. The color was bright.
       The necktie was loud.   The child was bright.
    c. The pencil was pointed.   d. The work was hard.
       The remark was pointed.   The ice cream was hard.
    e. The knife was sharp.   f. The sweater was yellow.
       His eyes were sharp.   The fighter was yellow.

8. Make a list of ten qualifying adjectives that can be used to describe people. Make a similar list of adjectives that can be used to describe concrete objects, and another that can be used to describe abstract concepts. Study any words that may appear in two or more of these lists. Do they have the same meaning when they are used to modify different types of concepts? Are the meanings of these words more general or more specific than the meanings of words which can be used to modify only a single type of concept? Can you determine which of the meanings are literal and which are figurative? Are all adjectives used freely in both the attributive (before the noun) and the predicative positions? Do any change form when placed in a different position?

9. As we have already observed, the basic patterns for linking verb statements are:

    (1) *Noun†Subject + Linking Verb + Noun Classifier*
    (2) *Noun Subject + Linking Verb + Noun Identifier*
    (3) *Noun Subject + Linking Verb + Adjective describing the Subject*

† A substitute for a noun may appear in any position in these formulas in which the word *noun* appears.

Write a series of generalizations describing the use of noun determiners with these patterns. In doing this, consider all the forms of nouns (singular, plural, genitive) and all the types of nouns (common, proper, generic, and so forth).

10. List as many verbs as you can that may be used in the patterns noted in question 9. Do you find any that can be used with only one of these patterns? Are there any which may be used with two of the patterns, but not with the third? To which of these verbs is it quite customary to add the infinitive *to be?* What occurs when we use *to be* with other verbs? Consider the following examples:

   a. She seems to be happy.
   b. He continues to be a widower.
   c. That remains to be seen.
   d. He hopes to be the candidate.
   e. She has to be careful.
   f. He ought to be a doctor.
   g. She wants to be a teacher.
   h. He appears to be a friend.

11. Does the situation mentioned in question 10 exist with linking verbs other than *to be?* Do you find a similar situation in any of the following sentences?

   a. He likes to appear the doting father.
   b. She expects to become a mother.
   c. She hopes to remain his secretary.
   d. The soup began to smell good.
   e. She continues to look a fright.

12. What conclusions do you draw? Can the concept of linkage be expressed in a sentence in which the verb is transitive? Do the sentences in questions 10 and 11 fit the patterns provided in question 9?

Exercise 14-2

1. Consider the two groups of verbs below. Which group appears to indicate the manner of motion and which the direction of motion? Can the verbs in either or both groups be used intransitively? Can they be used transitively? All of them?

A. come   B. walk
    go   run
    arrive   dance
    depart   crawl
    rise   swim
    sit   drive
    lie   fly
    fall   shake

2. What difference can you note between the verbs presented in the following groups? Can all of the verbs in either or both groups be used intransitively? Can all of the verbs in either group be used as transitive verbs? Do the verbs in either group seem to *imply* objects? Can you add other pairs to these short groups?

A. look   B. see
    listen   hear
    talk   speak

3. When some word or words are added to the *Subject + Verb* pattern of the intransitive nonlinking verb statement, what function does the word or unit serve? Does it ever modify the subject? Does it ever take the form of a singular noun? Of a plural noun? When it consists of a group of words, what form or forms can they take?

4. The basic patterns for nonlinking intransitive verb statements are:

(1) *Noun† Subject + Verb*
(2) *Noun Subject + Verb + Modifier of Verb*
(3) *Noun Subject + Modifier of Verb + Verb*
(4) *Modifier of Verb + Verb + Noun Subject*
(5) *Modifier of Verb + Noun Subject + Verb*

† A noun substitute may be used in place of a noun in any of these formulas.

Provide examples of each of the above patterns. What type of words can appear as the modifier in pattern 4? Can a prepositional phrase be used in this pattern? Are the verbs which can be used in this pattern taken from any of the groups provided in questions 1 and 2? Could any verb from either group be used? Could all verbs from any group be used? Are there other verbs not in these groups which may be normally used in pattern 4?

5. Do pronouns appear to be used more commonly than nouns in any of these patterns? Does there appear to be any basis for

choosing pattern 4 or pattern 5 when we have a noun or a pronoun subject?

6. Are infinitives ever used as modifiers in any of these patterns? Can these infinitives themselves be modified? Can they take objects? Are they sometimes followed by adjectives? Provide examples.

Exercise 14-3   Basic Patterns

1. Consider the six short groups of verbs below. Which of these verbs will take only one object and which will take more than one? Do any take more than two objects? Are the verbs which can take more than one object ever used with just a single object? Can any of these verbs be used intransitively? Is there any perceivable difference in the type of objects that may be taken by verbs in group *B* and those in group *C*? What relationship exists between the verbs in group *D* and their objects? Can the two verbs in group *E* be used in exactly the same ways? If two nouns (or a noun substitute and a noun) are used after the verbs in group *F*, what relationship exists between them? Can a modifier be substituted for the second of these nouns? What other verbs among the lists could be used in this pattern structure? Try adding verbs to each of the groups. To which groups is it most difficult to add more verbs?

A. hurt	*B.* offer	*C.* teach
break	give	show
D. build	*E.* marry	*F.* elect
dig	introduce	call

2. The basic patterns for transitive verb active voice statements are:

(1) *Noun† Subject + Verb + Noun Object*
(2) *Noun Subject + Verb + Noun Object + Noun Object*
(3) *Noun Subject + Verb + Noun Object + Prepositional Phrase Object*
(4) *Noun Subject + Verb + Noun Object + Noun Objective Complement*
(5) *Noun Subject + Verb + Noun Object + Modifier Objective Complement*

† A noun substitute may be used in place of a noun in any of these formulas.

Provide at least one example for each of the patterns noted above. At what point or points could modifiers of the verb appear in each of these structures?

3. Identify the pattern used in each of the following sentences. To which group does the verb of each sentence belong?

a. Mary has a book.
b. John hurt himself.
c. Lois sang a song.
d. Helen knitted a sweater.
e. The class brought the teacher a gift.
f. We showed the book to George.
g. The movers raised the house high above its foundations.
h. Frantically, we dug the well deeper.
i. They made George the scapegoat.
j. The medicine made him sick.
k. I introduced John to Mary.

4. Do we have one object or two in the sentences provided below? How does this structure differ from the ordinary object structure? Do we need a separate pattern for such sentences? Can these object words serve as subjects of verbs in the active voice? Can these sentences be put into the passive voice?

a. They hurt one another.
b. They dislike each other.

5. Can we use a noun instead of a noun substitute as object in the sentences given below? What patterns are represented by these sentences? Do we normally use the passive form of these constructions?

a. I blame myself.
b. The girl drove herself crazy.
c. The man bought himself a sun helmet.
d. I am going to get me a three point average this term.

6. Can we use a pronoun instead of a noun as the object in either of the sentences provided below? If so, what quality is lost by using it? What pattern is represented in each of these sentences? Is the identification of the object type a part of the pattern?

a. The class sang a song.
b. The boys ran the race.

7. Is the relationship between the verb and the object in each

of the sentences below a result of the sentence pattern? If not,
how do we identify this relationship?

   a. The boys built the fire.
   b. The man grew a beard.

   8. Do we have objects in each of the following sentences? How
do we determine whether we do or not?

   a. He works Mondays.
   b. He hates Mondays.
   c. He works everyone Mondays.
   d. He works everyone hard.
   e. He hates everyone Mondays.

   9. Summarize, as well as you can, the types of information
which are normally provided by (1) sentence patterning, (2)
lexical meaning, and (3) context.

   10. Do we normally put sentences of the type provided below
into the passive voice? Is this true of all verbs which indicate
possession, or is it a peculiarity of the verb *have?* Are there any
other verbs—some expressing concepts other than possession—
which are used transitively in the active voice, but which are not
used at all in the passive? Is such usage ever related to the type
of object which appears with them? Are the two sentences provided below identical in pattern? Do we have a form comparable
to "My head aches" which we could use as a substitute pattern for
the second? Of what is the object word of the first sentence compounded? Does this suggest anything? Write some sentences containing objects which are constructed by compounding other parts
of speech. Are there other ways of expressing the ideas of these
sentences?

   a. I have a headache.
   b. I have a pencil.

        Exercise 14-4   Basic Patterns

   1. A rule which is often repeated in elementary grammars states
that the passive voice is formed by using some form of the verb
to be with the past participle of another verb. What do the following examples suggest about the validity or completeness of

this rule? Do all of these sentences contain passive voice verbs? Must the agent of the passive voice be expressed? Must it be introduced by *by*? Can any linking verb be used with a past participle to form a passive? Construct sentences using linking verbs other than *to be* to form the passive voice. How many different verbs can you use?

a. The village remained stunned by the accident.
b. His mother became worried by his absence.
c. The mayor appeared horrified by the situation.
d. The sick girl seemed relieved by the medicine.
e. The boy got bit by the snake.
f. The prizes were awarded through the school.
g. The child was crushed in the crowd.
h. The girl grew frightened when the lion roared.

2. The basic patterns for passive voice statements are provided below. Wherever the word *noun* appears, we could use a pronoun or some other form of noun substitute.

(1) *Noun Subject + Linking Verb + Past Participle ± (Preposition + Noun Agent†)*
(2) *Noun Subject + Linking Verb + Past Participle + Retained Noun Object ± (Preposition + Noun Agent†)*
(3) *Noun Subject + Linking Verb + Past Participle + Preposition + Retained Noun Object ± (Preposition + Noun Agent†)*
(4) *Noun Subject + Linking Verb + Past Participle + Retained Objective Complement‡ ± (Preposition + Noun Agent†)*

† Note that the agent phrase does not have to be present in the passive patterns.
‡ Note that the objective complement may be either a noun or a modifier.

Provide sentences illustrating each of the above patterns. At what point or points could modifiers of the verb appear in each of these structures?

3. To which of the patterns listed in question 2 does each of the following sentences belong?

a. John was designated captain by the coach.
b. The group were bored by the proceedings.
c. The rain is retained in the measuring cup.
d. The class was made happy.
e. The house was painted quickly.
f. The hole was quickly enlarged by the borer.
g. The girl was made sick by the sight.

h. During the summer, ice is made artificially.
i. Mr. Truman was declared President.
j. The child was disturbed by the change in diet.

4. What relationship exists between the verb and the subject when the verb is in the passive voice? Does the same relationship exist when the subject represents an object as when it represents a person? What relationship exists between the verb and the subject in the sentences provided below? Who or what is the actor in each of these sentences? What is the form of the verb? Is this a passive voice pattern? Is it in any way related to the passive?

a. The game began at 2:00 P.M.
b. The play will open on the 16th.
c. The car parks easily.
d. The war started in 1912.

5. What differences, if any, do you perceive in the modifying relationship expressed in the sentences below? Can either or both of the modifiers be moved to another position in the sentence?

a. The well was dug deep.
b. The well was dug quickly.

6. What difference exists in the functions of the nouns that follow the verbs in the sentences provided below? Can any of them be used as the subject of a different passive voice sentence expressing the same idea? Can all of them?

a. The girl was taught Chinese.
b. The girl was chosen treasurer.
c. The girl was frightened yesterday.

7. Is the meaning of the verb identical in the two sentences given below? Can both of these sentences be put into the active voice? Do we have other concepts which we express only with the passive voice structure? Provide examples. What is the complete verb in each of these sentences?

a. The secretary was engaged by the manager.
b. The secretary was engaged to the manager.

8. Is the verb *laugh* normally used transitively or intransitively? In the sentence "I was laughed at," do we use an active or a passive voice pattern? What is the complete verb in this sentence? Is this in any way related to either of the sentences in question 7?

Suggested Readings

SECTION 14

Francis, W. Nelson, *The Structure of American English,* Chap. VII. New York: The Ronald Press Company, 1954.

Fries, Charles C., *The Structure of English,* Chap. VIII. New York: Harcourt, Brace & World, Inc., 1952.

Roberts, Paul, *Understanding English,* Chap. XII. New York: Harper & Row, Publishers, 1958.

Whitehall, Harold, *Structural Essentials of English,* Chap. III. New York: Harcourt, Brace & World, Inc., 1951.

Basic Sentence Patterns
—Questions

As soon as we begin to look at the interrogative forms in English we discover that they are of different types. One method of classifying questions is based upon the type of response the questions elicit. When we ask a child "Is your mother home?" we expect a reply in terms of "Yes" or "No," but we will think he is not very bright if he provides such a response for the question "What's your name?" Questions that demand a "Yes" or "No" response begin with a verb. If the verb is *be* or *have*, it may stand alone as the only verb in the question. If the verb is an auxiliary (including *be* and *have*), one or more other verb forms will appear after the subject. If more than one auxiliary is used, the subject will appear between the first and second auxiliary. Therefore our patterns for such questions are:

(1) *Verb + Subject + Complement or Complements*
(2) *Auxiliary + Subject + Verb ± Complement or Complements*
(3) *Auxiliary + Subject + Other Auxiliary or Auxiliaries + Verb ± Complement or Complements*

Some examples of these patterns would be:

Is John home?
Have you a book?

Is John going?
Has George bought a car?
Did Mary understand you?
Could George do the job properly?
Has Mary been taking lessons?
Could George have been graduated so soon?
Could Mary have been gone?

Complements for such questions will be identical in type, form, and position with those used in the statement. If you are in doubt about these complements, review Section 14.

Many questions of this type are designed to elicit an action response in lieu of, or in addition to, the affirmative response. The action response, of course, would not normally accompany the negative verbal response. Such questions are requests or polite imperatives.

Shall we go now?
Will you open the window?
Would you drive, John?

Questions requiring a verbal response other than "Yes" or "No" begin with interrogative function words.

Who is he?
Who(*m*) did you invite?
What did they say?
Which boy threw that?
Where did you go?
When did her friend appear?
How do you know?
How much did it cost?
How many people were there?

As a cursory examination will show, these are also of two types: (1) those that make use of a single verb word, and (2) those that require an auxiliary as well as the main verb. In our examination of questions beginning with either the full verb or the auxiliary form, we found that only *be* and *have* are normally used without the auxiliary, in which case the verb form occupies the initial position in the sentence, preceding the subject. (*Was* she beautiful? *Has* she a boy friend?) Although *have* may be used in this manner, it is quite as likely to be used in a construction with an auxiliary. (*Does* she *have* a boy friend?)

When we investigate questions starting with interrogative function words, we find that a wide range of verbs may be used without auxiliaries in these structures.

Who *made* the pies?
What *caused* the flood?
Which (the cat or the dog) *ate* the salmon?
Whose *finished* first?
Which boy *did* that?
How many contestants *started?*
Whose dog *barks* so loudly?
How much sugar *spoiled?*

We should note that the question-asking word in each of these
sentences is either a pronoun serving as the subject of the verb
or a modifier of a noun subject. Interrogatives which cannot serve
one of these two functions cannot be used in such constructions.

We have another group of questions which superficially appear
to be identical with these, but a more careful inspection will show
that their structure is different. When we use questions such as
"Who is he," "Who am I," "Who are they," "Which is it," "Which
are they?" we find that the form of the verb agrees in number
with the word which follows it rather than with the word which
precedes it. We can say, therefore, that the word following the
verb in such sentences is the subject, and that the word preceding
the verb (since the verb is a link and the word preceding it is
a noun substitute) is a predicate nominative. Our pattern for such
sentences would be *Subjective Complement + Link + Subject.* In
statements, this type of structure is occasionally found in sentences
which begin with the predicate adjective type of complement,
particularly when the noun subject is followed by an adjective
clause. (*Many* are the hearts that are weary tonight.)

But by far the greatest number of questions initiated with interrogative function words make use of auxiliaries in their structure.
In such questions the subject appears immediately after the first
auxiliary; the interrogative functions as a complement of the verb,
as a modifier of a complement of a verb, or as the object of a
preposition. In the latter instance, the prepositional phrase functions as a complement of the verb.

Who(*m*) did you see?
What did he do?

When can you go?
How will she know?
Where was it placed?
Why should he work there?
Which book may I have?
How much sugar will you need?
How many children do you expect?
How could he have known that?
Where can she have gone?
When was he to have been ready?
To *whom* am I indebted?
For *what* was he indicted?
At *which* place were you to meet him?

In making analyses it is easy to confuse sentences of the type illustrated above with those of another structure which contains two verb words, neither of which functions as an auxiliary. In such sentences the first verb word to appear is the main verb; the second will be nonfinite in form and will function as a part of the complement of the main verb. The subject of the sentence will appear before the main verb if that verb is in finite form, or before the first auxiliary if the main verb is not in finite form.

What makes him do that?
Who caught him stealing?
Who wants her to go?
How many of you want them punished?
Who will want him to work for them?
What could have caused him to cheat on the examination?

In such sentences the entire structure following the main verb must be considered as a syntactical unit functioning as a complement of the verb. The noun or pronoun following the main verb tends to name the doer of the action expressed by the verb which follows it when that verb is in common or infinitive form or in the *-ing* form. When the final verb is in the form of a past participle, the noun or pronoun preceding it tends to express the receiver of the action expressed by the participle. The passive nature of this participle is easily noted; it is generally possible to insert *to be* before it without in any way changing the meaning of the sentence. (How many of you want them punished? How many of you want them *to be* punished?) The function of the participle is that of the adjectival objective complement. This may be seen more clearly by comparing two sentences utilizing the participle and the pure adjective forms respectively.

Did the exercise keep him *fatigued?*
Did the exercise keep him *healthy?*

At first glance, the formation of questions in English appears to consist of a very complex series of structures, but, as we have seen, these can be reduced to a few simple basic patterns. To convince yourself of the truth of this statement, develop each of these basic patterns before beginning the following exercises. Because every statement can be made into a question, a simple means of developing these question patterns is to work from the basic patterns you already have for statements.

Exercise 15-1   Basic Question Patterns

1. Is the verb linking, intransitive nonlinking, transitive active, or transitive passive in the sentences below? What is the subject of each sentence? What is its position in the sentence? Does this differ from its position in statements when similar verbs are used? Can all linking verbs be used in this position?

    a. Was Helen the secretary?
       Was the secretary Helen?

    b. Is John a student?
       Are the students honest?

2. Is the verb *to be* used in the same manner in the following sentences as it was in the sentences for question 1? If not, what is the difference in the usages?

    a. Was he home?
    b. Were you there?

3. How is the verb used in the sentences provided below? Can other verbs which take objects be used in this pattern?

    a. Has he a book?
    b. Have you a car?

4. What pattern has Browning used in the quoted lines on page 209? Is this a normal pattern for English? If not, in what way does it differ from the normal?

Irks care the crop-full bird?
Frets doubt the maw-crammed beast?

5. Using the examples from Section 14 as models, construct the formulas for the patterns illustrated above in questions 15-1 through 15-3. Do we use any of these patterns when we have two objects? Do we use any of them with objective complements? Is the position of the modifier of the verb variable in any of these patterns?

6. In what manner is the verb used in each of the sentences below? What is the position of the subject in each sentence? What type of complement, if any, is found in each? What form of the main verb is used in the first three sentences? What forms of the main verb appear in the other sentences? To what type of pattern noted in Section 14 are the last three sentences related?

    a. Can you be the chairman?
    b. Will she become a bore?
    c. Should it be sweet?
    d. Is she going?
    e. Has he gone?
    f. Shall I sing?
    g. Ought we to go?
    h. Is the game beginning?
    i. Has the play begun?
    j. Did the motor start?

7. How are the verbs used in the examples which follow? Is transitivity related to the main verb or to the auxiliary? Compare the types and positions of complements in these sentences with those in the examples of transitive verb statements in Section 14. What do you find? Compare the positions of modifiers. What does the word *honestly* modify in sentence *i*? At what point do the patterns for these sentences differ from the patterns for statements? When more than two verb words are used to form an analytical tense, what is the normal position for the subject? What forms of the verb appear in these sentences? Compare these with the forms found in statements.

    a. Is she taking the medicine?
    b. Have you studied the text?
    c. Do you know her?
    d. Could you show him the difference?
    e. Did he give her the candy?
    f. Will that make John a martyr?
    g. Could this keep you honest?

   h. Did they treat you well?
   i. Honestly, do they really treat you well there now?
   j. Will that be to eat?
   k. Would he have studied?
   l. Do you have to go?
   m. Would he have been gone by then?
   n. Should I have been looking for you?

8. Construct the formulas for any new patterns illustrated above.

'   *Exercise* 15-2   Basic Question Patterns

1. Which word is the subject in each of the following sentences? Do we have one pattern or more than one pattern represented here?

   a. Who am I?
   b. Who is she?
   c. Who are you?
   d. What are they?
   e. Who is beautiful?
   f. Which girl is happy?
   g. How many boys are brave?
   h. How many boys áre there?
   i. How many boys are thére?
   j. How hungry are you?
   k. Where are the boys?
   l. What is that for?
   m. How tired are you?
   n. Why are the pickles sour?

2. Construct pattern formulas similar to those provided in Section 14 to summarize the varied patterns represented by the sentences in question 1. Does the question function word have any additional function in these sentences? If so, what is its syntactic function in each of them? Can all of the following sentences be fitted to one of the formulas you constructed for the sentences in question 1? If not, construct additional formulas for these sentences.

   a. What time is it?
   b. How many boys went home?
   c. Which is the Sophomore?
   d. Whose cat is a Siamese?

e. Who is ambitious?
f. Which flowers smell sweet?
g. How many officers were colored?
h. What have you there?

3. With what type of pattern do you have most difficulty in determining the subject? What is characteristic of this pattern in statement form? Does the form of the verb provide any clue as to which word should be the subject?

4. What is the subject of each of the sentences which are provided below? In what manner is the verb used? What type of complement, if any, is found in each of them? Do the relative positions of the subject and the verb appear to be related to the manner in which the verb is used (linking, intransitive, transitive)?

a. Who are you?
b. Who came?
c. What is it?
d. What happened?
e. Which candy tastes good?
f. Which boy left?
g. How many boys are intelligent?
h. How many boys remained?
i. Who hit me?
j. What hit me?
k. Which fool did that?
l. How many boys made the team?
m. What have we here?
n. How many classes have you?

5. In what way do the sentences below differ from those we have considered earlier in this exercise? Is there a difference in meaning expressed by the first and second sentences? What is the syntactic function of *leader* in each of these sentences? What causes us to hesitate between the choice of *who* or *whom* in some of these sentences? What is the voice of the verb in the last two sentences? Would you use *whom* in the first of these two? Why or why not?

a. Who can be the leader?
b. Who can the leader be?
c. Whose dog will be the winner?
d. What butterfly will that worm become?
e. When is he arriving?
f. Where have you been?

   g. Why did he leave?
   h. How does it smell?
   i. What does he need?
   j. Who(m) did you ask?
   k. Which would she like?
   l. What was John given?
   m. Who(m) are we entertaining?
   n. What have you given her?
   o. Who(m) did she give it to?
   p. To whom did she give it?
   q. When can he finish the job?
   r. Why do you distrust him?
   s. Who was taught French?
   t. What was given to Mary?

6. Is *make* used as an auxiliary or as a full verb in the following sentences? If we were to use a case-determining pronoun in the fourth sentence, what case would it represent? Is *does* a full verb in the third sentence? What occurs if you substitute the verb *cause* for the verb *make* in these sentences?

   a. What makes it smell?
   b. What makes him smell?
   c. What does he smell?
   d. What makes it beautiful?

7. What is the subject of the sentence "Why have them play?" What function does *them* serve? Is this sentence in any way related to such sentences as "What keeps her going?" or "What makes you tired?" To what structure of complementation are these questions related? What kind of complements do we have in these sentences?

8. Construct pattern formulas to summarize any new patterns for questions that you have learned. In what situations does the subject appear before the verb in questions? In what situations does it appear after a single-word verb? In what situations does it appear after the first auxiliary? When do we find objects appearing before the verb? In what situations do we have other types of complements before the verb?

9. Can we use all the varied types of complements with questions that we use with statements? Are their respective positions in the question different from the positions they would occupy in the statement? Is this true of all question patterns, or only of some?

Suggested Readings

SECTION 15

Brown, Dona Worrall, Wallace C. Brown, and Dudley Bailey, *Form in Modern English*, pp. 121-26. New York: Oxford University Press, Inc., 1958.

Jespersen, Otto, *The Philosophy of Grammar*, pp. 302-5. London: George Allen & Unwin, Ltd., 1924.

Roberts, Paul, *English Sentences*, pp. 223-25. New York: Harcourt, Brace & World, Inc., 1962.

SECTION 16

Basic Sentence Patterns
—Imperatives

We must consider two aspects of the imperative: (1) the formal structures of the command, and (2) the possibilities of expressing the ideational concept of command or request with structures other than that of the formal imperative. The command form of the imperative makes use of only one form of the verb—the common or naming form (*be, have, run, stop*); this form may be used either in the affirmative or the negative. The negative imperative makes use of the function verb *do* and the negative particle *not* or the contraction for these two (*don't*).

The imperative is found only in the second person, and hence there is no need to express the subject, which would invariably be *you*. The verb form may be preceded by a noun of address indicating the referent for the *you*, whether or not the pronoun itself appears. (*Mary*, go to the door.) The verb may also be preceded by the function word *please*. If both *please* and the noun of address are used, the noun of address will normally appear in the initial position. The noun of address is always set off by a juncture pattern in speech and by a comma in writing. Because the imperative has but one form, any indication of present or future time must be expressed by a temporal adverb. (Do it *now*. Do it *tomorrow*.) The nature of the imperative idea excludes the past.

214

The imperative verb may be followed by other nonfinite verb forms. When the imperative verb is *be*, the verbs seem to become a part of the verb phrase; with other verbs, they seem rather to be complements of the verb. (*Be gone. Be working* when he comes. *Begin writing* now. *Go to see* him. *Stop teasing* her.) Certain verbs, such as *go* or *run*, often appear with another verb in the common form immediately following them. Whether this should be considered as a coordinate structure or as a verb followed by an infinitive complement is a moot question. (*Go stop* the washing machine. Go (and/to) stop the washing machine. *Run get* Susie. Run (and/to) get Susie.) The imperative verb may be followed by any of the postverb complements that are found in statement or question structures.

The imperative idea (telling someone to do something) can be expressed in statement form. Auxiliaries expressing compulsion normally appear in such statements. (*You must* begin right away. You will *have to* start tomorrow.)

Normally, however, we prefer to soften the imperative and make a request rather than a command. The function word *please* is one of our means of softening the imperative, but more commonly we use a question form for this purpose. *Please*, of course, can be made a part of the question. The question would naturally be of the type that would elicit an action response.

We have two ways of developing this softer or more polite request. One is by the simple expedient of making it longer through using more words in the sentence. (Go! Please go. Would you go? Would you please go? Would you mind if I were to ask you to go?) Actually, what we are doing in using such forms is moving from the direct method of making our request to methods which are more and more indirect.

Indirection is also involved in our second method of softening requests. Here we use the first or third person instead of the second. When we use the first person, we make use of the plural pronoun which includes the speaker and the person to whom he is speaking. (Could *we* have the house finished by the first of the month?) When the third person is used, we make use of either the singular form of one of the indefinite pronouns or of the plural form *they*. (Can *someone* type this for me? Could *they* put in new sparkplugs while I wait?)

It is, of course, possible to combine these various forms in differing combinations. (Please, would it be possible for someone to put in new sparkplugs for me while I wait? I would greatly appreciate it if someone could install the new sparkplugs while I wait.)

Exercise 16-1   Imperatives

1. What grammatical person is represented in the following sentences? Can these same ideas be expressed in any other person? Why or why not? What types of verbs are used? Is there any subject present? Could a noun or pronoun be used as subject?

   a. Be a man.
   b. Appear a fool if you must.
   c. Go home.
   d. Open the door.
   e. Make John the chairman.
   f. Cut the neckline lower.

2. What structural difference exists between the sentences for question 1 and those provided below? What is the difference between a request and a command? Which group represents commands? Which of the sentences in either group is likely to elicit a response in terms of action? Which is likely to elicit a verbal response? Would any be likely to elicit both types of response? Are there sentences in either group which might elicit a verbal response when the speaker desired an action response?

   a. Can you be a man?
   b. Must you appear a fool?
   c. Will you go home?
   d. Would you open the door?
   e. Should we make John the chairman?
   f. Could you make John the chairman?
   g. Can you cut the neckline lower?
   h. Can we cut the neckline lower?
   i. Can they cut the neckline lower?

3. Can imperative sentences be put into any of the past tenses? Can the simple imperative be used in a future time situation? If we use the analytical future tense forms for requests, is the resulting structure imperative or interrogative? In the third example sentence of question 2, which would you use to express the imperative rather than the simple question—a rising or a falling ter-

minal? What do we indicate when we use an exclamation mark after a sentence form such as "Will you go home!"?

4. For what do we use the word *please?* Is this usage in any way related to our use of the interrogative in place of the imperative? Can we use *please* with an interrogative? What is the result? Can you think of any situations in which *please* or the interrogative pattern or both might be used as part of a strong imperative? Would the oral pattern differ from the normal oral patterning in such situations? Would the stress pattern differ? What do we mean by *sarcasm?* How do we recognize it? Might this be an example of it?

5. Do we make use of the passive voice in the imperative? Is "Be gone!" a passive imperative? Is "Get lost!"? What do we have in the sentence "Come and be entertained by the children"?

6. What syntactic function is served by the first unit in each of the imperatives provided below?

    a. Company, Halt!
    b. Forward, March!
    c. To the rear, March!

7. Compare and contrast the structures of the examples in question 6 with those of the following sentences.

    a. Children, stop your noise.
    b. Go to the attic.
    c. Drive more slowly.

8. Construct pattern formulas to fit all of the situations illustrated by the sentences below. Can we use the question form with passive imperatives? If so, would the patterns for it differ from the patterns for other interrogatives?

    a. Be a man.
    b. Be the secretary.
    c. Be good.
    d. Go!
    e. Go faster.
    f. Eat your meat.
    g. Give me a drink.
    h. Give the book to Helen.
    i. Teach the class the theorem.
    j. Teach the theorem to the class.
    k. Nominate Jane chairman.
    l. Make the pie sweet.

  m. Do the job quickly.
  n. Be warned by my experience.
  o. Be taught caution by this.
  p. Be thought insane, if you must.
  q. Be treated cruelly, if you enjoy it.

9. Would you say that we make frequent or infrequent use of the passive imperative in English? When we do use it, is it normally accompanied by a clause of condition?

Suggested Readings

SECTION 16

Brown, Dona Worrall, Wallace C. Brown, and Dudley Bailey, *Form in Modern English*, pp. 127-29. New York: Oxford University Press, Inc., 1958.

Jespersen, Otto, *The Philosophy of Grammar*, pp. 313-15. London: George Allen & Unwin, Ltd., 1924.

Basic Sentence Patterns .
—Negatives

In English the concept of negation is expressed in many different ways. With verbs used as auxiliaries or as substitutes for other verbs, and with the finite forms of *be* and *have*, we have the choice of using either the full form of the verb followed by *not* or of using a contraction representing these two forms. When we use the contractions we make a number of phonetic changes in speech, some of which are reflected in orthographic changes.

The most common of the phonetic changes is the addition of the suffix /ənt/, generally spelled *n't*, to the verb or to the auxiliary. This suffix is used with the auxiliaries *could, should, may, might, would, ought, dare, need, have,* with the forms *does* and *did* of the verb *do,* and with the forms *is, are, was, were* of the verb *be.* The suffix *n't* is similarly used with any of these finite forms of *be* and *have* when it appears as the only verb word in the clause. However, when any form of *have* is followed by an infinitive, we seldom find the contracted form. In some dialects the use of the contraction with *ought* is not considered the best usage. *Must* also takes the /ənt/ *n't* suffix, but it differs from the others in speech in that the /t/ is dropped before the suffix is added. An archaic negative form of *dare* /dæsənt/ is found commonly in the speech of children and in some dialects, but it rarely appears in modern writing. Standard English has no contracted form for *am,* but substandard dialects make use of two forms for this, *ain't* /eynt/ and *hain't* /heynt/. These forms are also used as substitutes for the *isn't, aren't* forms of standard English. In like manner, /warǝnt/ is sometimes substituted for the *wasn't, weren't* forms in some dialects.

The forms used with other auxiliaries vary considerably. *Can* simply adds /t/ in speech and *'t* in writing (/kæn/ *can*, /kænt/ *can't*). *Do* changes its sound from /uw/ to /o/, and adds the nasal /n/ and the alveolar /t/; in writing, the vowel letter remains unchanged and the *n't* is added (*do*, /duw/, *don't* /dont/). *Shall* loses its final consonant and adds the /n/ and the /t/ in speech; in writing, it loses its two final consonant letters and adds the *n't* (*shall* /s̆æl/, *shan't* /s̆ænt/). *Will* loses all sounds and letters except the initial *w* /w/ and adds the vowel *o* /o/, the nasal *n* /n/, and the alveolar *t* /t/ (*will* /wil/, *won't* /wont/).

When the full word *not* is used with any of these auxiliaries, they retain their full forms in both speech and writing.

When the contraction is used, it is attached to the first verb form appearing in the clause. If more than one auxiliary is used, the contraction is attached to the first of them. This is also the normal position for the full form *not,* but this form is occasionally shifted to some other position in the verb phrase to provide a different emphasis. (He could *not* have been chosen. He could have been *not* chosen.) When it is used in the nonnormal position in speech, the *not* receives primary stress; in the normal position, *not* normally receives no stress stronger than secondary. The suffix used in the contraction is always unstressed.

In sequential sentences or clauses, *not* is frequently used as a pronoun substituting for a complement or for a clausal referent which appears in the earlier clause or sentence. (He called me a *thief.* I protested that I was *not.* He asked me *if I thought he was a fool.* I said *not. Are you going?* I think *not.*) In older usage the *not* was often used after full verbs to express negation. (Consider the lilies of the field; they toil *not,* neither do they spin. Waste *not,* want *not.*) In modern usage, whenever the affirmation contains no auxiliary, we make use of *do* as a negative auxiliary. (I *do not* doubt it. She *does not* plan to go. We *did not* believe it could happen.) This construction may be used with all verbs except the modal auxiliaries, though its use with *be* is somewhat limited. (If he *does not be* kind to her, she will leave him. She *did not have to go.* She *doesn't dare* tell him. They *don't need* help.)

In addition to the *not* forms, we have a series of adverbs which express different degrees of negation. The adverb *never* is one of the strongest negatives in the language. *Never* refers to all time periods—past, present, and future. Like *not*, the normal position for *never* is after the first auxiliary verb in an analytical tense form; unlike *not*, it appears before the main verb in the simple tense form. It may also be used as an emphatic form before most auxiliaries, but is seldom found in this position when *may, might,* or *must* is used as the auxiliary. (We could *never* believe him. She *never* thought he would go. They *never* will see him again.)

A few other adverbs expressing relative negativity are used in a similar manner. The most common of these are *rarely, scarcely,* and *hardly.* In standard usage none of these words is used in the same structure with *not.* Words of this group may appear as the initial word in a clause. When they do, they are followed by an inversion of the verb and subject if the subject is either a pronoun or a proper noun. (*Never have I* heard him speak so eloquently. *Rarely has John* been known to lie. *Hardly had he* arrived when he had to leave.) When the subject is a common noun or an indefinite pronoun such as *anyone,* the subject and verb remain in normal positions. (*Scarcely a voice was* heard. *Hardly anyone came.*) When *never* is used in such a construction, it conveys the meaning of "Not a single one." (*Never* a man had moved.)

Negating words may serve as modifiers of the noun determiner, in which case they appear before it. (*Not one* boy was lost. *Scarcely any* books were available. *Hardly* a [one] passenger was aware of the danger.) When *no* or *not* modifies a determiner which indicates an indefinite number or amount, the combination expresses a weak affirmation. (*Not many* people understand this. *No few* boys were hurt. *Not much* sugar was left.)

Negatives also appear as modifiers of the noun. (*No boy* was chosen. *Neither girl* won a prize.) It takes little imagination to see that words such as *nobody* and *nothing* have developed from such usage. In like manner, the negative plus the word *one* (no one) is found in our pronoun *none.*

Certain of our conjunctions have negating forms. Some of these appear in correlative pairs to furnish emphatic negatives. (*Neither* John *nor* Mary could go.) Some are used to provide a transition from one negating statement to the next. (They are *not* successful. *Nor* are they ambitious.) Others are used in correlation with affirmative conjunctions to provide contrasts. (He *not only* paints; he *also* does sculpturing.)

Negative Affixes

To indicate negation, English uses numerous prefixes such as *dis, un, in, il, im, ig, ir, non, anti,* and *a.* These prefixes express several nuances of negation. *Non* generally means simply *not* or "the opposite of" (*non*participant, *non*-Christian), but it may also express the idea of *without* or "the absence of" (*non*belief). The most common meaning of the *a* prefix is that of "not concerned with" (*a*moral). This prefix also has an *an* form that is used before vowels (*an*esthetic) and an *ag* form that may appear before *n* (*ag*nostic). *Anti* may express such concepts as *against* (*anti*labor), "the reverse of" (*anti*toxin), or rivalry (the *anti*pope). *In, ig, il, im, ir* are all forms of the *in* prefix, and are used to express such concepts as "the opposite of" (*in*active, *il*legal, *in*significant) or "without" (*in*corporeal). *Un* may express "the lack of" (*un*happiness), "the opposite of" (*un*truth), a "reversal of action" (*un*chain), *not* (*un*-American), a mere intensification (*un*loosen), or "the removal from" (*un*hair). Most of these same concepts may be expressed by *dis* (*dis*advantage, *dis*bar, *dis*entangle, *dis*ease). These different meanings, varied though they may be, tend to shade into one another; it is therefore difficult to assign any one meaning to a prefix until the word on which the prefix is found is put into at least a sentence context, and even then it is often still difficult. Too frequently we tend to think of negation as meaning "the opposite of" when it actually represents some degree of oppositeness along a continuum stretching from absolute affirmation to absolute negation. We must also recognize that the application of a negative to a word does not necessarily produce the antonym. *Stop* and *start* would generally be considered antonyms, but the application of *don't* to either of them would introduce the general idea of *to continue*—that is, "Don't stop!" would be a command to continue whatever it was one was doing, and "Don't start!" would be a command to continue doing nothing.

Negation is used to express degree along the *all-none* continuum. Consider: *Everyone* was there. *No few* were there. *Not many* were there. *Nobody* was there. And, of course, such concepts as "the absence of" are quite different from "the opposite of." An *amoral* person is neither *moral* nor *immoral.*

We also make use of *-less* as a negative suffix. It generally takes the meaning of *without* (home*less*, value*less*, doubt*less*, relent*less*).

In addition to the concepts we have already explored, the negative is sometimes used to express simple contrast (I like meat, *not* vegetables) or the exclusion from a class (That color is *non*white).

The Multiple Negative

The general statement that double or multiple negatives are prohibited in standard English is only partially true. The use of certain types of double or multiple negatives is characteristic of substandard dialects, but other types are commonly found in the language of even the most precise users of English. The types that are generally prohibited in standard English dialects are those that involve the use of two or more negatives beginning with the /n/ sound, the use of a contraction of *not* in the same structural unit with a negative beginning with /n/, and the use of any of the /n/ negatives or of contractions of *not* with decrescent adverbs such as *hardly, scarcely, rarely,* and so forth.

Even such rules need further qualifications, for certain ideas require (or at least permit) the use of more than one /n/ negative. (He did*n't* just do *nothing;* he took some positive action. We ca*n't* possibly consider that of *no* value. He is *not* a man of *no* consequence.) Such negatives may provide a form of litotes expressing a mild affirmation or may be used to express two different negative concepts, such as the negation of action or state and the absence of some quality. It is this type of meaning which is generally expressed when we make use of a *not* negative and a negative prefix, suffix, or preposition in the same structure. (That is *not un*likely. She was*n't il*legitimate. He is *not* a *non*believer. This ca*n't* be use*less.* He is *not without* friends.) There are also certain English verbs such as *deny, doubt, refuse, reject, veto,* and so forth which tend to imply negation. When a negative is used with these, the structure may express something between affirmation and negation. "I do not deny" does not mean that "I admit," for one can say, "I neither deny nor admit my guilt."

One aspect of negation may sometimes be expressed by antonyms.

Each member of such a pair of words theoretically expresses a meaning opposite to that of the other. With many antonyms, however, we find it is difficult to establish a clear dichotomy, for, as has been noted, they represent degrees along a continuum rather than a purely dichotomous situation. Thus *hot* is an antonym of *cold,* but when something is *warm,* we would say that it is *not hot.* *Not hot* therefore expresses one concept from among a series of concepts, most of which are quite different from *cold,* though it is possible that *cold* might be included as one of them. We may even find a middle ground for concepts such as *inside* and *outside,* though at first glance these appear to be completely antonymic. In the story of "Grip, The Rat," which is frequently used in phonetic classes, the shirker Grip was found dead, *half in* and *half out* of his hole. The only antonym we have for many words is a negation. When this is so, we can use another negative form with this negating antonym to express mild affirmation.

When the negative is used in an exclamation which is in the pattern form of a question, it generally expresses a strong but indefinite affirmation. "What dídn't he do!" is the equivalent of "I can't tell you all the things he did," or "He did everything you can name."

The use of negations in questions is normally purely stylistic. The same idea is expressed by "Can you go?" and "Can't you go?"

Exercise 17-1　　　Basic Negative Patterns

1. Using contractions, express the following sentences orally in the negative. What phonetic variations do you find in these contractions? Write each of your negative sentences in phonemic transcription. Recheck your original findings.

    a. I can.
    b. We do.
    c. She shall.
    d. He will.
    e. We could go.
    f. We should take him.
    g. We must go.
    h. We must take him.

2. Recall other verbs normally used as auxiliaries. Are there any

phonetic variations found in the negative contractions with these verbs which are not included in the examples from question 1? In what type of phonetic situation do we simply add a /t/ sound? What situations involve the loss, change, and/or addition of either a vowel or consonant or both? What situations require the addition of a syllable? Does the syllable begin with a vowel sound or a consonant sound? Does the syllable end in the same sound in all situations?

3. With which single-word full verbs do we use either *n't* or *not?* Under what circumstances do we use word groups such as "I can't" or "He would not" as full sentences? Under what circumstances do we use *not* after nonauxiliaries such as *think* (I think *not*)? What syntactic function does *not* have in such sentences? How do we normally form the negative of such verbs as *become, believe, hurt, think, want?* What position does the negating word take in such situations?

4. Make a list of the negative prefixes that we attach to words. To what parts of speech do we attach these prefixes? On what basis do we choose among such prefixes as *ig, il, im, in, ir?* Is anything in addition to simple negation expressed by these prefixes? What differences in meaning are conveyed by the forms *unmoral, immoral,* and *amoral?* Do we make use of any negating suffixes?

5. Which, if any, of the following sentences would you consider to be negations? Which contain negatives?

   a. He found himself at a disadvantage.
   b. He is a non-Christian.
   c. They thought him an antichrist.
   d. We disagreed violently.
   e. She untied the box.

6. Does negation represent the opposite of affirmation? Consider the following pairs of sentences.

   a. Stop!   Go!
   b. Stop!   Don't stop!
   c. The room is cold.   The room is hot.
   d. The room is cold.   The room isn't cold.
   e. He is powerful.   He is powerless.
   f. We have some.   We haven't any.
   g. Somebody came.   Nobody came.
   h. Something happened.   Nothing happened.
   i. We always knew.   We never knew.
   j. Few people came.   No few people came.

7. What is the effect of such combinations as *no few* in the last

sentence of question 6, or *no small* in "That is no small amount"? Is anything similar represented in the sentences below? Do these sentences express a negation or an affirmation?

    a. We not only went; we stayed.
    b. We ate nothing but the cabbage.
    c. We liked all but him.

    8. Is negation or affirmation represented in each of the sentences provided below? Which of these would be considered substandard usage? Would all of them be classed as substandard?

    a. We can't never do nothing.
    b. I can't hardly wait.
    c. That story is not unlikely.
    d. It has never been illegal.
    e. She is not a nobody.
    f. We can't consider that as nothing.
    g. No one never told me.
    h. He is not a never-give-in type.

    9. Which of the substandard forms in the sentences for question 8 have only one negative? Which of the acceptable forms have more than one negative? What do you conclude about plural negation? Can the negative particle *not* or a similar negative word (*never*) be used in a sentence containing an object expressing negation? Can it be used in a sentence in which a negative adjective modifies a predicate noun? Can it be used with modifiers that express the general concept of "less than" or "infrequency" (*hardly, scarcely, rarely*)? Can it be used with a substantive expressing a negative class?

    10. What is the position of the negative contraction in questions that begin with a single verb? What change of position occurs when we use the full word *not* instead of the contraction? What is the position of the negative particle when the question begins with an auxiliary verb? Can it take more than one position? What is its position or positions in questions that begin with interrogative function words?

    11. Construct formulas representing the various patterns used when one or more negatives are present in a sentence. Do this for statements, imperatives, and questions.

12. What type of idea is expressed by the following sentences? In what circumstances would we be likely to use such sentences?

    a. Where don't you see him!
    b. What didn't he want to do!

Suggested Readings

SECTION 17

Jespersen, Otto, *The Philosophy of Grammar*, Chap. XXIV. London: George Allen & Unwin, Ltd., 1924.

Roberts, Paul, *English Sentences*, pp. 225-29. New York: Harcourt, Brace & World, Inc., 1962.

Expansion of the Noun

We have already noted that the noun serves several primary syntactic functions within the sentence—as subject of the verb, as object of the verb, as object of the preposition, and as identifying or classifying subjective and objective complements. In addition to these, it has some secondary functions—as the modifier of another noun, as an adverb, and as an appositive.

In many sentences the noun stands alone in these functions; in others it is subject to one or more types of modification. When it appears in modified form, we say that the head word of the unit is the *simple* (subject, object, or whatever its function is at that moment) and that the noun plus all of its modifiers would constitute the *complete* subject, object, complement, and so forth.

Because modifiers of the noun may appear either before or after it, we must discuss these pre-positional and postpositional modifiers one at a time. Among the pre-positional modifiers of the noun, we commonly find the noun determiner, the adjective, the noun adjunct, the verbal noun, the verbal adjective, the genitive noun, the genitive adjective, and, somewhat less commonly, locational words which are frequently classified as prepositions or adverbs. We rarely find prepositional phrases or any type of clause in the position before the noun that they modify; however, even these occur with sufficient frequency to warrant considering them as possible English patterns.

Any of these types of modifiers which precede the noun may appear in multiple units. Although these multiple units are often in a coordinate structure, they do not necessarily have to be so. For example, let us consider the noun adjunct as a noun modifier. We can put two or more noun adjuncts together in coordinate structure (the *stone* and *brick* house), or we can use more than one—each of which represents a different type of concept—in a structure which is not coordinate (the *Saturday mail* delivery, the *brick hearth* room). However, whenever we find three or more nouns grouped together in such a manner, we also find that in our oral patterning we tend to group these and thus treat two or more of them as single words. We might have, for example, the *brick-hearth* room or the brick *hearth-room*. In either case, we would apply the primary-tertiary stress pattern to the grouped unit. When four or more appear in a sequence, more possibilities of grouping are open to us. Thus we could group *Michigan State University Union* in the following ways: *Michigan-State University-Union, Michigan State-University-Union,* or *Michigan-State-University Union.* This grouping may also be indicated by the positions in which we apply the genitive inflection: Michigan State's University Union, Michigan's State University Union, or Michigan State University's Union.

There is also a definite patterning of pre-positional modifiers of nouns according to types. Nearest to the noun being modified will come the noun adjunct modifier. The descriptive adjective type will stand before the noun adjunct modifier. Before the descriptive adjective we may have a numeral or quantifying modifier, and before that, a determiner. The determiner itself may be preceded by a predeterminer, and this, in turn, may be preceded by an intensifier. Such a string of modifiers is represented by the subject in the following sentence.

Nearly all the seven old lawn mowers were destroyed.

It should be noted that while no variation in the position of these is permissible, it is possible to insert others of similar types at the adjective and noun adjunct positions; it is also possible to add normal modification to these units or to others that may be inserted.

Nearly all the seven *very* old *broken-down green* lawn mowers were destroyed.
Nearly all the seven very old broken-down *leaf-mulching dull* green lawn mowers were destroyed.

Only *all* or *both* will serve as predeterminers, and of these two *all* alone may be intensified. In effect, then, we can expand the prepositional modification of the noun head only in postdeterminer positions.

Inspection will also show that some of these modifiers may be moved to postnoun positions if we put them in the forms of prepositional phrases or clauses. *Lawn* cannot be separated from *mowers;* hence, this noun adjunct cannot be moved. We can move *green* to postposition, but if we do, it will carry any modifiers it may have with it (lawn mowers *of dull green*). If we move *leaf-mulching* it becomes either *for mulching leaves* or *for leaf-mulching*. *Broken-down* will retain its form except for the hyphen, but in postposition it will appear in its true passive voice clause, "which were broken down." *Old* and its intensifier *very* may also appear in the predicate position of a modifying clause, "which were very old." The others will remain in prenoun position. If we were to make all these possible changes from prenoun to postnoun positions, we would, of course, end up with a most awkward sentence, particularly if we did not coordinate some of the modifiers.

> Nearly all the seven lawn mowers of dull green, for mulching leaves, which were broken down, and which were very old, were destroyed.

This can be improved somewhat by using coordinate modifiers instead of modifying clauses, but even so, the sentence will leave much to be desired.

> Nearly all the seven lawn mowers of dull green, for mulching leaves, which were very old and broken down, were destroyed.

A few small patterns may also be perceived here. Prepositional phrase modifiers of the noun appear between the noun and any clausal modifiers that it may have. Noun modifiers of the noun appear between the noun and any noun substitute modifiers (in our example sentence, a gerund). A check of a few other examples will serve to confirm this.

> the piece *of plywood to cover the hole*
> a machine *of steel for cutting glass*

Remember that those placed nearest the noun in pre-position will remain nearest the noun in postposition.

Finally, we should note that when it is possible to interchange the position of the pre-positional noun modifiers, we can coordinate these modifiers in postposition.

seven *old broken-down* lawn mowers
seven *broken-down old* green lawn mowers
seven green lawn mowers which were *old and broken down*

Actually, the pattern for noun modification may be stated very simply: The more exact or specific the nature of the information provided by the descriptive modifier, the closer to the noun it appears. This rule can best be observed in a series of modifiers, all of which represent the same general type of concept.

the Oscoda school gymnasium stage lights
the lights on the stage of the gymnasium in the school at Oscoda

Whenever we have modifications of equal exactness, the position of the modifiers may be interchanged.

ladies' *white faille cotton* dresses
ladies' *white cotton faille* dresses
ladies' *cotton white faille* dresses

One major exception to this generalization appears in our handling of dates. We can say either "It was Thursday, *the seventh of June* in 1865" or "It was Thursday, *June 7, 1865.*"

Numerals are rarely modified. When they are, the result is to make them less exact rather than more exact.

Nearly all the *seven or so* old lawn mowers
Some six people appeared.

The noun appositive presents another type of expansion of the noun through modification. In most situations the appositive construction will consist of one noun which names a class and another which is a member of that class. In general, the class-naming noun will be accompanied by a determiner and the member-indicating noun will appear without a determiner.

the plumber, Smith   Smith, the plumber
the material, silk   silk, the material

When both nouns are accompanied by determiners, the class-naming noun will be preceded by a determiner of the *a/an* type and the member-indicating noun by one of the *the/his* type.

my dog, a dachshund

If, however, the function of the appositive is that of identification rather than classification, both nouns will be preceded by determiners of the *the/his* type.

> *Her* flowers, *those* roses, were welcome.
> *My* dog, *the* dachshund, received a blue ribbon.
> *That* house, *our* home for many years, was burnt.

In the structure of apposition, the first noun is considered the head word and the second furnishes some type of explanatory information about it. The second noun, the appositive, will normally be set off from the head noun by a juncture pattern in speech and by commas in writing. It is this difference in oral patterning, reflected by our punctuation patterning in writing, that enables us to distinguish the appositive structure from the *Noun Adjunct + Noun* structure. Any native speaker will easily recognize the different oral patterning in these two constructions by using the following phrases as tests.

> *The old dog, Tray, ate from the old dog tray.*

We are also aided by the fact that the noun adjunct will normally not be accompanied by a determiner of its own, but will appear between the noun head and *its* determiner.

> those *stone* houses
> an *iron* pail
> his *rubber* boots
> two *walnut* desks

Nouns of measure, however, may have a number-indicating determiner attached to them even when they appear in the noun adjunct position.

> his *ten*-gallon hat
> a *five*-dollar bill

Postpositional modifiers of the noun will retain the characteristics of their original word-class. For example, a verbal modifier of the noun may be accompanied by objects and/or adverbs; a noun in apposition may be accompanied by modifying adjectives, and so forth.

> A resolution *to eliminate racially discriminatory clauses from the constitution of Greek organizations on the U. of Kansas campus* was passed by the Student Congress Wednesday.

Although the phrasal and clausal types of noun modifiers normally appear after the noun they modify, they are occasionally found in pre-position.

His *off the record* remarks were enlightening.
Her *I-don't-give-a-damn-what-you-think* attitude was disturbing.

Here again, it should be noted that oral patterning would be used to indicate that we are to take the entire word group as a unit modifier.

Exercise 18-1   Expansion of the Noun

Earlier we learned that the noun may function in the following syntactical manners: (1) as the subject of the verb, (2) as subjective complement, (3) as the object of the verb, (4) as the object of a preposition, (5) as an objective complement, (6) as a modifier of another noun (noun adjunct or appositive), (7) as a modifier of a verb, (8) as a modifier of an adjective. We will now look at the possible expansion of the noun when it is used in each of these situations.

1. What is the subject of the headline "BOY WINS PRIZE"? What do we normally add to such a sentence to put it into natural English? What is added to the subject in each of the following emendations?

a. The boy wins the prize.
b. The Swedish boy wins the prize.
c. The Swedish boy, Jan, wins the prize.
d. The blue-eyed Swedish boy, Jan, wins the prize.
e. The blond blue-eyed Swedish boy, Jan, wins the prize.
f. The young blond blue-eyed Swedish boy, Jan, wins the prize.
g. Jan, the young blond blue-eyed Swedish boy in the brown coat, wins the prize.
h. The young blond blue-eyed Swedish boy who is wearing a brown coat and sitting in the corner wins the prize.
i. The young blond blue-eyed Swedish boy who is sitting in the corner and wearing a brown coat despite the hot weather wins the prize.
j. The young blond blue-eyed Swedish boy, who, despite the hot weather, is wearing a brown coat while he sits in the corner, wins the prize.

2. In what two positions do you find expanders of the subject? What is characteristic of those in each position? When we expand a noun subject in this way, do all of the additions become direct modifiers of the simple noun subject itself? Are those that are not direct modifiers of the simple subject a part of the complete subject? Are all possible types of modification represented in the sentences for question 1? If not, what types are missing? Supply examples of each of these missing types used as modifiers of the noun subject.

3. What syntactic element is represented by the expanded parts of each of the sentences provided below? Identify at least one example of an expanded noun used in each of the eight functions noted in the introductory paragraph. Identify the type of expansion used in each.

   a. They bought a new deepfreeze unit.
   b. His coal-soot black face was very animated.
   c. He goes to Chicago nearly every Monday.
   d. Henry, the sewage disposal plant designer, was a nice fellow.
   e. George Washington was elected the first President of the United States of America.

4. Can all types of expansion be used in every possible function of the noun? Construct pattern formulas to represent the types of expansion that can be used with the noun in each of its functions. Provide a sample sentence with each formula.

Exercise 18-2   Modification of the Noun

In Exercise 18-1 we observed some of the ways in which the noun may be expanded through modification. It might be well to recall that the primary function of most modification of the noun is to provide more exact meaning through limitation or description. As a means of refreshing our memory, let us consider a single sentence:

A poor family bought two old abandoned Pere Marquette passenger cars, which had been dismantled years ago, to use as a home.

1. What is the simple subject of this sentence? Does this subject have any modification? What is the simple object? What types of modification does it have? What parts of speech are represented by *Pere Marquette* and *passenger*? How are they used here? What modifier requires the plural form *cars*? Why aren't *Pere Marquette* and

passenger pluralized? What type of syntactic structure is represented by *which had been dismantled years ago?* To what word is this unit related? What type of syntactic structure is represented by *to use as a home?* To what word is this unit related?

2. Assuming that the same people are represented in all four of the following sentences, which sentence expresses the idea most exactly? Which expresses it least exactly? Describe the subject of each sentence.

    a. They were happy.
    b. The children were happy.
    c. John and Mary were happy.
    d. The children, John and Mary, were happy.

3. Is coordination, as it is used in the sentences below, in any way related to the expansion of the noun by modification?

    a. The house and the rooms in it were large.
    b. The house was large and roomy.
    c. The large roomy house was comfortable.

4. What syntactic patterns are used to add new elements of meaning to each of the following pairs of sentences?

    a. John is going.
       John and his father are going.
    b. The old house was deserted.
       The old stone house was deserted.
    c. The old house was deserted.
       The old stone house was dirty and deserted.

5. Is any new element of meaning added by coordination in the second sentence provided below? What is accomplished by coordination in this sentence?

    a. The family got along well with the neighbors.
    b. The family and the neighbors got along well.

6. Can new elements of meaning be added through coordination of the nonadditive varieties? Provide sentence examples of contrastive, alternative, and conditional coordination which add new meaning to sentences. Are all of these freely usable as expanders of the noun? Is coordination merely a substitute for modification? Cite examples to support your response to this last question.

7. Can coordination be used with the noun in all its possible functions? How is it used in each of the given sentences?

   a. She was elected secretary and treasurer.
   b. The dog belongs to Mary and John.
   c. They painted the house and the barn.
   d. We work Wednesdays and Fridays.
   e. The steel and concrete structure withstood the earthquake.
   f. The sleet- and snow-laden wind cut through us.

8. List the different means we have of expanding the noun. Supply examples for each.

Suggested Readings

Section 18

Lees, Robert B., *The Grammar of English Nominalizations*, Appendix A. Bloomington, Indiana: Indiana University Research Center in Anthropology, Folklore, and Linguistics, 1960.

Roberts, Paul, *Understanding English*, pp. 185-94. New York: Harper & Row, Publishers, 1958.

Expansion of the Verb

The verb may be expanded in either of two ways: (1) the simple
tense form may be changed to an analytical tense form, or (2) the
verb, whether it be in simple or analytical tense form, may be complemented by adverbs, objects, or adverbial objects. (The addition
of the preposition/adverb to the verb normally results in a new
verb, so it is not here considered to be an expansion of the verb
head form.)

In the development of analytical tense forms in which we use two
or more verb words, we can note, first, that only the nonfinite forms
of the verb are used in any position after the initial one, and
second, that not all nonfinite forms may be used after all verbs.
Some will take but a single form, some will take two of the three
forms, and a very few will take all three forms.

Let us look at a short list of verbs which may appear with one or
more of the nonfinite forms following them. For the time being we
will not concern ourselves with the question of whether these nonfinite forms are being used as a part of the verb phrase or whether
they are functioning as some other word-class in the sentence. Before we begin, we should observe that the common or infinitive form
of the verb appears after some verbs without its sign *to,* whereas
other verbs will require the sign when the infinitive form follows
them. We can thus make four distinctions: (1) those verbs followed

by the infinitive form with *to*, (2) those followed by the common form without *to*, (3) those followed by the *-ing* form, and (4) those followed by the past participle form.

Verb followed by	Infinitive with *to*	Common form	*-ing* form	Past participle form
anticipate			x	
appear	x			x
be	x		x	x
begin	x		x	
can		x		
continue	x		x	
could		x		
dare	x	x		
desire	x			
do		x		
expect	x			
get	x		x	x
have	x			x
hope	x			
may		x		
might		x		
must		x		
need	x	x		
ought	x			
recall			x	
regret	x		x	
remember	x		x	
seem	x			x
shall		x		
should		x		
start	x		x	
try	x		x	
will		x		
wish	x			
would		x		

If we look first at those which may take the infinitive with its sign, we find that one of these verbs, *ought*, has but a single form. All others, if they appear in initial position, will be conjugated as though they were full verbs. A little experimentation will show us that *ought* is used only in initial position in most standard dialects. (Some dialects may permit constructions such as *had ought, should ought,* and so forth.) The other verbs in this group, however, may be placed in any position in the verb phrase in any standard dialect.

Of those verbs followed by the common form without *to*, the nine one-form verbs (*can, could, may, might, must, shall, should, will, would*) will appear only in initial position; the others may appear in any position.

Two verbs, *dare* and *need*, appear both with and without the *to*. *Need* takes the common form only when *not* or *n't* appears between it and the following verb. (You need *not* go. You need*n't* try. You need *to try*.) *Dare* is also followed by the common form in these constructions, but it may take the common form in other constructions. (You dare not *do* it. I dare *say*. Do you dare *do* it?) In most constructions either form may be used with *dare*. (I dare *try*. I dare *to try*. Do you dare *do* it? Do you dare *to do* it?) Note that it is not the presence of negation which demands our use of the common form after such verbs as *dare* or *need*, but rather the position of the negating element. If we use a *do* construction negative we may use either form after *dare*, but only the *to* form after *need*. (You do not dare *do* that. You do not dare *to do* that. You do not need *to do* that. You need not *do* that.) These two verbs are anomalous in another respect. When they are used initially in the third person singular, they take the *-s* inflection in affirmations; in this they are like all other verbs except the ten single-form verbs we have noted above. In negatives, and in questions in which they appear as the initial verb, they may omit this inflection. (He *dare* not talk. She *need* not go. *Dare* she do it? *Need* she be told?) The usage of *dare* is slightly more flexible than that of *need*. Neither may take the *-s* when the contracted *n't* is used (He *daren't* talk. She *needn't* go), but *dare* may take the *-s* before *not* (He *dares* not talk), though it is certainly more normal for us to use "He does not dare to talk" or "He dare not talk."

Such variability in usage should lead us to question whether we have more than one verb in *dare* or in *need*. We have numerous examples of homonymic verbs in English—the auxiliaries *can* and *will* and the full verbs *to can* and *to will*, the verb *lie* (to prevaricate) and the verb *lie* (to recline), and so forth. We also have numerous examples of auxiliaries whose basic concept may be expressed by other forms—*can, to be able to; will, to be going to; must, to have to. Dare* and *need* appear to combine some qualities of both groups.

The only other verb on our list that precedes the common form without the *to* is the verb *do*. This verb also has multiple usages. As a function word auxiliary, it is commonly used in forming questions and negations (I know him. I *do* not know him. *Do* you know him?) and in forming the emphatic verb (I *do* know him). In addition to these usages, it frequently appears as a substitute for some other verb (Who broke the window? I *did*) or as a substitute for the verb and any complements the verb may have. (Do you take this woman to be your lawful wedded wife? I *do*.) In this last usage, it is operating like *be, have,* and the one-form modals, which may also stand as substitutes for the verb or for the verb and its complements.

The infinitive which may follow the initial forms of *be* is sometimes a part of the verb and sometimes a complement to the verb— most frequently one expressing purpose. When it is a part of the verb, with the present tense forms, it expresses future time. (I *am to see* him tomorrow. We *are to leave* Tuesday.) When the past tense forms are used, the construction implies that a planned action has not as yet been carried out. (I *was to see* him today. We *were to meet* them here.) In colloquial usage, these *was/were* forms sometimes appear as a substitute for *went.* When this occurs, the infinitive becomes a complement of the verb. It is also a complement of the subject whenever the subject is one that could not perform the action named by the infinitive. (That fruit is *to eat.* This meat is *to fry.*) It is a subjective complement whenever the infinitive can be used as a substitute for the subject. (His solution was *to run. To run* was his solution.)

The infinitive following *have* may be either a part of the verb phrase or a complement. When *have* is used as the auxiliary, the combination expresses the idea of compulsion; through the use of the past tense form *had,* it permits us to express that concept in the past as we cannot do with *must.* The *have* form of the auxiliary is commonly pronounced /hæf/ rather than /hæv/. When the infinitive following *have* is a complement, we do not use the /hæf/ pronunciation, and the infinitive generally expresses the concept of purpose. (What do we /hæftə/ eat? What *must* we eat? What do we /hæv/ to eat? What *is* there to eat?)

Get followed by the infinitive expresses a passive idea similar to "be permitted to" or "be able to." *Get* is sometimes used after *have* and before an infinitive. In this construction it is either redundant or slightly emphatic. (We *have got to work* hard.) The total construction expresses the compulsion concept.

Get also is commonly used as a substitute for other verbs. (We *got to work* about ten o'clock.) In such a construction *to work* may be a prepositional phrase rather than an infinitive, and it functions as a complement of the verb. But because *to work* could also be a verb (in which case the idea expressed would be "were able to start working" instead of "arrived at work"), the construction is potentially ambiguous.

Certain linking verbs, such as *seem* and *appear*, imply the possibility of a negation when they are used before an infinitive. (He seems to run well [but he may not be doing so].)

A sizable number of verbs expressing the general concept of desire are commonly found before the infinitive. When the present tense forms of these verbs are used, the construction expresses some lack of assurance concerning future action. Contrast "I will see you again" with "I hope to see you again." This same lack of assurance may be expressed when past tense forms are used in some situations, but in others the implication is that the action has not been completed. (I had hoped to meet her there.)

Closely related to these is a series of verbs which express the general concept of anticipation. Some of these, such as *expect* or *plan*, may appear before the infinitive. Others, such as *anticipate*, are not used in this construction. Future time is lexically inherent in such verbs.

Verbs such as *recall* or *remember* have past time lexically inherent in them. *Recall* is not used before the infinitive; *remember* may be when it is used in the sense of "not forgetting," but it is not so used when it implies *recall*. (He *remembers to call* me each week. He *remembers seeing* her last week.) Both verb forms are complements.

Verbs whose lexical meanings imply the inception, conclusion, or continuation of an action or state are often followed by an infinitive. Most of these verbs may also be used before the *-ing* form. At least one (*keep*) is not used before the infinitive. Another (*remain*) is quite commonly found before the passive infinitive (This remains *to be done*); when it is followed by an active infinitive, however, the infinitive tends to be a complement of the verb rather than a part of it. (They remained *to work*.) The same type of ambiguity mentioned earlier—that based on infinitive, verb; infinitive, complement; prepositional phrase—is likely to appear with such verbs.

The verb *try* is frequently found before the infinitive. In normal speech, *and* may appear quite as frequently as *to* as the sign of the infinitive following this verb. It is possible to consider such a structure as coordinate; we can also say that *and* may serve as the sign of the infinitive after verbs such as *try, come,* or *go*.

Only one third of the verbs provided in the sample list on page 238 normally appear before the *-ing* form when that form is actually a part of the verb phrase. *Be* is commonly used with this form to provide the progressive tenses; *get* is sometimes so used as a substitute for *begin* or *start*. (Get moving.) *Get* is also used with a *to* between it and the *-ing* form. (We *got to talking* about various things.) This *to* construction is also used with a few composite verbs. (I will *look forward to seeing* you.)

Most of the verbs which may be followed by the *-ing* form belong to the inception, continuation, conclusion group. In these constructions the *-ing* word and any complements it may have can be considered as the object of the preceding verb. Nonetheless, the idea expressed in most situations is definitely a verbal one. (I like [the act of] swimming.) We will return to these distinctions in the infinitive and the *-ing* forms after we have discussed the uses of the past participle in verb phrases.

The past participle is used in verb phrases in two different manners: (1) After some form of *have* to construct the perfect tenses. (I *have gone*. He *has written*. They *had believed*.) (2) After a linking verb to form the passive voice of a transitive verb. In this last usage the participle is often followed by a prepositional phrase denoting the agent or actor. (The work was accomplished *through the efforts of the committee*. The boy was hit *by the car*.) If the agent is not expressed, the past participle normally functions as a predicate adjective modifying the subject. (The boy was *tired*. The *tired* boy.) As we have already seen, the object of the verb in the active voice normally becomes the subject of the verb in the passive voice. When, however, the object is of a reflexive type, the subject of the active voice remains as the subject of the passive verb. (The prisoner incriminated himself. The prisoner was self-incriminated.) Also, when the verb is one involving a reciprocal action, either the subject or the object of the active voice verb may appear as the subject of the passive. (She met him at noon. She was met at noon by him. He was met at noon by her.)

Despite the fact that the passive voice is normally limited to transitive verbs, we sometimes find intransitive verbs used in what appears to be a passive construction. In older usage such constructions as "He is risen," "I am come," and "They are fallen," were fairly common; in modern English we find "She is gone," "I am resolved," "I am determined," "I am indebted to." Quite frequently the addition of the preposition/adverb to the verb will result in changing the verb from intransitive to transitive. (He *jumped*. He *jumped on* me. I was *jumped on.*) The passive voice construction is also used at times as a substitute for a linking verb. (She *became* a widow. She *was left* a widow.) In conclusion, we could say that the past participle should be considered to be a part of the verb phrase whenever an agent is expressed or whenever the participle itself cannot be moved to the attributive position without distortion of usage. At times, the presence or absence of a modifier may affect such usage. If we change the sentence "The house was built of wood" to *"The built* house was of wood," we have distortion; but if we use instead "The house was well built of wood," we can change the structure without distortion—"The *well-built* house was of wood." When no agent is expressed and when the participle may be moved to the attributive position without distorting usage, we must consider the past participle as being an adjective.

Let us return now to the infinitive and the -*ing* forms to see if we can find a basis for distinguishing their use as a part of the verb phrase from their use as a complement. As a beginning, let us take the infinitive noun and the prepositional phrase which are identical in written form. In the sentence "He went to work" we might have either construction. If we have a prepositional phrase here, we can insert a determiner between the *to* and the noun. (He went to *his* work.) In the idiomatic expression "He went to work" (He began working), we find a closer juncture between *went* and *to* in speech than we do in the structure in which the infinitive designates purpose. (He went in order to work.) In all three expressions the prepositional phrase or the infinitive is being used adverbially, and hence should be considered as a complement of the verb rather than a part of it. The infinitive may also serve as a complement to the subject. (His purpose was *to work.* I am *to blame.*) When the infinitive follows an object, the object often is the subject of the infinitive and the clause consisting of the infinitive and its subject is the real object of the verb. (I want *him to know.*) Note that in this example the meaning is neither "I want him" nor "I want to know." We must therefore consider "him to know" as being the structural unit.

Part of our difficulty in analyzing structures of this type stems from the fact that the *to* in modern English is often a part of the auxiliary verb rather than the sign of the infinitive. We find this particularly in forms such as *ought to, used to, have to.* This form also combines with verbs such as *get* and *go. Get to* is frequently followed by an *-ing* word. (We got to talking.) One meaning of *go to* is to begin or to start. (He immediately *went to work.*) One meaning of *be going to* is that of expressing simple future time. (I *am going to go.*) The test of meaning is the simplest method of determining whether the infinitive or common form of the verb is a part of the verb phrase or is serving some other function. The final verb word in any verb phrase provides the lexical meaning for that phrase. The auxiliaries provide structural meanings such as tense, mood, person, number, and so on. In the phrases "will have been eaten" and "will have been written," the lexical meaning rests in *eaten* and *written,* and the structural meaning in *will have been.* If we take the sentence "He will have been there," the lexical meaning is carried by *been* and the structural meaning by *will have.* If we reduce our verb phrase further to "He will have a pencil," *have* is no longer an auxiliary and now carries the lexical meaning of *possess. Will* carries the structural meaning of future time, and other structural meanings such as person and number are signaled by the pronoun subject.

In ordinary speech we normally vary our intonational patterns slightly to indicate such differences in structure and hence in meaning, but in my own speech, at least, this difference in patterning is so slight that I would hesitate to depend upon it to express the difference. In actual life, all utterances are a part of a larger context —verbal and/or situational—and we depend upon this context to provide such nuances of meaning. For example, consider "He is going to see the wizard" as the answer to the two questions "Where is he going?" and "Why is he going?"

We can also make use of structural tests of transformations to determine the final verb word in a transitive verb. If we take, for example, the sentence "I would have been delighted to have had to go to visit him," we can place this whole infinitive unit in subject position for the active voice transformation. "*To have had to go to visit him* would have delighted me." We can say therefore that this unit is the subject of the active voice verb or the agent in the passive voice construction. It is not a part of the verb phrase in either structure. As agent, however, it is a part of the expansion of the verb just as any other type of complement of the verb is a part of its expansion.

Because the *-ing* form, like the infinitive, may serve as a verb, noun, adjective, or adverb, the problem of distinguishing its use in a particular structure is almost identical with that of distinguishing the uses of the infinitive or common form. In addition to these uses, the *-ing* form is sometimes used as a preposition. (We worked *during* the afternoon. We were reassured *concerning* the payment.)

Expansion through Complementation

We have already looked at the adverb (pp. 118ff.), and at the various types of objects (pp. 156ff.), so we will concern ourselves here only with those adverbs and objects whose forms may be identical with verb forms in speech or writing. These consist of: (1) the common form of some verbs, which may be used as a noun (I will *push* him. I will give him a *push*); (2) infinitive forms which may serve as nouns, modifiers of nouns, modifiers of adjectives, or modifiers of verbs (The majority chose *to hunt*. We have rooms *to rent*. He was too backward *to learn*. He stretched *to see*); (3) *-ing* forms which may function as nouns, modifiers of nouns, modifiers of adjectives, or modifiers of verbs (She preferred *swimming*. We caught John *napping*. She was happy *playing*. They came *running*); (4) the past participle forms which may appear as nouns, modifiers of nouns, modifiers of adjectives, or modifiers of verbs. (I chose the *retreaded* [tire]. We saw the man *shot*. She is happy *married*. We arrived *tired*.)

We shall have to say that we have a verb word used as an adverb complement of the verb whenever we find it in postverbal position and expressing the concept of time, place, manner, or purpose. Some of these will be purely adverbial (He stretched *to see*. He came *running*), and others will seem to be quasi-adverbial and quasi-adjectival. This latter group will tend to modify the subject as well as the verb (We arrived *tired*) or the object as well as the verb (We used the hole *to peep*).

We shall have to say we have a verb word used as an object whenever it is possible to use it as the subject of the passive voice construction. (A *push* was given to him. *To hunt* was chosen by the majority. *Swimming* was preferred by her. The *retreaded* [tire] was chosen by me.) We must conclude that a verb word is an object when it appears in object position and may be preceded by a noun determiner. (I enjoyed *the walking*.)

Exercise 19-1   Expansion of the Verb

In an earlier exercise some attention was given to analytical tense forms and to the combination of the simple verb with the preposition or adverb. In this exercise we will return to our analysis of the analytical tense forms and the ideas expressed by them.

1. What time area is expressed by the verb in each of the sentences provided below? What tense form is used? If we were to substitute the word *today* for the word *tomorrow*, would we still be speaking of the future?

   a. He leaves tomorrow.
   b. He will leave tomorrow.
   c. He is to leave tomorrow.
   d. He is going to leave tomorrow.

2. What concepts other than time are represented in the following sentences?

   a. He has to leave tomorrow.
   b. He should leave tomorrow.
   c. He may leave tomorrow.
   d. He can leave tomorrow.

3. What form of the verb do you find following modal auxiliaries? What form or forms of the verb follow *be* when it is used as an auxiliary? What form or forms follow *have*? What form or forms follow *do*? Are any forms other than the present participle, the past participle, and the common or infinitive form ever used after auxiliaries? Make a list of all the commonly used auxiliaries and of the form or forms of the verb that may appear immediately after each of them.

4. Where the same form of the verb may appear after more than one of the auxiliaries, is the meaning changed by our choice of an auxiliary? Always? Consider the following examples.

   a. The road has divided.   The road is divided.
   b. She has to come.   She is to come.
   c. We should go.   We ought to go.
   d. I must go.   I have to go.
   e. We may go.   We might go.
   f. The boy is trying to learn. The boy keeps trying to learn.

5. Do we have the same form of the main verb in all four of the sentences given below? How did you arrive at your answer?

  a. John has hurt someone.
  b. John has to hurt someone.
  c. John is hurt.
  d. My finger does hurt.

6. Do the generalizations you have arrived at apply when more than one auxiliary is used in the expanded verb? Consider units that have two auxiliaries. Do we ever use more than one modal auxiliary in expanding a verb? Do we ever make use of the same auxiliary twice? Do we ever use *do* as an auxiliary in the same structure in which we use a modal? Do we have any analytical tenses that make use of more than three auxiliaries? When we use both *have* and *be* as auxiliaries in the same expanded verb, which appears first? When there is a number-person distinguishing form, on which of the verb words does it appear?

7. Do any of the verb words commonly used as auxiliaries ever combine with a preposition or an adverb? Are they ever used as auxiliaries in this form?

8. Do we have any substitutes for auxiliaries? How about *how about?* In what ways do we use this expression? For what can it substitute? Consider the following examples. Do they cover all the possible usages of this expression? Would you consider any of them to be abnormal or substandard English?

  a. I voted; how about you?
  b. How about some more peas?
  c. How about a movie tonight?
  d. How about going with me?
  e. How about John? Would he be satisfactory?

9. Make a list of at least ten expanded tense forms that you would normally use. What concepts in addition to the temporal concept can be expressed by each of the forms on your list? Determine whether these concepts result from the use of the combined form, from the choice of the auxiliary, or from the lexical meanings of the main verb. Note the following examples, but do not include any of the two-form units that are analyzed here as a part of your list. You may, if you wish, use the unanalyzed three- and four-form tenses that appear here as a part of your list.

Two-form Tenses	Time	Concepts Expressed
is eating	present-future	Action concurrent with time of speech if unmodified; with time of modifier if modified.
should go ought to go Should he go, . . .	present-future	Obligation, and/or doubt if action will be completed. *Should* also expresses condition when (a) the subject follows the auxiliary, and (b) the clause is not in itself a question.
have to eat	present-future	Compulsion expressed by tense form of *have* plus infinitive.
has battered	past	Reiterative concept inherent in main verb.

Three-form Tenses
has been gone
will be eating

Four-form Tenses
will have been gone

10. Do you find any differences in the uses of multiform tenses of transitive verbs and those of intransitive verbs? What is peculiar about the usage of the verb *use* as an auxiliary? Do we ever make use of a construction such as "He has been suffering for some time now"? Is this a passive voice? If not, to what is it related? What time problems are raised by constructions such as this one? By such a construction as "He will have been sleeping for some time by now"?

Exercise 19-2   Modification of the Verb

1. In Section 18 we saw that one of the primary purposes we have in expanding the noun through modification is that of limiting or making more exact the meaning expressed by the noun. What types of concepts are expressed by modifiers of the verb in the sentences below? What form (word, phrase, and so on) does each of the modifiers take? Do any of these modifiers limit the meaning of the verb in the same manner that modifiers of the noun limit its meaning? If not, how do they limit it? You will find that some of these modifiers express an inexact or an approximate concept, and some a concept that is relative to some fixed meaning. Does this in

any way parallel the types of modification which can be provided for the noun?

    a. The train will arrive at 10:00 P.M.
    b. We flew for a while.
    c. Our guests should arrive soon.
    d. I saw him twice.
    e. We meet them now and again.
    f. We will expect you often.
    g. We rented the cottage for a week.
    h. We had been planning it for some time.
    i. That will not last long.
    j. He went home.
    k. We traveled here and there.
    l. The house is near the school.
    m. They went North.
    n. He wobbled back and forth.
    o. They started in a northerly direction.
    p. That much gasoline will take us ten miles.
    q. We continued for some distance.
    r. We should go far.
    s. He came running.
    t. They worked hard.
    u. He studied to learn.
    v. He worked because he needed money.

2. What parallel do you see in the following pairs of sentences?

    a. That is a hart.
       He battered the door with his fist.
    b. That is a male deer.
       He struck the door repeatedly with his fist.

3. Which of the modifiers in the examples for question 1 can themselves be modified? Does this modification of the modifier always modify the verb-modifying unit, or does it sometimes modify a subunit within the verb-modifying unit?

4. Can any of the concepts provided by verb modifiers in the sentences for question 1 be used in a sentence with any other type of modifying concept? Can more than two of them be used to modify a single verb? If two or more are used to modify a single verb, do they have any fixed positions in the sentence with relation to one another? Which of the following sentences represent the more normal patterns for English?

    a. He went home early.   He went early home.
    b. They worked hard to learn.   They worked to learn hard.

5. Is the object of the verb ever used to clarify the meaning of the verb or to make the meaning more exact? Consider the following sentences. Do they represent substandard usage?

a. He drove a hard bargain.　　He drove a Chevrolet.
b. She set a fine example.　　　She set a fine table.
c. We took a whirl at it.　　　　We took a friend with us.

6. Summarize your conclusions about the forms, functions, positions, and lexical concepts of verbal complements.

Exercise 19-3　　　Coordination of the Verb

1. Which of the following examples represent true coordination of the verb? What do the others represent?

a. Try and stop me.
b. Run and play.
c. Come and meet him.
d. Go and get it.
e. Eat and drink all you want.

2. What do you find when you try to substitute *to* for *and* in the examples for question 1? What do you find if you change these sentences into statements with *he* as the subject? Do any of them appear to fit both situations?

3. Can linking verbs be coordinated with intransitive nonlinking verbs? Can they be coordinated with transitive verbs? Can active and passive voice constructions be coordinated with one another? Provide examples to support each affirmative response.

4. Is there any limitation we must observe in coordinating tense forms? Can we coordinate past with present, present with future, past with future? Can we coordinate simple tenses with progressive tenses? Simple tenses with perfect tenses?

5. Can we coordinate verb forms representing different moods?

6. Can we coordinate verb forms representing different persons?

7. Can we coordinate verb forms representing different numbers?

8. Consider the sentence "He gets angry and beats her frequently." Could we change the position of *angry* or *her* in this sentence? What conclusion do you draw about complements of coordinate verbs? Is this true of all complements? Could *frequently* be said to complement both verbs? What type of verbs are used in this sentence?

9. At what point in analytical verb tenses can coordination take place? What problems do you find with the following attempted coordination? Can auxiliaries ever be coordinated?

   a. He has and is hurt.
   b. He has and is mistaken.
   c. He ought and used to work.

10. Are there any situations in which coordination of the verb serves as a substitute for modification of the verb? Are there any situations in which we use coordination of the verb to achieve a type of emphasis? Is coordination ever used to provide such concepts as iteration? Provide examples.

11. Summarize your findings about the uses of coordination with verbs.

Suggested Readings

SECTION 19

Francis, W. Nelson, *The Structure of American English*, pp. 252-68. New York: The Ronald Press Company, 1954.

Jespersen, Otto, *The Philosophy of Grammar*, pp. 254-89. London: George Allen & Unwin, Ltd., 1924.

Roberts, Paul, *Understanding English*, pp. 194-203. New York: Harper & Row, Publishers, 1958.

A Further Look
at Modification

Earlier we defined the adjective as a word which limited the meaning of the noun and which appeared in either the attributive position before the noun or in the predicate position after the linking verb. In either position, it could be intensified by one of the words in the *very* class or limited by one of the words in the *scarcely* class. We found that certain adjectives could be classed as base adjectives and that others were derived from different word-form bases through the use of a large number of derivational suffixes. We also found that many adjectives show degree either by adding the inflections *-er* or *-est* or by making use of such function words as *more, most, less, least.* Finally, we learned that not all modifiers of nouns are adjectives and that some words might appear either as adjectives or as members of some other word-class without undergoing any change in form.

Although our position test pattern is very useful, it is by no means definitive. We find, for example, that whenever an adjective and a noun have been combined to represent a unit concept, we cannot separate them to put the adjective in predicate position. As we have seen, these combinations may be written as separate words, hyphenated, or written solid. The unit concept words will not take intensification either. Many unit concept words exist in both forms, identical in writing but with a varying stress pattern in speech. (The hót dôg (wiener) was cold. The hôt dóg (canine) was panting. The panting dog was *very hot.* The hígh châir was old. The *very* hîgh (tall) chaír was old.)

We also find that certain adjectives express a concept that is discrete rather than relative. Idiomatic usage for such words varies considerably. Some words, such as *perfect, round, square,* should logically be discrete, for they express the ultimate of their particular qualities. Usage, however, permits us to treat such words as though they expressed relative degrees of their qualities, and so we find such constructions and forms as *more perfect, rounder,* and *squarest.* Words of this group may also be used as predicate adjectives.

Another group of adjectives which express comparably discrete concepts may be used only in the attributive position and are never accompanied by degree function words or degree inflections. Some examples of this group are *chief, main,* and *principal.* In general, spacially or temporally locative adjectives are used only attributively and do not take function words or inflections for degree (a *nasal* infection, a *natal* injury). But some of these may express relative qualities when they are used with certain nouns. Thus, we can speak of a *very nasal tone* or a *more nasal tone,* but *not* of a **very nasal infection.* In such instances it is not the form, but the type of concept we are expressing, that determines whether or not we may add further modification. When, subjectively, we feel that the concept is discrete, we may not add further modification; when we feel that it is relative, we may.

Most noun modifiers of other nouns may appear either before the noun they modify or in a prepositional phrase following it. Thus we have a *stone* house, a house *of stone;* a *dining* room, a room *for dining;* the *Chicago* fire, the fire *in Chicago;* the *family's* doctor, the doctor *for the family;* my *uncle's* home, the home *of my uncle.* When we find widely different meanings expressed by the noun adjunct and the genitive noun, we also find that the concept expressed by the noun adjunct cannot be expressed in prepositional phrase form. (The *child's* mother, the mother *of the child;* but the *child mother.*) Closer scrutiny will show that this type of noun adjunct structure represents a unit concept similar to the unit concepts represented by hót dôg or greénhoùse, that it also takes the same stress patterning as the adjective-noun units do, and that the modification is of a reciprocal nature, such as we find in the appositive (the mother who is a child, the child who is a mother; Sam, who is my barber, my barber, who is Sam).

Except for the infinitive, verb modifiers of nouns may appear either before or after the noun they modify; they cannot be intensified. The infinitive is normally found only in the position after the noun it modifies (the rúnning bôy, the bôy rúnning; the accepted decision, the decision accepted; the man to see). Both the present and the past participle of some verbs may appear as participial adjectives. In this structure they may be expanded by intensifiers or by degree-indicating function words, and they may take the normal positions of the adjective. (A very chârming gírl. No occasion could be more fitting.) The gerund modifier of the noun (also an -ing form) cannot be moved from its position before the noun it modifies (a díning roòm), but the unit concept expressed by such a construction may be modified in the same way any other normal noun (a beautiful díning roòm); it can also appear in a phrase (a room for dining).

When we find adverbs modifying the noun, they most frequently take the position following the noun, but a few may be used either before or after it. (The above notation, the notation above.) Most adverbial modifiers of nouns are locative in space or time and referential in nature, as can be seen from the type of phrasal or clausal structures which may be substituted for them. (The time now is six o'clock. The time at this moment is six o'clock. The boy there is my brother. The boy on the davenport is my brother. The bibliography below is incomplete. The bibliography which is provided below is incomplete.) Such modifiers may be expanded to provide more precise information. (The river below looked like a tiny brook. The river two thousand feet below looked like a tiny brook.) Positional or directional adverbs of this type cannot be modified by intensifiers directly, but they may be modified by other adverbs expressing relative concepts, and these, in turn, may be modified by intensifiers. (The river very far below looked like a tiny brook.) Expanding such modifiers also gives them greater mobility. In the sentence we have been using as an example, the simple modifier below is quite fixed in its position following the noun, but in its expanded forms we can move it to various positions within the sentence. (Two thousand feet below, the river looked like a tiny brook. The river looked like a tiny brook two thousand *feet below.* The river *very far below* looked like a tiny brook. The river looked like a tiny brook *very far below.*)

When we look at modification closely, we find that it is relatively rare for the total modifier to be modified by another modifier. What occurs more often is that some element of the original modifier becomes the head word or unit for further modification. One common exception to this is the clausal modifier which is itself modified by another word-group modifier. In the sentence "It was late when we took the girls home after the dance," we have a clausal modifier, *when we took the girls home,* modifying the main clause and, in turn, being modified by the phrase, *after the dance.* More commonly we find a series of modifiers, each of which modifies a specific word or unit in the foregoing modifier. (He lived *in a small room at the rear of the fourth floor of a house on 87th Street.*) In the example just cited, each prepositional phrase except the first is a modifier of the noun head of the preceding prepositional phrase.

Let us consider another example: "John experienced difficulty in repairing the motor rejected by the mechanics because its cylinders were scored." The clause *because its cylinders were scored* has as its head the participle *rejected;* the phrase *rejected by the mechanics* has as its head the noun *motor;* the phrase *in repairing the motor* has as its head the main clause *John experienced difficulty.* In sentences such as this we are not dealing with expansion, but rather with substitution, or contraction of some of the units through the medium of modification. Our main ideas in this sentence are:

The motor contains cylinders.
The cylinders were scored.
The mechanics rejected the motor.
Repairing the motor was difficult.
John experienced the difficulty.

We can combine these ideas in many different ways:

The scoring in the cylinders of the motor rejected by the mechanics made it difficult for John to repair.
The motor which the mechanics rejected because of its scored cylinders was difficult for John to repair.
John found it difficult to repair the scored-cylinder motor which the mechanics had rejected.
The repairing of the cylinder-scored motor which the mechanics had rejected was difficult for John.

Though each of these sentences differs from the others in structure, the basic linguistic device of substituting contracted modifiers for full sentences is common to all of them.

It is easy to see that if we used no modifiers or substitutes our language would be exceedingly dull, monotonous, and inexact. The kind of modifying substitutes we have considered here, however, is but one type of substitution we commonly use. In the next section we shall consider some of the other general types of substitutions available to us and shall try to note their potentials and their limitations.

Exercise 20-1   A Further Look at Modification

1. A dozen phrases consisting of modifier and noun are provided below. In what position or positions in the sentence can each of these modifiers be used? With what types of verbs can they be used? Can any of these modifiers appear as objects of prepositions? Can any of them be used as modifiers of the verb? Are there any distinct formal characteristics for the modifiers which can be used to modify either the noun or the verb?

bitter medicine	fast car	hard luck
brighter skies	good boy	slow train
clean sheets	greatest emphasis	soft music
early bird	happy children	sweet tooth

2. In what ways do the modifiers in the following phrases differ from those provided for question 1?

national budget	friendly person
hopeful suitor	aesthetic experience
helpless children	wooded lot
boyish grin	three-drawered desk

3. How do the modifiers in the phrases below differ from those in question 1 and those in question 2? Apply the same questions to these that you applied to the modifiers in questions 1 and 2. Do you find any difference in usage?

working agreement	restrained feeling
playing children	sunken boat
seating chart	rooms to rent
tired boy	something to eat

4. What is illustrated by the following sentences?

a. The children, playing roughly, were reprimanded by the teacher.
b. The children reprimanded by the teacher were playing roughly.

5. In what way do the modifiers provided below differ from those for questions 1, 2, and 3? Apply the same questions to these that you applied to the modifiers in those lists. What do you note about variations within this group? For example, *brick house* can be expressed by *a house of brick,* but what happens when we attempt to develop parallel constructions with the others in this group? What type of modification—the noun adjunct or the prepositional phrase—normally provides us with the clearest meaning? In an earlier exercise we noted some of the different types of concepts that may be expressed by the noun adjunct type of modification. Is there any relationship between the type of concept expressed and our ability to substitute a prepositional phrase for the noun adjunct? Can a clause be substituted for a noun adjunct modifier? For those expressing all types of concepts? Is there any relationship between the type of concept expressed by the noun adjunct modifier and the choice of preposition or prepositions that may be used in phrasal modifiers substituted for it?

brick house	everyday occurrence
family doctor	north wind
Washington correspondent	kitchen furniture
barn roof	treasury surplus
Sunday paper	quart jar
child mother	signal tower

6. What differences do you find in the usage of the noun adjunct modifiers below and those provided for question 5? What difference do you note in the nouns being modified? What occurs when you change these to prepositional phrases? Can you add others to these?

lotus eater	lawn sprinkler
woman hater	dog trainer

7. Do all the modifiers listed below operate in the same way? What basic differences do you find? Add to these lists. Are there more types than are indicated here?

ten-ton load	brick-veneered house
ten-gallon hat	silver-plated teapot

8. Are such words as *blue, white,* and *yellow* adjectives or nouns? On what basis did you make your decision? Do they have plural forms? Can *very* be used with them as an intensifier? Can they show degree? Can they be used as subjects and objects? Can they appear in all the positions of the adjective in the sentence? Can they appear in all the positions of the noun in the sentence?

9. Apply the questions concerning noun adjuncts in question 5 to genitive nouns expressing parallel ideas. What do you find? Is there any situation expressed by the noun adjunct and the noun it modifies that parallels the double genitive (a friend *of mine,* a friend *of* my *father's*)? Can this double genitive be used with all types of concepts expressed by genitive nouns? If not, with which types may it be used?

10. In conventional grammars the various types of noun-determining function words are often designated as adjectives. What do you find about our usage of them? Do they all operate in the same manner? What do we have, for example, in constructions such as "The stars in her hair were *seven*" or "A committee of *three* was appointed"?

Exercise 20-2

1. What function is served by the italicized words in the sentences provided below? Can any of these words be shifted to a different position in the sentence?

    a. She was *very* good.
    b. They were *extremely* happy.
    c. There was *scarcely* enough.
    d. She was *rarely* dejected.
    e. He had *hardly* gone when the explosion occurred.

2. Do the italicized words in question 1 belong to one class or two? What occurs to the subject and verb when we use one of the mobile group as the initial word in the sentence? List as many words as you can that may be used in the same manners as the words *very* and *rarely.* Write sentences illustrating the use of each word in each of your lists.

3. When we use single-word modifiers, we sometimes have a fairly fixed word order for them. For example, we say "He left East Lansing Monday," but we do not say *"He left Monday East

Lansing." When we substitute phrases for these, we find we can say "He left on Monday from East Lansing." Another example of fixed word order is "the Lansing Auditorium stage curtains." Write five sentences containing two or more single-word modifiers of the noun and five sentences containing two or more single-word modifiers of the verb. Try placing these modifiers in different positions within the series. Formulate your conclusions about their fixity or variability, then change each of these into prepositional phrases and again draw conclusions about the fixity of their positions with regard to one another.

4. When we use a prepositional phrase to modify a noun, what is its normal position with relation to the noun? When we use a prepositional phrase to modify a verb, what position or positions may it take in the sentence?

5. Consider each of the clausal modifiers in the sentences below. Which of them can be reduced or contracted in form? What kinds of verb tenses do we have in those clausal modifiers which may be expressed in contracted form? Are there any other tense forms that can be contracted as modifiers?

    a. The boy who sits in the corner is my son.
    b. The boy who is sitting in the corner is my son.
    c. The boy who is seated in the corner is my son.
    d. The boy who sat in the corner is my son.
    e. The boy who will sit in the corner is my son.
    f. The boy who has been seated in the corner is my son.
    g. The boy who is being seated in the corner is my son.
    h. The boy who will be sitting in the corner is my son.
    i. The boy who will be seated in the corner is my son.

6. Make a list of the types of ideas or concepts that can be expressed by single-word modifiers of the verb (include infinitives). Provide an example of each used in a sentence.

7. Make a list of the ideas that can be expressed by prepositional phrase modifiers of the verb. Provide an example of each used in a sentence. Can all the ideas that may be expressed by single-word modifiers also be expressed by phrasal modifiers? Are there any ideas expressed by phrasal modifiers that cannot be expressed by single-word modifiers?

8. Make a list of the concepts that may be expressed by clausal modifiers of the verb. Give an example of each used in a sentence. Can all of the ideas or concepts expressed by single-word or

phrasal modifiers also be expressed by clausal modifiers? Are there any ideas or concepts expressed by clausal modifiers that cannot be expressed by the other types?

9. In certain situations we feel that the modifier is modifying the entire main clause rather than the verb. What kinds of ideas or concepts are presented by such modifiers? What form or forms (word, phrase, clause) can they take? Do they have any fixed position or positions in the sentence?

Suggested Readings

SECTION 20

See the readings suggested for Section 9.

SECTION 21

Semantic Substitution

Many of us, when we think of substitutions in English, think only of structural substitutions such as the passive voice for the active voice, the use of a noun phrase or noun clause in place of a simple noun, or the synonymic type of substitution at the part-of-speech level. Actually, we make use of substitutions at all levels. At the phone level, we noted the possibility of substituting one phone for another at any point at which free variation occurred—for example, the vowel /i/ for the vowel /ə/ in the forms /wantid/ /wantəd/. We also have substitutions at the morph level—for example, the bound morph /ənt/ for the free morph /nat/. Our concern here, however, will be with structural substitutions which provide either semantic identity or close semantic similarity (in other words, different manners of expressing the same idea). We need to study these because English sentence structure and style appear to be built upon them. The discussions and examples will by no means cover all of the possible substitutions that could be made, nor even all of the possible types of substitutions; they are designed only to provide a procedure which may be used in making further observations.

Our approach will be in terms of structural forms. We will look first at (1) some words which are commonly substituted for others; (2) words which may be substituted for phrases, or phrases used in place of single words; (3) the substitution of words for clauses or clauses for words; (4) phrases which may be substituted for other phrases; (5) phrases which may be substituted for clauses or clauses which may be substituted for phrases; and (6) clauses and sentences which may be substituted for other clauses and sentences. Many of these have already been noted in the earlier discussion, so there will necessarily be some repetition.

Among the most commonly used substitutions of one word for another is that of the pronoun used to replace a noun. The general principle of all semantic substitutions—that the referent must be unmistakably clear—is easily observed here. The English personal pronouns of the third person are substitutable for eleven different classes of noun referents. Their corresponding genitive adjectives or noun determiners are also used to identify the same classes.

1. Nouns for which no plural form exists. For these we can use only the *it* forms (*it/its*). (The *traffic* was heavy. *It* delayed us.)

2. Nouns for which no singular form exists. Here we can use only the *they* forms (*they/their/them*). (His *trousers* were dirty, so he sent *them* to the cleaners.)

3. Nouns representing male human beings only. For these we can use the *he* forms for the singular and the *they* forms in the plural.† (*Father* was so angry that *he* struck me. Our *fathers* were glad when *they* found us.)

4. Nouns representing female human beings only. We can use the *she* and the *they* forms.† (*Mother* smiled when *she* saw me. Mothers are nearly always proud of *their* children.)

5. Nouns which represent things. For these we make use of the *it* forms and the *they* forms. (The *box* was large, but *it* was light. The *boxes* were heavy, but the man could lift *them*.)

6. Nouns representing nonhuman female beings, nations or other political structures, boats or machinery, and certain celestial bodies (for example, the moon). For these we make use of either the *she* or the *it* forms for the singular and the *they* forms for the plural. (The *moon* sheds *her/its* light on the just and the unjust. The *cow* is fresh; *she/it* gives a lot of milk. *France* expects *its/her* soldiers to do their duty. The *Rotterdam* was not due until this morning, but *she/it* docked last night. My *Rambler* is old, but *it/she* still runs well. The *mares* were frightened; *they* galloped madly about the pasture.)

7. Nouns representing nonhuman male beings or certain celestial bodies (for example, the sun). Here we use either the *he* forms

† See also classes 8, 10, and 11.

or the *it* forms for the singular and the *they* forms for the plural. (The *sun* follows *its/his* course across the sky. The boar is lazy; *it/he* sleeps all day. *Boars* are lazy; *they* sleep a lot.)

8. Nouns representing either male or female human beings. For these we use the *he* or the *she* forms for the singular and the *they* forms for the plural. Because these nouns do not designate the sex of the individual being referred to, the substitute furnishes a type of information that the noun itself cannot furnish. This group is made up of non-sex-designating nouns such as *parent,* and includes all the professions. When a profession is commonly associated with one sex, we feel the necessity for modification if the opposite sex is indicated (male nurse, woman taxi driver). If such modification is not provided, we sometimes doubt the validity of the pronoun signal, and hence feel the sentence to be ambiguous. (The [woman] *doctor* was angry with the [male] *nurse; she* told *him* he didn't know *his* business. The *patient* sighed as *he/she* took the medicine. The doctor's *patients* recovered or *they* died.)

9. Nouns representing groups which may be considered either as a unit or as individuals. We may substitute either *it* or *they* forms for the singular and *they* forms for the plural. In addition to the normal words of this group, such as *audience, congress, team,* and so forth, we have some *-s* form nouns which are used either as singulars or as plurals in some dialects. The British generally consider these collectives as plural, and use the *they* forms (The *government* are determined that *they* will achieve *their* goal); in most American dialects these collectives are felt to be singular (The *government* is determined that *it* will achieve *its* goal). When we have the *-s* forms, our usage is frequently based upon our feelings of multiplicity or unity. (The *woods* are beautiful as *they* change color in the fall. The vinegar *works* is down near the river; *it* is in a large gray building.) Some people would consider the preceding example substandard. (The class rose to *its/their* feet. The *classes* rose to *their* feet.)

10. Certain compound words, generally listed as pronouns, but which form their genitives by using the noun inflection. The first element of such words represents a plural concept and the second represents a concept of unity. These words represent more than one being, but the second element is never pluralized. With this class we sometimes use the *he* forms, sometimes the *she* forms, sometimes both the *he* and the *she* forms, and sometimes the *they* forms. (*Everyone* has to hold *his/her/his or her* own ticket. *Everybody* was there; *they* all had *their* tickets in *their* hands.) Our usage of the *she* forms for these words is confined to those situations in which all members of the group are feminine. For mixed groups, we use either the *he* forms or the *he or she* or the *they* forms.

11. Certain compound words, again generally listed as pronouns, and certain nouns representing animate beings whose sex is either not easily discernible or not immediately determined. The nouns representing insects, most reptiles, and many animals fall into this class. For these words we use the *it* forms, the *he* forms, or the *she* forms for the singular, and the *they* forms for the plural. (*Someone* was lost; *it/she* was a little girl. The *baby* is wet; *it/he/she* is uncomfortable. The *turtle* lays *its/her* eggs in the sand. When *babies* are wet, *they* are uncomfortable.)

In addition to these distinctions, we observe a different type of distinction among the relative pronouns. Careful usage dictates that we use *who/whose/whom* and *that* in referring to people, and the *which/whose* and *that* forms in referring to nonhuman beings and to inanimate things. In less precise usage, the *who* forms are frequently used to refer to animals. Some examples of these usages are:

The *man who* was here is back again.
The *men who* were here are back again.
The *man that* I saw is gone.
The *door which* was locked was broken.
The *cat who* is frightened is dangerous.

All of these distinctions provide signals which are of great importance to us in the use of our language. A careful use of these substitute words and of their referents is essential if we wish to speak or write clearly. Whenever we make use of a substitute word that may have two or more referents, we produce a sentence with ambiguous meanings. (The *teacher* told the *girl she* could go.)

In addition to the pronouns, nouns of reference frequently appear as substitutes for other nouns. The term *noun of reference* is rather a broad one; it must include any word functioning as a noun in a sentence and having as a referent some other word or word-group unit in that sentence or in some nearby sentence. Normally the referent will precede the noun of reference, though in some cases the nature of the noun of reference is such that it will dictate that the referent or referents must follow it. Some of these nouns of reference, such as the *former,* the *latter,* the *first,* the *second,* the *last,* the *following,* are merely position indicators; others are full nouns representing a concept somewhat broader than the concept expressed by the unit for which they are substituting. (As a *prize*, John was offered either a *clock* or a *radio;* he chose the *latter.* Grace inherited her father's *home;* this *property* is in Lansing. As a result of the fire, the labels were washed off the *canned goods*, and the *frozen fruits* were defrosted. Some of this *stock* was sold at greatly reduced prices, and the *rest* destroyed.) It may be well to note here a second principle of reference: the reference word must express a broader or more general concept than its referent; the referent itself supplies the narrower or more exact meaning that the substitute word is to express in this particular context.

The synonym is not a word of reference in this sense. Most English words may be used to express more than one meaning. When we find two words that happen to have one of their meanings in common, we have a synonymous pair, and we have the alternative of using either to express that particular meaning. The other member of the pair need not be present in the passage. Thus we can speak of a *creed* or of a *belief;* we can describe a situation as being *sanguine* or as being *hopeful;* we can likewise speak of a battle as being *sanguine* or as being *bloody,* but we cannot use *bloody* as a synonym for *hopeful.*

We have a similar type of alternative which allows us to choose a gerund or an infinitive for a noun subject of the verb, for the noun object of the verb (in some instances), and, in a few instances, for the noun object of a preposition. (*Dancing* was his ambition. *To dance* was his ambition. He hated *going.* He hated *to go.* We had the choice of *eating* or *swimming.* We had the choice of *to eat* or *to swim.*)

The auxiliary frequently serves as a *verb of reference.* When it is the type of auxiliary that requires the sign of the infinitive, the *to* is included as a part of the verb of reference. (He asked if I *could go,* and I told him I thought I *could.* They want to know if we will *come.* I think we *ought to.* They want us *to visit them.* Do we *have to?* I said I would *go* and I *shall.*)

Certain adverbs are so general in nature that, if they are to be clear, they must have some referent either in the context of the sentence or in the context of the situation. (He went *home. There* he knew he would be welcomed. We bought this turkey *Thanksgiving.* It was not expensive *then.*)

Words of reference need not be of the same form-class or part of speech as their referents. Modifiers are frequently used as substitutes for their head words. (The *poor* are always with us.) We may also have a shifting within the types of modifiers that are used. (She sings *well*, doesn't she? Yes, she is very *good*.)

Most modifiers used as words of reference will have a word-group rather than a single word as referent. The prepositional phrase is a most common type of referent. (He was *in Chicago in 1951*. Why was he *there then?*) Structures of complementation, such as the verb and its complement or complements, may serve as the referent for the auxiliary. (Who *pumped all that water? I did.*) So and *not* often have clauses as referents. (*Did they collect the garbage this morning?* I think *so/*I believe *not.*) When participles or infinitives appear as substitutes for modifying phrases or clauses, the information provided by the tense or mood forms of the verb used in the phrase or clause is generally lost. (The man [whom] *you/he/she should see/ought to see/will have to see/* [and so forth] is Mr. Jones. The man *to see* is Mr. Jones. The man who *was/is/will be/* [and so forth] *dining* was my boss. The man *dining* was my boss. The boy who *has been/was/is/is being/is to be/will be/* [and so forth] *chosen* will receive a scholarship. The boy *chosen* will receive a scholarship.)

We often substitute phrases for other phrases simply because we do not want to repeat the same words. Here again, the referent phrase will supply a more exact meaning than does the phrase of reference which is substituted for it. (He went to Chicago *in 1951. At that time/in that year*, he worked for Household Finance Corporation.) Sometimes, however, we simply choose between phrases which represent different degrees of specificity. (He worked for them *for some time*. He worked for them *during May and June*.) Frequently we employ both types of phrases, one providing rather general information and the other more specific information. (He worked for them *for a while during May and June of 1951*.)

When phrases are used as substitutes for clauses, we often find the same type of mood-tense loss that we find when words are substituted for clauses. The phrase may have the clause as a referent, or we may simply choose the alternative of using the less specific phrase instead of the more specific clause. Occasionally one may be about as specific as the other, and in such cases we merely choose between alternative structures. (During the summer *he worked in a gas station. By doing this,* he earned enough to go to the university. He worked for them *when he was a student.* He worked for them *as a student.* Before *he was elected,* he promised many things. Before *his election,* he promised many things.)

The clause generally contains within itself all of the elements needed for the complete expression of thought; therefore we seldom find clauses which have other clauses as referents, though we commonly find clauses or sentences which have words or phrases within them which are clarified by referents in nearby clauses or sentences. We do, of course, have many clauses or sentences which may serve as alternative methods of stating the same idea. We shall deal with alternative structures more specifically in the next section. Now let us look at a piece of unified prose to see how referents and words or phrases of reference are used to provide coherence and movement of thought. We will use the *Gettysburg Address,* which was delivered by President Lincoln at the National Cemetery on November 19, 1863. Words or phrases having a referent in the situation are printed in capital letters; those having a referent in the context itself are italicized. Those which have referents in both situation and context are underscored. Try to locate the referent for each word or unit so indicated.

Fourscore and seven years AGO OUR FATHERS brought forth on THIS CONTINENT a new NATION, conceived in liberty, and dedicated to the proposition *that all men are created equal.* NOW WE are engaged in a great civil war, testing whether *that nation,* or any nation *so* conceived and *so* dedicated, can long endure. WE are met on a great BATTLEFIELD of *that war.* WE have come to dedicate *a portion of that field,* as a final *resting place* for those *who* here gave *their* lives that *that nation* might live. *It* is altogether fitting and proper that WE should *do this.* But, in a larger sense, WE cannot dedicate—WE cannot consecrate—WE cannot hallow—this ground. The brave men, living and dead, *who* struggled here, have consecrated it, far above OUR poor power to add or detract. The world will little note, nor long remember, that WE say here, but *it* can never forget *what they did* here. *It* is for US the *living,* rather, to be here dedicated to the unfinished *work which they who* fought here have THUS FAR so nobly advanced. *It* is rather for US to be here dedicated to the great *task* remaining before US—that from *these* honored *dead* WE take increased devotion to *that cause* for *which they* gave *the last full measure of devotion*—that WE here resolve that *these dead* shall not have died in vain—that *this nation,* under God, shall have a new *birth* of freedom—and that government of the people, by the people, for the people, shall not perish from the earth.

The large number of referents found in such a short passage gives some indication of the importance of referents to our language. In addition to those that are noted, we also have some allusive referents. The clause "that all men are created equal" might carry no overtones to an Oriental who happened to read Lincoln's speech, but any American should certainly recognize the allusion to our *Declaration of Independence.* We find a similar allusive reference in Lincoln's "government of the people, by the people, for the people" to the statement in the *Declaration of Independence* that "governments derive their just powers from the consent of the governed"; this impression is reinforced by the opening statement of our Constitution: "We the people . . . do ordain and establish this Constitution for the United States of America."

Lincoln makes use of repetition to gain his effects. Note how often some form of the word *dedicate* appears. He also makes use of contrast in such forms as "little note nor long remember . . . never forget . . . ," but his principal contrast is through his use of active and passive voice to change the thinking of his audience from the initial notion of "dedicating the cemetery" to his central theme of "dedicating themselves" to the cause. He helps assure the unity of his speech by beginning and ending it with allusions to the beginning of life: "Our fathers *brought forth* . . . a new nation. . . ." ". . . This nation . . . shall have a new *birth* of freedom. . . ."

Exercise 21-1   Substitutions

1. The examples below are arranged in pairs. The second example of each pair contains a substitution for something in the first example. Identify the substitute and the unit for which it is substituted.

a. /mauntən/	/mauntin/
b. /ai kud hæv gɔn/	/ai kud əv gɔn/
c. He does not know Mrs. Jones.	He doesn't know her.
d. That style is prettier.	That style is more pretty.
e. Do you want to go?	Yes, I do.
f. Will he be here?	I think so.

2. What type of grammatical information (degree, gender, mood, number, person, tense) is provided by the italicized word in each of the following sentences? Is this the only word in the sentence that signals some or all of this particular information?

    a. *She* died last week.
    b. *He* does study a lot.
    c. I should go if I *were* you.
    d. *It's* a cute baby.
    e. The teacher was glad *she* had talked to the boy's mother.
    f. *Who* are they?

3. What word or what construction provides a referent for the italicized word in each of the given sentences? Does the italicized word serve as a substitute in all of them? Does it in any of them?

    a. John received an A in English, *which* pleased his mother.
    b. The man had acquired first editions of all of Swift's works. This *collection* was willed to the library.
    c. One of his *oddities* was to drink brandy before breakfast.
    d. He worked because he wanted *to*.
    e. Have you ever met him? I think *not*.

4. For what grammatical element in the first sentence of each pair provided below can the italicized element or elements in the second sentence substitute? What is accomplished by using the substitute in each example?

    a. He was convinced in advance that the man was crazy. *This* interfered with his judgment of that *individual*.
    b. He worked there for many years. He worked *in the Sonora radio factory* for *seven* years.
    c. His work took him to Managua for a year. At first, he did not like it *there*.
    d. She was given the choice of apologizing or leaving. She chose the *former*.
    e. There are four reasons for this. The *last* is the most important, but the *others* should not be overlooked.

5. Find as many words or phrases of reference as you can in the short passage quoted below, and identify the referent for each of them.

An abbey in Brittany became vacant; at a hint from Duke Conan, which may well be supposed to have been suggested from Paris, the monks chose Abélard as their new abbot, and sent some of their number to Suger to request permission for Abélard, who was a monk of Sant-Denis, to become Abbot of Saint-Gildas-de-Rhuys, near

Vannes, in Brittany. Suger probably intimated to Abélard, with a certain degree of authority, that he had better accept. Abélard, 'struck with terror, and as it were under the menace of a thunderbolt,' accepted. Of course the dignity was in effect banishment and worse, and was so understood on all sides.

—Henry Adams, *Mont St. Michel and Chartres*, XIV[1]

Suggested Readings

SECTION 21

Lee, Irving J., *Language Habits in Human Affairs*, Chap. III. New York: Harper & Row, Publishers, 1941.

Philbrick, F. A., *Understanding English: An Introduction to Semantics*, Chap. XII. New York: The Macmillan Company, 1944.

[1] Henry Adams, *Mont St. Michel and Chartres* (Boston: Houghton Mifflin Company, 1913), p. 343.

Syntactic Substitution

In our consideration of the basic patterns for English sentences, we set up what amounted to formula patterns for sentences—such things as *Subject + Verb + Object, Subject + Verb + Predicate Noun,* and so forth. A careful re-evaluation of such patterns will show that when one of them is used, we will recognize the word sequence as an English sentence even though it expresses sheer nonsense—for example, "The ig will oodle the att." But such a re-evaluation will also show that while these patterns may serve as blueprints for English sentences, we cannot use actual words haphazardly in making our sentences according to these patterns. Thus the word group "The stone ate the goldfish" satisfies our pattern condition of *Subject + Verb + Object,* but we would deny its validity as a statement because it contradicts our experience. Yet despite the fact that the idea expressed is invalid, we would still recognize it as being an English sentence, whereas "Ate goldfish stone the the" would not be so recognized because it conforms to no pattern which is normal to English. In like manner, "The fish is tall" would constitute an English sentence of the *Subject + Link + Predicate Adjective* type, but *tall* is not a qualifier which we would apply to *fish.* We could, however, have many sentences based on this pattern which would make use of either *fish* or *tall.* (The tree is tall. The boy is tall. The fish is thin. The fish is flat, and so forth.)

A complete analysis of English would set up numerous sub-groups for each word-class and describe exactly the condition or conditions under which each would be used. For example, the verbs *eat* and *drink* normally require subjects that are symbols for animate beings—a very small proportion of the total noun-class—and these verbs are likewise limited in the type of objects that they can take. *Eat* will normally take as an object only those nouns that represent solid foods, and *drink* will take as an object only those nouns that represent liquids.

Though considerations of this sort severely limit the type of conclusions we may draw, we can still begin our study of syntactic substitutions with some of these basic structures. Our problem is simple: Given any particular basic sentence structure, what other structure or structures may be substituted for it to express the same idea? In other words, do we have more than one way of expressing any idea in English and, if so, what structures can we use?

Let us begin with the simplest type of sentence—*Subject + Verb*. Certain of these sentences begin with a genitive adjective type of noun determiner, followed by a noun naming some part of the body, which in turn is followed by a verb expressing a state or condition. A common example is "My head aches." There are a number of changes that can be made in structure without basically changing the idea expressed by such a sentence.

> My head aches.
> My head is aching.
> I have an aching head.
> I have a headache.
> I am suffering from a headache.

The first of these changes, from the simple present to the present progressive tense form, can occur with any *Noun + Verb* sentence. (Harry runs. Harry is running. The stone falls. The stone is falling.) Past tense forms or future tense indicators may also be substituted with equal freedom. (My head ached. My head was aching. My head will ache. My head is going to ache. My head is going to be aching.)

The number of sentences which can undergo the second type of change is much more limited. Only those *Noun + Verb* sentences which begin with a genitive determiner can be changed in this manner, for a required part of the change is that what was formerly the genitive adjective now becomes the substantive subject. (*John's* head aches. *John* has an aching head. *My* head aches. *I* have an aching head.) In addition, the original subject has retained its noun form, but it is now functioning as the object of the middle transitive verb *have,* which has been added, and it has a classifying type of determiner rather than the genitive type of the original sentence. The form of the verb, which became a modifier in our first change, remains the same, but its position as modifier has been shifted. In the first shift it might have been quite legitimate to describe *aching* as a verb, but now that it has been placed in the attributive position its function has become clearly adjectival. It can also be intensified in this position.

In the third change (I have a headache), we have the same type of subject shift and the addition of the same transitive verb, but here the original noun subject and its verb have become a compound noun object. This change, in contrast to the previous one, admits the pluralization of the noun object. (I have headaches.)

It should be noted that the original verb, *ache,* is descriptive of a state or condition. The fourth change also requires a verb of this type, which can then be modified by a prepositional phrase in which the object is a noun compounded from the original subject and verb. Concomitant with each syntactic shift we find morphological shifts. Thus *ache* appears in one sentence or another in each of its morphological variations—*ache, aches, ached, aching* —and it may function in the sentence as any one of the four major word-classes—noun, verb, adjective, or adverb.

With the *Subject + Link + Predicate Noun* type of sentence, we have two variants: the identifying type of predicate noun indicated by the *the/my* type of determiner and the classifying type of predicate noun indicated by the *a* type of determiner. The types of changes that may occur in these differ when the clause is used as a sentence in itself and when it is used as a noun clause object. As a full sentence, the identifying type is frequently changed by the simple expedient of transposing subject and predicate noun. (John is the culprit. The culprit is John.) As a noun clause, however, it may undergo other changes.

I thought John was the culprit.
I thought John to be the culprit.
I took John to be the culprit.
I took John for the culprit.

Because the noun lacks case forms, the complete changes in the above sentences are not as clearly indicated as they would be if we used a pronoun as subject of the clause.

I thought he was the culprit.
I thought him to be the culprit.
I thought him the culprit.
I took him to be the culprit.
I took him as/for the culprit.

In this group of sentences the linking nature of the infinitive *to be* is still clear. We can shift the position of the subject and the noun following it just as we could when a finite form of *to be* was used. (I thought him to be the culprit. I thought the culprit to be him.) The same type of transposition is possible when the infinitive is omitted. (I thought him the culprit. I thought the culprit him.) This transposition can even occur when the prepositional phrase is used. (I took him as/for the culprit. I took the culprit for him.) Either *him* or *culprit* may provide a subject for the passive voice construction, and the verb *to be* may appear between the main passive verb and the retained object of that construction. (He was thought [*to be*] the culprit. The culprit was thought [*to be*] him.)

Additional variants of this sentence can be developed by using the noun clause as subject, as object of transitive verbs which take the -*ing* form rather than the infinitive, or as object of the preposition.

That John was the culprit is now established.
I recall that John was the culprit.
I hate to think that John was the culprit.

Each of these sentences may be changed to forms in which we use the genitive form of the subject noun and the -*ing* form of the verb.

John's being the culprit is now established.
I recall John's being the culprit.
I hate to think of John's being the culprit.

In addition, under certain circumstances, we may find the uninflected form of the noun or the objective form of the pronoun standing before the -*ing* form.

> I recall John being the culprit.
> I hate to think of him being the culprit.

The linking nature of the copula is still clear, for the position of the two nouns may be transposed. (I hate to think of John being the culprit/the culprit being John.) It should be noted that even such a simple transposition is not ordinarily made when one of the nouns is in the genitive. A transposition can be made, but the noun or pronoun preceding the verb will take the genitive form and the pronoun following the verb will take the objective form. (I recall *his* being the culprit. I recall the *culprit's* being *him*.)

In some situations similar ideas may be expressed by using either the linking verb structure or a passive voice structure. A change in the selection of the verb is essential, because links do not have the quality of voice.

> She became a widow.　　She was left a widow.
> Jones became Mayor.　　Jones was elected Mayor.

Two things should be noted about such sentences. (1) We do not feel the same freedom to transpose the linking verb sentences even when the predicate noun is of the identifying type. "*The widow became she" and "*The Mayor became Jones" are certainly structures we would avoid using. (2) When these ideas are expressed by a passive voice construction, the words that were predicate nouns in the link construction become retained objective complements rather than retained objects. In other words, they cannot serve as possible subjects for the passive voice verb.

The *Subject* + *Verb* + *Object* structure lends itself to a number of different types of changes. Most sentences based on this structure can be put into the passive voice; however, as we have already seen, certain middle verbs are transitive but have no passive form, and others have a passive form only in certain restricted senses. The verb *have*, for example, normally has no passive form. ("The pencil was owned by the boy," but *not* *"The pencil was had by the boy.") Modern American idiomatic usage has, however, developed the passive *to be had* in the restricted sense of *to be defeated* or *to have something disagreeable happen* to the speaker or subject. In general, this passive suggests that an irrevocable action has occurred.

With the normal transitive verb the passive merely provides an alternative means of expressing an idea. Because the passive does not require that the actor be named, the use of this structure may result in an obscure sentence. For this and other reasons, many handbooks decry the use of the passive. It should be pointed out, however, that one can achieve equal obscurity with certain active voice structures. A structure such as "It is said that . . ." is no more vague than the active voice "They say that. . . ." Studies of the writing of recognized stylists show that they make use of the passive voice in about 15 per cent of their transitive verb structures.

With many transitive verbs we may develop a third structure by making use of *have*. This structure is in the active voice, but we retain the passive participle and may also retain the passive agent. Thus we can say:

> The doctor examined my eyes.
> My eyes were examined by the doctor.
> I had my eyes examined by the doctor.

In terms of meaning, this third form adds a slight element of causation. We can see this more clearly in a different example.

> I had him arrested.
> I caused him to be arrested.

Many transitive verbs may serve as nouns without having any derivational suffix added to them. A considerable number of this group may serve as the direct object of verbs which normally take two objects.

> He shoved me.
> He gave me a shove.
> He punched me in the stomach.
> He gave me a punch in the stomach.

It should be noted that the direct object of the original sentence becomes the indirect object of the revised sentence.

In a few pairs of sentences, we find a situation in which the object of the verb in one sentence may serve as the subject of the verb in the other without changing either the voice of the verb or the meaning of the sentence. The verb in such sentences expresses a reciprocal action.

John met Mary.   Mary met John.
John was met by Mary.   Mary was met by John.

Similar to this is the situation in which the verbs used tend to be antonymic. Fries' classic examples of these show that the passive voice of one verb expresses a meaning equivalent to that expressed by the active voice of the other.[1]

The water wet the sponge.   The water was absorbed by the
                                   sponge.
The sponge absorbed the water.   The sponge was wet by the water.

The *Subject + Link + Predicate Adjective* type of construction may be expressed in phrase form by placing the adjective in attributive position and dropping the link. (The boy was happy. The happy boy.) When a clause of this type is used as the main clause of a sentence containing a subordinate clause, we not infrequently invert the main clause, particularly if we wish to emphasize the adjective.

Happy is the man who is solvent.
Many are the hearts that are weary tonight.
Gone are the days when my heart was young and gay.

When the word following the link is the past participle of a transitive verb, we always have the possibility of the structure being a passive voice; hence it may appear in the active voice structure as well. (The boy was tired [by the exercise]. The exercise tired the boy.)

The mobility of the adverb makes possible a wide range of sentence variants. In a three-unit sentence (*Subject + Verb + Adverb*) any type of adverb may appear in final position. (Remember that we have already excluded intensifiers from the adverb class.)

[1] Charles C. Fries, *American English Grammar* (New York: Appleton-Century-Crofts, Inc., 1940), p. 190.

For some types of adverbs this is the only position; for others it is strongly normative; for some it is but one of a number of alternative positions. Most flat adverbs (John worked *hard*/ drove *slow*) appear only in this position in the three-unit sentence, but they may be followed by other adverbial modifiers or preceded by objects. (John worked *hard at the office.* John hit *the ball hard.*)

Spatially locative adverbs provide us with information about location, direction, or distance. All three of these may be expressed by the noun functioning adverbially. In some situations the noun is unaccompanied (She went *home.* They drove *north.* We walked *miles*); in others it may be the head word in a prepositional phrase, and/or may be accompanied by a determiner. (She went *to church.* We walked *two miles.* They drove *to the West.*) For the main part these are found only in final position, though we may put some of them in initial position in the sentence when we wish to emphasize them strongly. The unaccompanied noun *home* is commonly found before a noun object as well as after it. (He took *home* a book. He took a book *home.*) Derived adverbs such as *backwards* or *crosswise,* but not those with the *-ly* suffix, have almost the same limited mobility we find in the adverbial noun.

Words which are normally classified as basic adverbs, such as *away,* may be used finally or initially with the three-element sentence. In a four-element sentence with a pronoun object, they are confined to the final position; they may either precede or follow a noun object. (They strolled *away.* *Away* went the train. *Away* he went. We put *it away.* We put *the book away.* We put *away the book.*)

Most directional words which are used sometimes as prepositions and sometimes as adverbs follow much the same patterns, but, as we have already noted in our discussion of the verb, many of these are actually a part of the verb unit. Even when this is true, mobility is possible for some of them. Those that are mobile may appear either before or after noun objects, but only *after* pronoun objects. None of those that are a part of the verb may appear as the initial word of a sentence; but when these are used as prepositions, they may introduce prepositional phrases which begin the sentence. (*Look after* the baby. *Turn* your books *in.* *Turn* them *in.* *Turn in* your books. We *turned in* at nine o'clock last night. *In the bed,* we *turned* and tossed.)

Temporal adverbs provide us with information about location in time, direction and relative location in time, or duration of time. Exact location and duration may be expressed by nouns (*Wednesday*, an *hour*). Adverbs expressing such concepts are generally reference words (*then, now*), and hence depend upon their referent in the sentence or in the situation to provide exactness of meaning. Direction and relative location in time are most frequently expressed by prepositional phrases (*before ten o'clock*), though they may be expressed by adverbs (*before, after*). Again, the noun may appear unaccompanied or in prepositional phrase form to indicate location in time. (He worked *today*. He worked *on Tuesday*.) Duration is normally expressed by the prepositional phrase or by the noun with a numerical determiner. (He worked *for hours*. He worked *two hours*.)

The temporal noun used as an adverb normally appears last in the sentence. It may, however, appear in initial position in the sentence, set off by a comma in writing and by a significant juncture and terminal pitch pattern in speech. (*Saturday*, we will begin our vacation.) Time directional adverbs follow the same patterns. In general, durational adverbs appear initially only in prepositional phrase form or in clausal form, but occasionally we place a single-word durational adverb at the beginning of a sentence to give it additional emphasis. (*Long* may it wave.)

The infinitive (or a prepositional phrase including either an infinitive or a noun clause) is commonly used to express purpose. These structures may be used in either initial or final position. (He had to work *to win*. *To win*, he had to work. He took the job *in order to eat*. *In order that he might eat*, he took the job.) The infinitive may, of course, be complemented. (He worked *to win the* prize.)

Basic adverbs expressing frequency and most derived adverbs in *-ly* expressing frequency or manner have greater mobility. They are commonly found in initial and final positions, in the position between the subject and the verb, in the position after the first auxiliary, and occasionally between the sign of the infinitive and the infinitive itself. (He approached the bridge *slowly*. *Slowly*, he approached the bridge. He *slowly* approached the bridge. He will *often* tell the story. We used to *often skate*.) Participles are sometimes used in a semiadjectival semiadverbial manner. Their normal position in such usage is final, but now and then we find them in initial position. (He finished the race *crawling*. The boy began the job *exhausted*. *Crawling*, the boy finished the race.)

When we were working with modification we learned that many so-called adverbial concepts could be expressed by modifiers of the noun. We can also observe that many words, phrases, and clauses may modify either a verb or a noun without undergoing any change in their forms. (He came *here*. The boy *here* is my brother. They left *Wednesday*. The *Wednesday* concert was exceptionally good. They live *on the corner*. The house *on the corner* is theirs. He goes *where there are jobs*. Towns *where there are jobs* attract workers.) We should expect, therefore, in many instances to find that the same idea may be expressed through modification of the noun or through modification of the verb. In other words, these units may shift their functions. We also find function shifts accompanying structural changes in the synonymous expression of an idea, and most of these function shifts involve structural changes in the words whose function is being shifted—that is, we find it necessary to add or remove derivational suffixes.

In his *Philosophy of Grammar*[2] Jespersen provides ten examples of such changes which will serve well to illustrate our point. In each case, we will work from an original sentence "He moved astonishingly rapidly." The following symbols will be used to indicate structure:

A = adjective	O
$\overset{A}{(\quad\quad)}$ = adjective unit	$\overset{O}{(\quad\quad)}$ = object unit
Av = Adverb	P = preposition
$\overset{Av}{(\quad\quad)}$ = adverb unit	S = subject
C = conjunction	$\overset{S}{(\quad\quad)}$ = subject unit
D = determiner	V = verb
O = object	V/N = verbal noun

Where we have need for other terms, such as *Link*, they will be given in full. The ten sentences that Jespersen provides do not encompass all the possible changes which could be made in these

[2] Otto Jespersen, *The Philosophy of Grammar* (London: George Allen & Unwin, Ltd., 1924), p. 91.

synonymous expressions, but they will provide enough examples to serve our purpose. It may be well to state again that each change is described in relation to the original sentence: "He moved astonishingly rapidly."

1. He moved astonishingly fast.
   Change: substitution of synonym.
2. He moved with astonishing rapidity.
   Changes: Av *rapidly* becomes O of P
            Av *astonishingly* becomes A
         Structure: S V Av, Av becomes
                         Av
             S V (P A O)

Before going on, it may be worth while to reinterpret the symbols we have used to indicate these two simple changes. In change 1 the adverb *fast* was substituted for the adverb *rapidly*. The change therefore involved the substitution of one synonym for another, but no structural change. In change 2 the adverb *rapidly* is changed to the noun *rapidity*, which then serves as the object of the preposition *with;* also, the adverb *astonishingly* is changed to the adjective form *astonishing* and is used to modify the noun *rapidity;* the structural result of these changes is that what was originally two adverbs—one modifying the other—has now become a prepositional phrase which is used adverbially.

3. His movements were astonishingly rapid.
   Changes: V becomes S (move—movements)
            S becomes D (He—his)
            Av becomes A (rapidly—rapid)
            Link added
         Structure: S V Av Av becomes
                D S Link Av A
4. His rapid movements astonished us.
   Changes: V becomes S
            Av becomes A
            Av becomes V
            O added
         Structure: S V Av Av becomes
               D A S V O
5. His movements astonished us by their rapidity.
   Changes: V becomes S
            S becomes D
            Av becomes V

Av becomes O of P
O, D, and P added
Structure: S   V   Av   Av   becomes
                                        Av
            D   S   V   O   (P̄ D̄ Ō)

6. The rapidity of his movements was astonishing.
   Changes: V becomes O of P
              Av becomes A
              S becomes D
              Link and P added
              Structure: S   V   Av   Av   becomes
                                                     A
                          D   S   (P̄ D̄ Ō)   Link   A

7. The rapidity with which he moved astonished us.
   Changes: Av becomes S
              Av becomes V
              Main clause becomes modifying clause
              D, P, O, and relative added
              Structure: S   V   Av   Av   becomes
                                                     A
                          D   S   (P̄ Ō S̄ V̄)   V   O

8. He astonished us by moving rapidly.
   Changes: Av becomes V
              V becomes O of P
              O and P added
              Structure: S   V   Av   Av   becomes
                                                     Av
                          S   V   O   (P̄ V/N̄ Āv)

9. He astonished us by his rapid movements.
   Changes: Av becomes V
              Av becomes A
              V becomes O of P
              P, O, and D added
              Structure: S   V   Av   Av   becomes
                                                     Av
                          S   V   O   (P̄ D̄ Ā Ō)

10. He astonished us by the rapidity of his movements.
    Changes: Av becomes V
               Av becomes O of P
               V becomes O of P
               O, two P's, and two D's added
               Structure: S   V   Av   Av   becomes

$$ S \quad V \quad O \left(\frac{\overline{Av}}{(\overline{P\ D\ O})} \quad \frac{\overline{A}}{(\overline{P\ D\ O})} \right) $$

It should not be necessary to make similar analyses of sentences more complex than those used here, for in actuality we have used all the elements that appear in English sentences—subjects, verbs, modifiers, objects, and function words such as the determiner, the preposition, and the conjunction. As a matter of fact, it is not at all important that we be able to make such detailed analyses of the changes that may take place in the form of a sentence. What *is* important is that we recognize that we have available to us such widely different means of expressing the same general idea. It is also important to realize that some of these would be more suitable than others in a particular situation, and that some of them provide nuances of meaning which are not present in others. Finally, we must also remember that although we may have a wide range of possible structures for the expression of an idea in English, that range is nonetheless limited, and the choice of any structure outside the limits will result in an unclear expression of the idea. When we consciously choose one form of expression rather than another, we have made a beginning toward using our language as a precision tool.

Exercise 22-1   Syntactic Substitutions

We have in earlier exercises already looked at the basic sentence patterns used in expressing statements, commands and requests, questions, and negations. We have also looked at patterns for compounding and modifying the various elements which make up the basic sentences. The time has now come to pull together the various bits of information we have gleaned, to look at some of the possible variations in patterns which may occur in English sentences, and to see which of these patterns can be used to express similar ideas.

1. Construct formulas for each of the sentences provided below. Are any of these compound sentences? Is it possible to have a compound subject for an imperative sentence? How is *John and Mary* used in the second sentence of group *a?* Do we have a compound subject in the fourth sentence of group *a?* Is the use of a singular form of the verb acceptable in such a sentence? What do you note about the types of verbs compounded in the sentences of group *c?* Could we mix the verb types for sentences similar to those

in group *d?* Are there any compounds in these sentences for which we could use one-word substitutions? Provide examples.

    a. John and Mary went to the store.
       John and Mary, stop that noise.
       Did John and Mary come?
       Neither John nor Mary was there.

    b. That bothered John and Mary.
       Give John and Mary some teaspoons.
       Did you see John and Mary?
       Did you see either John or Mary?

    c. John sat and visited for an hour.
       John met Mary and took her home.
       John stopped and tried on a suit.
       John was happy and told Mary so.

    d. John and Mary came and went.
       John and Mary were and are happy and good.
       John and Mary eat and drink native foods and beverages.

2. How do the sentences below differ from those provided for question 1? Why are these called compound sentences? What kinds of elements make up a compound sentence? Is it possible to have compound units within one of the simple units of a compound sentence? Is it possible to have modifying clauses within one of the simple units of a compound sentence? Can we substitute words, phrases, or subordinate clauses for any of the coordinate elements found in these sentences?

    a. John cooked and Mary sewed.
    b. Mary spanked the child and it cried.
    c. John and Mary read, but Helen and George watched television.
    d. John and Mary read, but Helen and George sat and talked.
    e. John and Mary read, but Helen and George sat and watched the neighbors and their children.

3. In what way is each of the clauses provided below like a sentence? In what way does it differ from a sentence? Which of these could be used as questions without change in word order? What changes would appear in the oral patterning if these were used as questions?

    a. That he would come.
    b. That he be here.
    c. Who was here.
    d. Which was broken.
    e. Whom we knew.

    f. Where he lives.
    g. When he arrived.
    h. While we were away.
    i. Why he came.
    j. How he did it.
    k. Because he needed it.
    l. Though you believe that.
   m. Whenever you wish.

4. What syntactic function does each clause of the types provided in question 3 serve in the following sentences? In which could the connecting word be omitted? Construct some generalizations to describe the situations in which we may omit the connecting word. In which of these could the clausal unit appear in a different position in the sentence? Would this also be true of a single word serving the same syntactic function as the clausal unit? Can the concepts expressed by any of these sentences be expressed in coordinate or compound sentence form?

    a. That he will come is certain.
    b. I know that he has been there.
    c. He can be whatever he wishes to be.
    d. Give it to whoever comes.
    e. Give whoever comes the message.
    f. You made me what I am today.
    g. That man, whoever he is, is responsible.
    h. Give him whatever he asks.
    i. It is certain that he will come.

5. How do the clausal units in the following sentences differ from those in the sentences for question 4? In which of these may the connecting word be omitted? Do the generalizations you developed for question 4 apply here also? What syntactic function does each clausal unit serve? In which of these sentences could the clausal unit appear in a different position? Could these or similar clausal units appear after nouns serving functions other than that of subject of the verb? Provide examples. Can any of these sentences be rewritten, either as compound sentences or as simple sentences containing compound elements?

    a. The boy who was here has gone.
    b. The bow which was broken was discarded.
    c. The girl whom he knows won the prize.
    d. The house where he lives is being repainted.
    e. The hour when he arrived was inauspicious.

  f. The reason that he gave was false.
  g. The years while we were away passed quickly.
  h. The reason why he came was never clear.

6. How do the clausal units in the sentences below differ from those that are provided for question 5? Are there any ideas expressed by modifying clauses that cannot be expressed by single-word or phrasal modifiers? Construct formulas for each type of complex sentence (those containing a main clause and a dependent or subordinate clause).

  a. I am happy that you could come.
  b. She was certain that they were married.
  c. It is sweet because it has so much sugar in it.
  d. I came as soon as I could.
  e. They left after we did.
  f. We moved before the war started.
  g. We live where the two routes meet.
  h. We swim whenever we can.
  i. He divided it as equally as he could.
  j. It appeared to fly higher than a kite normally flies.
  k. She was more dejected than she realized.
  l. The star disappeared more quickly than we had anticipated it would.
  m. If the shoe fits, put it on.
  n. Should anyone ask, we will go.
  o. Never has he been around when he was needed.

7. In what manner do the sentences below differ from the other sentences we have considered in this exercise? Is there any justification for applying the term *compound-complex* to them? Construct formulas for each type illustrated here. What other variants *might* there be? Provide examples.

  a. John read and Mary sewed while the dinner was cooking.
  b. John was helpful and Mary was kind to us when we visited them.
  c. The potatoes boiled dry while John read and Mary sewed.
  d. We had a wretched time, though John was helpful and Mary was kind to us.

8. In what manner or manners do the sentences provided below differ from those we have considered so far? Do any of the sentences from question 6 belong to this group? What name would you give to such constructions? Find as many variants within this type of construction as you can. Provide examples and construct formulas for each of them.

a. They asked John if he could come when the harvest was over.
b. The boy who was here when we arrived has left.
c. The girl who he knows won the prize denies winning it.

9. Is there any apparent difference between the type of sentences provided for question 8 and the following sentence? Compare their patterns.

They asked if John could come because they needed a fourth at bridge.

10. Does the group of words provided below represent one sentence or two? If one sentence, does it fit any of the patterns we have considered to date? What is the relationship between the position of the negative and the anticipated response to such a sentence? What response would you expect from this sentence? How would you change it if you hoped for a negative response?

You are going to the movies, aren't you?

Exercise 22-2

1. Under what circumstances do we find a single word standing as a sentence? In what way or ways do the single-word sentences of group *B* differ from those of group *A*? In what way or ways do those of group *C* differ from those of the other groups?

A. Go!	B. Ouch!	C. Certainly.
Look!	Hey!	Yes.
Run!	Hello.	No.
Stop.	Danger!	Hardly.

2. Is each of the following units from a telephone conversation a sentence? Is the meaning of each clear? Is the total meaning clear? Why not?

a. This is Mrs. Jones speaking.
b. Why, hello, Holly, how are you?
c. No, I hadn't heard that.
d. What is she going to do?
e. That's too bad.
f. Did he really say that?
g. I'll tell John when he comes home, but I don't know what he can do.
h. It was nice of you to call and tell me.

3. Are sequence sentences found only in conversations? Is the

meaning of the following sentence clear? If not, what is needed to clarify it?

"Some of them are purely traditional, formulated a century or two ago on theoretical grounds by teachers and writers who had no adequate knowledge of the history or phonetics of English; and they have been reverently copied and taught by later writers and teachers without a knowledge of either their ultimate origin or their validity."

4. The sentence that began the paragraph and immediately preceded the sentence quoted in question 3 reads as follows:

"Some of the rules are well founded, no doubt; but many of them are quite without foundation in the usage of past or present."

When we place these two sentences in their proper order, do they express the writer's thought clearly? What is added when this final clause from the preceding paragraph is provided?

". . . we accept rules of pronunciation as authoritative without inquiry into either the validity of the rules or the fitness of their authors to promulgate them." [3]

5. Read the following paragraphs carefully. The sentences are numbered within each paragraph for ease of reference.

THE FOUNDATIONS OF ARTISTIC COMMUNITY[4]

(1) When I was a child, there used to be hung above the dining room table in the Christmas season, as the festive token that its celebrations were in progress, an ingenious device which would nowadays be described as a mobile. (2) It was to me then, and shall always seem, the strangest and most curious of fabrics, made of thread, of a few tenuous wire rods, and of pieces of colored glass and ceramic angels, all delicately strung together in a sequence of suspensions, which floated the rods in space and produced, by deviations from the horizontal, a splendid series of apparent imbalances, angels soaring and sinking as rods rose and fell. (3) Collapsed in the box in which it was stored, it was an insensate tangle of debris. (4) Suspended aloft, lighted, touched, it was a little universe in miniature, which would move with an eerie majestical precariousness for an hour long before regaining its static equilibrium again. (5) Its motion had the intellectuality of music, a music of pure

[3] The quoted material is taken from John Samuel Kenyon, *American Pronunciation*, 6th ed., rev. (Ann Arbor, Mich.: George Wahr, Publisher, 1935), Introduction, p. 3.
[4] John F. A. Taylor, "The Foundations of Artistic Community," *The Review of Metaphysics*, XIII, 2 (December 1959), 235f.

silence, whose tones were shapes, whose melody was change, whose intricate harmony was enough to addict a childish heart, if it had known Pythagoras, to affirm devoutly the harmony of the spheres of heaven.

(1) The hanging of the mobile aloft was annually performed with a solemnity and care suited to so important a matter. (2) For each year, as it was resurrected from its storage place, it hung foolishly askew, demoralized by vicissitude, like a drunkard's hat crushed out of shape. (3) Not that it had not still an equilibrium, a static balance, which it would assume and, if disturbed, would assume again, as if to declare idiocy alone immortal. (4) It did not wait, in order to have an equilibrium, for an artful hand to give it one. (5) Such equilibrium as it had, from the accidental concert of its parts, it had with the indifferent equanimity of all things merely physical. (6) Beauty was its accident, as idiocy also was its accident. (7) It was as innocent of virtue as it was innocent of sin: it knew no propriety, therefore deserted none. (8) I admired in it only what I demanded of it, a virtue of which it knew nothing. (9) Yet, for my part, I permitted myself no such egotist reflection. (10) I regarded it all as the contrivance of the hand which adjusted it. (11) In my child's world, that was the secret of my mother's hand, which no other sought to compete with, much less to penetrate. (12) She knew, at least her hand knew, that of all the possible equilibria which were available equally for choice, there was one special equilibrium needed, only one which was alive, resonant, essential to the production of that effect to which it intricately ministered. (13) That equilibrium was indispensable to the music which the mobile gave forth, its beginning and its end, the poise from which its movement issued, the cadence in which it came with perfect finality to rest.

(1) The indispensableness of that equilibrium I learned when at last, the usual hand grown quiet, I tried to hang the mobile unassisted. (2) There it was, the same mobile, the same in all its elements. (3) No element was wanting. (4) The effect only was wanting. (5) It was an offense to the eye, crippled, disproportioned, grotesque, the dead corpse of what it was capable of, and I took it down. (6) Who was demoted, it or I? (7) I, surely, for the partisanship, the predilection, was, like the disappointment, in me, not in it. (8) The demand which conferred rightness on it, like the incapacity which could not set it right, was mine. (9) Therefore I was desolate, not because of what it was, but because of what it failed to be, because of what I wanted of it and had not the craft to produce in it.

(1) In such simple incident lies the image of all art. (2) Let that equilibrium which was needed in order that the mobile should work its desired effect be described as the *normative equilibrium*. (3) That equilibrium will be the rightness of that structure, that which is sought after whenever any adjustment is made of it. (4) By reference to the normative equilibrium of the structure one may then mark a

distinction between a right adjustment of it and a wrong adjustment of it, between a valid essay and an invalid one.

What do the words and word groups in each of the following groups have in common? What purposes do such units serve in the paragraph? (The numbers refer to the sentences in which the units occur in paragraph 1.) What word or word groups in paragraph 1 are related to the concept of balance? What figures of speech does the writer use in sentence (5)? What function does repetition serve in this paragraph? How does the writer achieve movement from one idea to another? What function is served by the contrast of sentences (3) and (4)? What is the relationship between (4) "universe in miniature" and (5) "harmony of the spheres"?

A. When I was a child (1)   B. token (1)
    nowadays (1)   device (1)
    then, and shall always   mobile (1)
        seem (2)   the strangest and most
                                            curious of fabrics (2)
                                        an insensate tangle of
                                            debris (3)
                                        a little universe in
                                            miniature (4)
                                        it (2, 3, 4)

6. What function is served by the phrase "The hanging of the mobile" (1) in paragraph 2? How many times in paragraph 2 is *it* or *its* used to refer to the mobile? How many words or word groups are used to express the concept of equilibrium in paragraph 2? What words or word groups in paragraph 3 are substitutes for the word *equilibrium* or refer to the concept of equilibrium?

7. What is indicated by the first sentence in paragraph 4? How is this sentence related to the title? What is now suggested about the meaning of the word *community* in the title? Could you predict the theme of the entire article from these four introductory paragraphs? say:

8. John Dewey, in writing on the subject of thought,[5] has this to say:

> The story is told of a man in slight repute for intelligence, who, desiring to be chosen selectman in his New England town, addressed a knot of neighbors in this wise: "I hear you don't believe I know

[5] John Dewey, *How We Think* (Boston: D. C. Heath & Company, 1910), pp. 2-3.

enough to hold office. I wish you to understand I am thinking about something or other most of the time." Now reflective thought is like this random coursing of things through the mind in that it consists of a succession of things thought of; but it is unlike, in that mere chance occurrence of any chance "something or other" in an irregular sequence does not suffice. Reflection involves not simply a sequence of ideas, but a consequence—a consecutive ordering in such a way that each determines the next as its proper outcome, while each in turn leans back on its predecessors. The successive portions of reflective thought grow out of one another and support one another; they do not come and go in a medley. Each phase is a step from something to something—technically speaking, it is a term of thought. Each term leaves a deposit which is utilized in the next term. The stream or flow becomes a train, chain, or thread.

Does the thought in "The Foundations of Artistic Community" appear to be reflective? Point to specific examples to prove your point.

9. Are the twin principles of "reversion to concepts already stated" and of "directed movement of thought" characteristic of all good use of language? How many times is the word *dedicated* or some substitute for it used in Lincoln's *Gettysburg Address* (pp. 267-68)? How many times is a first person plural pronoun used? How many times is the battlefield referred to? (Do not overlook *here.*) What is the central theme of the Address? Can you state it in three words?

Exercise 22-3   Rebuilding Sentences

Rewrite each of the following sentences in two or more different forms. You may change the form of words and the order of words, and you may add such function words as may be necessary, but try to preserve the idea presented in the original sentence.

a. In dealing with words and their forms, we must anticipate much that concerns the sentence as a whole.
b. Mulcaster's great virtue is his moderation.
c. The armies were appointed, consisting of twenty-five thousand horse and foot, for the repulsing of the enemy at their landing.
d. All languages, however different, have many things in common.
e. New thinking, new tools to work with, new materials to work on—this trinity accounts in part for the undeniable fact that language study is livelier today than it has ever been.
f. We English of the moment have agreed that "morbid" shall mean diseased, the Italians that morbid shall mean soft: so a feeble Italian is inclined to smile at our "morbid bones," as a feeble Englishman smiles at their "morbid velvet."

Suggested Readings

SECTION 22

Fries, Charles Carpenter, *American English Grammar,* Chap. VII. New York: Appleton-Century-Crofts, Inc., 1940.

Jespersen, Otto, *The Philosophy of Grammar,* Chap. VII. London: George Allen & Unwin, Ltd., 1924.

Roberts, Paul, *English Sentences,* Chap. XIV. New York: Harcourt, Brace & World, Inc., 1962.

Whitehall, Harold, *Structural Essentials of English,* Chap. VIII. New York: Harcourt, Brace & World, Inc., 1951.

Indirect Language

In the preceding section we noted that English sentence patterns were recognizable even when the idea expressed was sheer nonsense or when it represented something which was completely contrary to experience. Yet, we all know that we use many sentences which represent a denial of experience, so we must seek an answer to the question: What is there that leads us to reject as a denial of experience a sentence such as "The brick ate the fish," and at the same time to accept as a legitimate sentence one which our experience would equally deny—"John is a rat"? The answer is that in the second sentence we recognize an implied comparison, whereas in the first we do not.

In our everyday life we have constant need for making comparisons. To compare quantities and qualities, we normally use degree indicators such as the inflections *-er* or *-est,* or function words such as *as . . . as, so . . . as, more, most, less, least,* and so forth. However, these do not always provide us with a means of expressing the exact type of similarity or dissimilarity we wish to indicate.

Our simplest and unmistakably clearest means of expressing similarity and dissimilarity is to make use of such words as *like* or *unlike,* or such phrases as *similar to* or *dissimilar to.* When we use these words or phrases we are making use of a figure of speech

called a *simile*. More often, however, we make use of the *metaphor*.
The metaphor does not actually state the comparison to be made;
it merely implies it. Thus, when I say "John is a rat," I am implying
that John has some quality or qualities in common with rats. More
exactly, I am ascribing to John the disagreeable overtones that are
associated with the word *rat*. I am not implying that John has
the size, shape, coloring, or other such physical characteristics of
the rat. Such an implication would fall within the area of "denial
of experience" and would be rejected as untrue or ridiculous.

Such implied comparisons may take numerous grammatical forms.
I can say, for example, "He has a heart *of stone*" or "an *iron* will."
If I do so, I do not expect my hearer to interpret my words literally. In this situation I have used an adjective phrase or a noun
adjunct to imply the comparison. When Coleridge, in his *Rime of
the Ancient Mariner,* wrote "At one stride comes the dark," he
used a more complex structure than the classifying predicate noun
or the qualifying modifiers of our previous examples, and he implied a different type of comparison. Darkness, of course, cannot
stride. Men stride. So Coleridge's implication is that darkness came
quickly—as quick as a man could take a step. When we suggest
that abstractions such as darkness have human characteristics such
as the ability to stride, we are using a figure of speech called
personification. Personification is a specialized type of metaphor.
That we make great use of personification can be easily seen from
the numerous clichés which involve it. (Duty calls me. Love
conquers all. Hope reigns eternal in the human heart.)

Mankind is given to exaggeration, and gross exaggeration is frequently expressed through the use of stated or implied comparisons.
Thus we find Shakespeare writing in *Othello* (Act II, Scene 1,
lines 5-10):

> Methinks the wind hath spoke aloud at land,
> A fuller blast ne'er shook our battlements.
> If it hath ruffianed so upon the sea,
> What ribs of oak, when mountains melt on them,
> Can hold the mortise?

This short passage implies a number of comparisons. We have the
wind *speaking* and *playing the part of a ruffian.*
Ribs of oak also deserves our attention. The verb *to rib* originally

meant to *arch over*. When man learned something of his own anatomy, he applied the term *ribs* to those bones that arch over his chest cavity. In this passage, *ribs* is applied to those parts of the framework of a vessel that *arch under*. In all these uses, however, we have the central idea of a basic frame enclosing a cavity, so the comparison is a valid one.

"When mountains melt on them" provides us with an exaggerated comparison. The basic idea is, of course, that the waves are as large as mountains, but that they lack the solid quality of mountains in that they can *melt* over the boat. The technical name given to such exaggeration is *hyperbole*. Here again, we are not supposed to take a literal meaning from the passage, and few of us would.

We often use words as substitutes when the association between the two words and the concepts they represent should be clear to our readers or hearers. For example, the White House is associated with the President in the minds of most Americans. Hence we can say "The White House is less than enthusiastic about the bill" when we mean "The President has no enthusiasm for it." This figure of speech is called *metonymy*. Another common example of it is the use of *table* for *food* in "She sets a good table." *Synecdoche* is a particular type of metonymy. In using it, we normally substitute a word indicating a part for a word which would indicate the whole. Our use of *wheel* for *bicycle* is an example of this; so, too, is the use of *bread* for *food* in "He broke bread with them." The term *synecdoche* also encompasses the opposite practice of using a word indicating the whole to represent the part. For example, if your brother arrived home from military camp, you might announce him to the family by saying "The army is here."

In some instances proper nouns are associated with a particular concept rather than with a person or place—for example, *John Barleycorn* with whiskey, *Joe Miller* with old jokes, *Uncle Sam* with the government of the United States, *John Bull* with England, *Marianne* with France, and so on. Whenever this has occurred, these may be used as substitutes for the terms with which they are associated. It should be noted that these substitutions do not imply comparisons of any type. In this, they differ from the general area of metaphor.

Sometimes metaphors are extended to great lengths. *Pilgrim's Progress* is a book which literally tells a story about a man taking a journey, but its intent is to show how a man should avoid the temptations of life in order to achieve salvation. The controlling metaphor of the book is therefore "Life is a journey." The name given to such extended metaphors is *allegory*. Most fables are allegorical, and most allegories have as their aim the teaching of some moral or lesson. In order to understand the allegory, we must be able to associate the idea expressed with the idea that the speaker or writer had in mind.

Parody demands a different type of association—that of form. In general, the parodist is poking fun at the ideas expressed by some other person; he does so by using a form very much like the original writer's, but by making the content of his parody pure nonsense. Because he fears we may mistake or fail to recognize his clue of form, he often will give his work a title which will suggest the original. Note the close similarity of stanzaic form in the stanza from Cuthbert Bede's "In Immemoriam" and the stanza from Tennyson's "In Memoriam."

> We seek to know, and knowing seek;
> We seek, we know, and every sense
> Is trembling with the great intense,
> And vibrating to what we speak.
> —BEDE

> We have but faith: We cannot know,
> For knowledge is of things we see;
> And yet we trust it comes from thee,
> A beam in darkness: let it grow.
> —TENNYSON

By treating lightly a subject which the original writer treated seriously, the parodist expresses a mild contempt for that subject, or at least for the author's treatment of that subject. He does not expect us to take his own work seriously; he is simply pointing out that we should not take the original work seriously either.

In addition to simple figures of speech and such longer forms as allegory and parody, we have other forms of speech and writing which are not meant to be interpreted literally. In *sarcasm*, for example, we are likely to say the exact opposite of what we mean. If you are in the habit of arriving at class late, your instructor may pause some morning to remark that you are early today. If he does, he is being sarcastic. What he probably means is that you are later than you normally are. You understand his meaning because you know that, given the particular situation, he could not possibly mean that his remark should be taken literally.

It is often difficult to draw a line between sarcasm and irony or between sarcasm and sardonicism. In general, *irony* is a light type of sarcasm primarily intended to provide humor; a sardonic remark has quite a different intent—to wound the individual at whom it is directed by sneering at him or mocking him. What we normally refer to as sarcasm falls between these two poles. The term irony also appears in several other types of situations in which it has rather specialized meanings. We classify as ironical any situation in which something happens which is in a sense unexpected and possibly ridiculous—for example, a firehouse which burns to the ground, or a swimmer with medals for lifesaving who drowns in a small pool. Socratic irony occurs when one person draws another person out by pretending to be ignorant when he really is not. Dramatic irony occurs when the theatre audience possesses information which is not available to one of the characters on the stage; when this character makes a statement that presumably has a literal meaning for him, but which, in consequence of their knowledge, has a different meaning for the audience, we have an example of dramatic irony.

All of these terms have but one thing in common—they name different language situations from which we are not supposed to take literal meanings. Satire has in common with these the fact that it does not convey its meaning directly. It generally has, however, a more serious purpose than irony or sarcasm. Its purpose is to improve a situation, and it seeks to bring about this improvement through ridiculing certain aspects of the situation. *Gulliver's Travels* is a story about a shipwrecked sailor, but in the process of telling his story, Swift points out the ridiculousness of many human actions. In the fourth book, he finds a society of horses acting far more rationally than men normally do. Swift attempts to show us each of our faults—from our pride in physical beauty to our inability to achieve peace—with the hope that we will do something to correct them.

Many people like to play with words. Often they will consciously use a sentence which may have more than one meaning—"The teacher who can be replaced by a machine ought to be." Such a sentence represents a conscious ambiguity, and is quite different from the unconscious ambiguity that may be present in a sentence such as "The minister told the man he was wrong," in which *he* might refer to either *minister* or to *man*. Actually, the sentence that is consciously ambiguous in writing is not so in speech, for there we can differentiate our meanings by using different oral patterning.

Another common method of playing with words involves *metathesis* or the interchange of parts. Clichés and folk sayings frequently furnish the basis of humor with this method, for in order to recognize the metathesis we must first be familiar with the original form. A good example of this is the variation of the folk saying "All work and no play makes Jack a dull boy." In a modern version of this, we have "All work and no play makes jack." The pun is often dependent upon the familiar cliché. A good example of this is the story of the pilot fish who one day appeared without the whale that normally accompanied him. When one of the other fish asked, "Where's your fat friend?" he replied with another question, "Am I my blubber's kipper?" The pun is generally based upon our recognition of phonemic identity or approximation; or upon our recognition of the fact that two phonemically similar morphs are members of different morphemes. Occasionally, we find some that involve a change in the suprasegmental phonemes, but these are more rare.

Although we have not begun to discuss all the possible types of variants that go beyond the simple grammar and semantics of English, enough have been introduced to show that we must constantly be aware of the possibility of a meaning beyond that which is presented by the literal use of language. And, of course, if we are to become efficient and artistic producers of language, we must learn to make use of some of these devices too. The exercises following this section will review most of those devices which have been discussed, and will introduce you to a few others.

Exercise 23-1   Indirect Language

1. In the passage above we noted that we frequently imply comparisons by making statements which would obviously be untrue if we were to apply literal meanings to them. What is being com-

pared in each of the sentences provided below? On what point or base is the comparison made? What form, word, or words, if any, are used to introduce the comparison or to connect the two concepts? What is their syntactic function? What types of sentences are used? Are the two people, things, or concepts which are being compared always named? If they are not, how do we recognize them? Is contrast a type of comparison?

a. Mary looks like her mother.
b. But she is not so tall as her mother.
c. Her eyes are as blue as her mother's.
d. Her nose is shorter than her mother's.
e. She is the shortest member of the family.
f. I feel better.
g. You are becoming more beautiful every day.
h. They arrived earlier than we expected they would.
i. I used to run, but now I walk.
j. I studied while she wasted her time.

2. How do the comparisons in the sentences provided below differ from those in the sentences for question 1? Are different word-forms used? What part of speech is used to imply comparison in each sentence? Do any of these sentences contain more than one implied comparison?

a. George is a wolf.
b. Mary is a birdbrain.
c. The sun marched across the sky.
d. The enemy fleet was bottled up in the harbor.
e. The seaplane lands on water.
f. She wished him oceans of luck.

3. Do we have something other than comparison involved in the indirect language of the following sentences? If so, what? Do any of these sentences contain symbols?

a. The boy got on his wheel and rode away.
b. He bought ten head of cattle.
c. They lived three doors down the street.
d. The neighbors have another mouth to feed.
e. He has a good seat. (Said of a horseman)
f. Uncle Sam has made enemies as well as friends.
g. If he would stop using his fork, his doctor might avoid using his knife.
h. The water of life (see the etymology of *whiskey*) will be the water of death for him.

4. How do we know that the passages from Voltaire and George Jean Nathan which are reproduced below are not to be interpreted literally? Look up the word *humour* in Fowler's *Modern English Usage* or the word *humor* in Nicholson's *American English Usage*. Which of the terms distinguished there would you apply to each of the quotations in this question? Are there examples of more than one of these distinctions in either of the passages?

> The University of Coimbra had pronounced that the sight of a few people ceremoniously burned alive before a slow fire was an infallible prescription for preventing earthquakes; so when the earthquake had subsided after destroying three-quarters of Lisbon, the authorities of that country could find no surer means of avoiding total ruin than by giving the people a magnificent *auto-da-fe*.
>
> They therefore seized a Basque, convicted of marrying his godmother, and two Portuguese Jews who had refused to eat bacon with their chicken; and after dinner, Dr. Pangloss and his pupil, Candide, were arrested as well, one for speaking and the other for listening with an air of approval. Pangloss and Candide were led off separately and closeted in exceedingly cool rooms where they suffered no inconvenience from the sun, and were brought out a week later to be dressed in sacrificial cassocks and paper mitres.
>
> —VOLTAIRE, *Candide*[1]

> The Creator is imperfect deliberately, intentionally. Save He were given to imperfections, millions of His creatures would starve to death. He made the human eye imperfect that thousands of occulists might earn a livelihood; the human foot, that thousands of idiots might live by chiropody; the human fingernail, that thousands of females might substitute manicuring for streetwalking. Through His sapiently manoeuvered physical imperfections, thousands of doctors have jobs; through His shrewdly wrought mental imperfections, thousands of shyster lawyers get their bread and butter; through His all-wise manipulations of fatal imperfections He has guaranteed a living even to livery stable owners, florists, campstool manufacturers, black cotton glove merchants, clergymen, bad organists, worse singers, and undertakers.
>
> —GEORGE JEAN NATHAN, *The World in Falseface*[2]

5. What must we recognize before we can fully appreciate the humor of the following quotations?

> He slew the noble Mudjekeewis,
> With his skin he made them mittens;

[1] Voltaire, *Candide or Optimism,* trans. John Butt (Harmondsworth, Middlesex: Penguin Books, 1947), p. 36.

[2] George Jean Nathan, *The World in Falseface* (New York: Alfred A. Knopf, Inc., 1923), p. 307.

> Made them with the fur-side inside,
> Made them with the skin-side outside;
> He, to keep the warm side inside,
> Put the cold side, skin-side, outside;
> He, to keep the cold side outside,
> Put the warm side, fur-side, inside—
> That's why he put the cold side outside,
> Why he put the warm side inside,
> Why he turned them inside outside.
>   —GEORGE STRONG, *The Song of Milgenwater*[3]

> The skies they were ashen and sober,
> The streets they were dirty and drear;
> It was night in the month of October,
> Of my most immemorial year.
> Like the skies, I was perfectly sober,
> As I stopped at the mansion of Shear—
> At the Nightingale—perfectly sober,
> And the willowy woodland, down here.
>   —BRET HARTE, *"The Willows*[4]

Exercise 23-2   Indirect Language

1. What is meant by the word *pun?* Are the puns which occur in the example below all based upon the same type of linguistic substitution? If not, how do they differ? Does the pun differ in any way from the *double-entendre?* How do we realize that the writer does not want his language to be understood literally?

Marrulus: You, sir, what trade are you?
Cobbler: Truly sir, in respect of a fine workman I am but, as you would say, a cobbler.
Mar: But what trade art thou? Answer me directly.
Cob: A trade sir, that I hope I may use with a safe conscience, which is indeed, sir, a mender of bad soles.
Mar: What trade, thou knave? Thou naughty knave, what trade?
Cob: Nay, I beseech you, sir, be not out with me. Yet if you be out, sir, I can mend you.
Mar: What mean'st thou by that? Mend me, thou saucy fellow!

[3] George Augustus Strong, *The Song of Milgenwater:* Translated from the original Feejee by Marc Antony Henderson [pseud.] (Cincinnati, Ohio: Jones, Brown & Robinson, 1856).
[4] Bret Harte, *Complete Poetical Works* (New York: P. F. Collier and Son, n.d.), p. 294.

Cob: Why, sir, cobble you.
Mar: Thou art a cobbler, art thou?
Cob: Truly, sir, all that I live by is with the awl: I meddle with no
tradesman's matters, nor women's matters, but with awl. I am in-
deed, sir, a surgeon to old shoes. When they are in great danger,
I re-cover them. As proper men as ever trod upon neat's leather
have gone upon my handiwork.
—SHAKESPEARE, *Julius Caesar*
Act I, Scene 1, lines 9-30

2. If someone were to tell you that Russian summer resorts are
full of hot reds, would you recognize anything in the statement
beyond the literal meaning? Is this usage in any way related to
the pun? What kind of information do we need in order to appreciate a play on words? Do well-educated people ever consciously
misuse words? If you heard a professor of English use the sentences provided below, what would be your assumption about his
knowledge of and interest in the language? What kind of information would you need in order to understand his meaning? How
is this related to the character of Mrs. Malaprop in Sheridan's *The
Rivals?*

a. I would like to buy a house, but not at these exuberant prices.
b. My friend is an invertebrate bridge player.

3. Constructions such as "Twenty-three, skidoo!" and "You tell
'em, Pie, you've got the crust" were once common in American
English. What name do we give to such language? Is it normally
acceptable? Provide some examples of it from current American
English.

4. What is represented by the short passage below? How does
this differ from slang? Do most occupations have such languages?
Consult any bibliography of books and articles on language. Also
see the introduction to the *Shorter Oxford English Dictionary.*

As soon as you get some more quoins and furniture and lock up that
chase, put it on the bed and we'll be ready to roll. Don't move it until
you are sure it will lift; we don't want a lot of pied type around here.

5. Do you use freely all of the words provided in each of the
lists below? Are some of these terms new to you? What is represented by such variations? In what way does social approval or
disapproval affect our use of such terms?

A. fishworm	B. peanuts	C. cottage cheese
angleworm	goobers	Dutch cheese
earthworm	groundnuts	smearcase
redworm	pinders	pot cheese
dew worm		
nightcrawler		

6. What is your opinion of the use of /et/ as the past tense of the verb *eat?* Look up *eat* in Webster's *Collegiate Dictionary.* What does it have to say about this? How do the British feel about the use of the word *bloody* as an adjective? Do all speakers of English agree upon which words or expressions should receive social approval? Consult Markwardt and Walcott's *Facts About Current English Usage.* Do we sometimes approve of a particular usage at one period and disapprove of it at another?

7. In rapid speech most of us will use the sounds /əv/ as an auxiliary verb in such situations as "I should've gone." Would you want to use this form if you were giving a commencement address? Do you write *of* for *have* in your term papers? What is the difference between formal and informal English? How does Webster's *Collegiate Dictionary* define the term *colloquial?* Do you find similar definitions for this term in other dictionaries? When dictionary-makers apply this term to a word, should we consider the word to be socially unacceptable?

8. To what does the *hood* of a car refer in American English? Do what does it refer in British usage? What occupation does the term *chemist* represent in British usage? What was the meaning of the word *lewd* in medieval English? Do the words *undertaker* and *entrepreneur* have anything in common? Can the same word express quite different meanings to contemporaries who use the same language? Can the meaning of a word change quite radically over a period of time? Does this mean that anyone may use any word to express any concept? Why or why not?

Suggested Readings

Section 23

Brooke-Rose, Christine, *A Grammar of Metaphor,* Chap. I. London: Secker & Warburg, 1958.

Langer, Susanne, *Philosophy in a New Key: A Study in the Symbolism of Reason, Rite, and Art,* pp. 110-16. Cambridge, Mass: Harvard University Press, 1942.

Ogden, C. K., and I. A. Richards, *The Meaning of Meaning,* pp. 149-59. New York: Harcourt, Brace & World, Inc., 1923.

Philbrick, F. A., *Understanding English: An Introduction to Semantics,* Chap. IV, VIII, IX, and X. New York: The Macmillan Company, 1944.

Schlauch, Margaret, *The Gift of Language,* Chap. IX. New York: Dover Publications, Inc., 1955.

Index